Pursuit of the Ancient Maya

Pursuit of the Ancient Maya

Some Archaeologists of Yesterday

Robert L. Brunhouse

UNIVERSITY OF NEW MEXICO PRESS

Albuquerque

Manufactured in the United States of America.
Library of Congress Catalog Card Number 74-27443
International Standard Book Number 0-8263-0363-3
First edition

ACKNOWLEDGMENTS

The following persons generously provided aid in various forms during the research for this volume: Doris Antin, Anita Bayles, Junius Bird, Alice Blengsli, Gertrude Duby Blom, Gertrude Brown, Margaret Currier, Andrew Dees, Gordon Ekholm, Arthur E. Gropp, J.O. Kilmartin, Mary Le Blanc, Marjorie LeDoux, James Mundie, Ross Parmenter, Maurice Ries, Martha Robertson, Spencer Rogers, Stella Rosenblatt, Dennis Rowley, Linda Schele, Richard Schimmel, Harry L. Shapiro, Ailes Spinden, Doris Stone, Jane W. Stretcher, Michael Thomason, J. Eric S. Thompson, Richard Tracy, Doris Watt, Robert Wauchope, Eugene Wilson, Lee Woodward, Sue Woodward, Nathalie H. Zimmern, Margaret B. Zorach.

I am also indebted to the following libraries for the use of their resources: American Museum of Natural History, American Philosophical Society, Brigham Young University, Brooklyn Museum, Field Museum, Free Library of Philadelphia, Florida State University, Museum of the American Indian, Heye Foundation, Peabody Museum of Harvard University, Tulane University, University of Pennsylvania, University of South Alabama, University of Texas.

CONTENTS

Illustrations

Following page 118

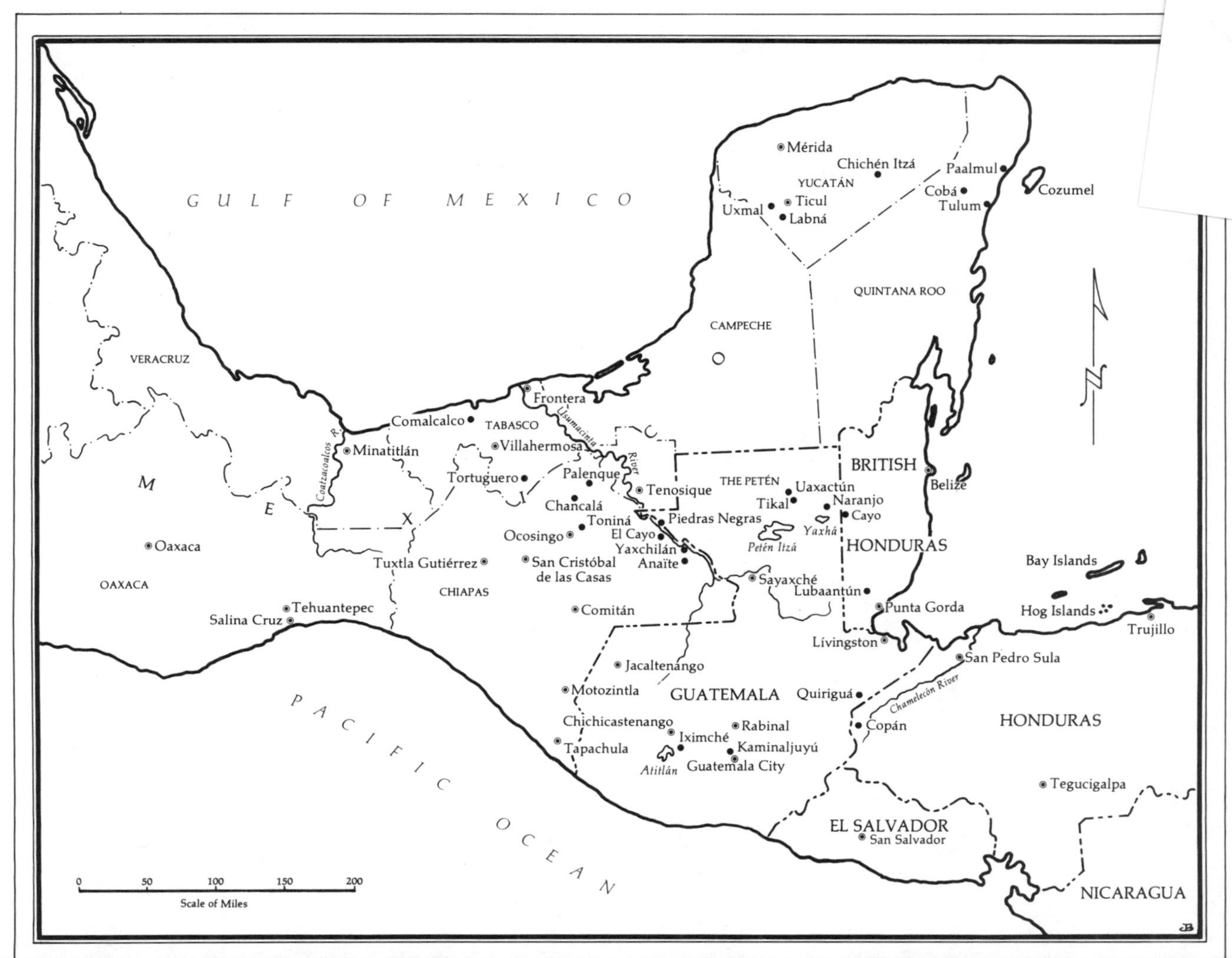
GULF OF MEXICO
PACIFIC OCEAN
Mérida
Chichén Itzá
YUCATÁN
Paalmul
Cozumel
Cobá
Tulum
Uxmal
Ticul
Labná
QUINTANA ROO
CAMPECHE
VERACRUZ
Frontera
Comalcalco
TABASCO
Usumacinta River
Coatzacoalcos R.
Minatitlán
Villahermosa
Tortuguero
Palenque
Tenosique
THE PETÉN
Uaxactún
Tikal
Naranjo
Cayo
Chancalá
Toniná
Piedras Negras
Ocosingo
El Cayo
Yaxhá
Petén Itzá
Yaxchilán
Anaïte
BRITISH HONDURAS
Belize
MEXICO
Oaxaca
OAXACA
Tuxtla Gutiérrez
San Cristóbal de las Casas
CHIAPAS
Sayaxché
Lubaantún
Punta Gorda
Bay Islands
Hog Islands
Trujillo
Tehuantepec
Salina Cruz
Comitán
Lívingston
San Pedro Sula
Jacaltenango
Motozintla
GUATEMALA
Quiriguá
Chamelecón River
Chichicastenango
Rabinal
Iximché
Kaminaljuyú
Copán
HONDURAS
Tapachula
Atitlán
Guatemala City
Tegucigalpa
EL SALVADOR
San Salvador
NICARAGUA
0
50
100
150
200
Scale of Miles

INTRODUCTION

Maya archaeologists may not be a unique breed of men, but many of them have been unusually interesting. It is profitless to argue whether the subject attracted curious personalities. There is no doubt, however, that a number of Maya archaeologists were remarkable people —sometimes resourceful, occasionally naïve, and frequently colorful.

This book presents the life stories of seven Maya archaeologists who worked in the late nineteenth and early twentieth centuries. The subjects have been chosen not only for their success or failure in enriching our understanding of the Maya but also for their singular personalities.

One would assume that a prototype of the archaeologist might emerge from these sketches. For example, Teobert Maler, Alfred Maudslay, Frederick Mitchell-Hedges, and Frans Blom were led into Maya archaeology by a youthful desire to see strange countries. Many of these men also appear to have had a gift for getting along well with people—their own associates as well as the natives of Middle America—but William Gates and, to a lesser degree, Maler stand out as the remarkable exceptions. All the men, of course, shared an interest in things Maya, though the degree of that interest varied from person to person.

These seven men did enjoy one common condition: the scholarly freedom both to choose the problems they wished to investigate and to determine the method of solving those problems. Only during the 1930s did the lack of institutional funds prevent Blom from making expeditions to Middle America. It should be added, however, that freedom of scholarly action did not necessarily assure brilliant results. The outstanding cases are Mitchell-Hedges and William Gates; although both men possessed independent resources to do as they pleased, neither made a marked contribution to knowledge of the Maya.

No stereotype emerges. If we wish to understand these men and what they did, it is necessary to consider each one as an individual. A brief review of their careers reveals the variations among them.

Teobert Maler was a loner. An expatriot by choice, he led a singularly isolated life, devoting several decades to the examination of Maya sites. No domestic ties held him in one place; no strong friendships enriched his daily life; and on endless expeditions through Yucatán and Guatemala, he had no informed companions with whom to share the excitement of his discoveries. Rarely did he visit the urban centers of scholarship in Europe or the United States. Of the enormous body of information he assembled, only a portion was published during his lifetime. In old age he nurtured hatred against some people and a distrust of mankind in general.

The perfectionist of the group was the old-school Englishman Alfred Maudslay. After the ruins attracted his attention, good judgment and self-confidence guided him in the self-appointed task of preserving the record for posterity. Fearing the loss of the original remains of Maya civilization, he photographed and molded the significant monuments, and provided drawings and maps to supplement the record. His *Archaeology* and the display of choice items in the British Museum represent the culmination of his work. The recent pillaging of Maya sites underscores the unique foresight of the man.

Sylvanus Morley's contribution ranged far beyond his establishment of a chronology for the major Maya sites. His highly charged personality opened doors, made friends and created goodwill, and spread news of the ancient Maya to the layman. He associated with Latin Americans, from peasants to high governmental officials, on their own terms. He loved the Maya past and present, glorying in the achievements of the ancient Maya and finding only virtue in their modern descendants. To

Morley, life was a vast drama of fascinating persons and intriguing events. Wherever he moved, everything was lively and dynamic. An interesting individual meant more to him than a political philosophy, and he preferred the emotional joy of gazing upon the great monuments of Chichén Itzá or Uxmal to studying the crude little archaic figurines which indicated a new extension of the prehistory of Middle America into the distant past.

The desire for personal adventure was the ruling passion of Frederick Mitchell-Hedges. A tall, self-confident man, he enjoyed expeditions to Central America, got along well with the natives, and usually returned with claims of great discoveries. He liked deep-sea fishing, and sometimes collected ethnological objects and archaeological artifacts. He also believed in Atlantis and crusaded unsuccessfully to revive male chauvinism in England.

Herbert Joseph Spinden brought an unusual mind to the profession. He advanced a number of hypotheses that fellow workers found useful frames of reference in their research; some of his ideas have survived for a half-century. He warned against the evils of specialization, and attempted to reduce elaborate factual data to satisfactory generalizations. Dedicated to humanistic values and appreciative of primitive man's adaptation to nature, Spinden applied his knowledge to contemporary culture, counseling regard for the earth, which sustains man, and recognition of the psychic forces that support a healthy society. Fellow archaeologists, quick to point out that some of his professional ideas were dubious, did not always appreciate the active mind in their midst.

In William Gates, we encounter a man who attempted to have the best of two worlds—private and professional—and failed. Imbued with theosophist ideals and searching for the expression of man's highest development, which he believed lay in the distant past, Gates struggled with the decipherment of Maya hieroglyphs as a route to that ancient knowledge. Although he spurned contemporary archaeologists, he vainly looked to them for recognition of his merits. His obsessive collecting of documents on Middle American linguistics gave him the sense of power he craved. On the other hand, an unconsciously defensive posture isolated him from fellow scholars and created difficult problems when he had to work with other people.

Finally, Frans Blom provides a fascinating study in personality. His heart was in the tropical forests of southern Mexico. When he could not return to those forests for spiritual nourishment, his spirits slumped. Administrative duties and the hard times of the 1930s drove him to desperation, and alcoholism appeared to end his career. But once more he wandered down to Mexico, where he met a spirited woman who gave him hope and encouragement to start a second career. Personal crisis, reevaluation, and the maturity which comes with age broadened his outlook and deepened his satisfactions. His love for the forests of Chiapas and his concern for the welfare of the natives brought him close to the fundamentals of existence.

Perhaps it will be easier for us to understand these men when we see how they responded to crises in their lives. And there were crises: a court in England stripped Mitchell-Hedges of all personal respectability; Spinden saw his prized correlation system repudiated by his professional friends; Morley was superseded as director of the project in Yucatán that he had labored mightily to establish; Gates imagined a host of enemies closing in to destroy his reputation; and Blom set out to raise $2 million and was fired.

The more we know about these men the better we can understand them as archaeologists.

1

Teobert Maler

Although Maler did not enjoy a very happy life, he could boast of varied experience. Born in Rome of German parents, he became an Austrian by choice; he studied architecture, fought for Maximilian in Mexico, and became a voluntary expatriot. Finally, he wandered into the Maya country with a camera, devoted two decades to reconnoitering ruins known and unknown, and lived out his last days in retirement and disappointment in Mérida.

The passage of time has made it clear that Maler played an important part in the development of Maya archaeology—a role that he did not fully comprehend in his day. Although he was untrained in archaeology—no formal training was available at that time—he became a learned amateur in Maya culture and did much to provide a solid groundwork for professional Maya archaeology, which emerged in the last decade of his life. Little concerned with the theories of the nineteenth century, he engaged unerringly in fruitful kinds of research which helped to introduce a new, important era in the study of the Maya.

The early decades of Maler's life gave no indication of his future career. He was born in 1842, in Rome, where his father was carrying out a mission for the Duchy of Baden. At the time his father was forty-three and his mother twenty-three. In the following year, however, his mother died on the trip home to Karlsruhe, and Teobert apparently grew up without the emotional security of a normal family life. His father became eccentric; he was gloomy, distrustful, miserly, and sometimes actually insane. Later on, Teobert put a good face on his early years by explaining that he had enjoyed the advantages of education and travel during his youth.

Although we know nothing about the travels he referred to, it is clear that he attended a technical school in Karlsruhe and trained in architecture and engineering. When he completed the curriculum at the age of twenty-one, he went to Vienna, became an Austrian citizen, and secured a job with Baron von Ferstel, a reputable architect of that day. Soon, however, wanderlust put an end to the career that beckoned. He gave up the job with the idea of traveling to Turkey and adjacent countries, and for a time he attempted to learn the languages of those nations.

Then events shifted the direction of his wanderlust from east to west. In 1864, Maximilian became emperor of Mexico, and Maler joined the French forces that were sent to the New World to support the emperor's regime. The young soldier landed in Mexico in January 1865 and spent a year and a half fighting for Maximilian's cause. In the army he rose from the rank of cadet to that of captain. When the empire collapsed and Maximilian ended his career before a firing squad, Maler chose not to return to Europe.

Free from the restraints of military life, he satisfied his craving for new sights and strange people by wandering from state to state over the mountains of Mexico. He photographed the colorful costumes of the natives and the quaint streets of the villages. We pick up his trail in Jalisco in 1873; then he moved down into Guerrero, and by 1876 he was in Tehuantepec, Oaxaca. At Mitla he made pictures of the old Zapotec structures with the intriguing mosaic decorations, and in Tehuantepec he bought two small gold objects which had come from a recently unearthed Zapotec tomb. There is no evidence of how he supported himself during these years of carefree travel. Possibly his father sent him remittances.

Then, in the summer of 1877, he traveled from San Cristóbal north to Palenque. The Indians who accompanied him had to open the road to the ruins with machetes. After exploring the entire site, he complained that previous visitors had not gone beyond the structures around the palace. He remained at Palenque for a week, living at the ruins; he sketched designs and decorations he found, photographed buildings, and decided to devote himself to Maya archaeology.

During the visit to Palenque, Maler met Gustave Bernoulli, whose name left a singular imprint on the story of Maya archaeology. Bernoulli was born in Berne, Switzerland in 1834. He studied medicine, but, like Maler, he yearned to visit strange lands. On the advice of the scientist Alexander von Humboldt, he settled in Guatemala in 1858. The management of a coffee plantation and the ownership of several pharmacies provided an income and allowed him time to explore the country for the study of botany. By the 1870s he showed some interest in Maya ruins, and accompanied by a young German, Herr Cario, he visited Palenque in July 1877, when Maler was also there. "We interchanged a great deal of information concerning this country and became very good friends," Maler explained later. Bernoulli collected botanical specimens, and after ten days set off with Cario for Tikal. "Dr. Bernoulli was at that time already suffering greatly from weak lungs. He was amply supplied with funds," observed Maler, "but I feared he would not be equal to the difficulties of the journey. . . . "[1] At Tikal the botanist took a fancy to a magnificently carved lintel in one of the temples and had it removed and sent to his home city of Basel.

Does Bernoulli deserve to be considered a vandal who robbed Guatemala of a fine work of art? In view of the recent pillage of Maya monuments in Central America, it is natural to consign him to the rogues' gallery of cultural culprits. Maler, however, supplied details that put a different face on the incident. Some months after the visit, Bernoulli informed Maler that "he had obtained permission from the government of Guatemala to take out" the carved lintel "and send it to Europe, and he sent money to the alcaldes of San José and San Andrés to cover the expenses of removing the beams and transporting them."[2] Bernoulli followed the best ethics of his day in securing official permission to take the carving. A century ago, moreover, foreigners believed that they were bringing unappreciated art works to the attention of the learned world by rescuing them from the tropical forest. Maudslay used the same method to obtain the superb panels now in the British Museum. Latin Americans, justifiably incensed today over the loss of many of their antiquities, must remember that their own governments willingly cooperated in sending relics to foreign lands. In the case of Bernoulli, it is interesting to realize that Maler, who later became almost fanatical in denouncing any desecration of Maya monuments, did not condemn Bernoulli's action.

The story has a final chapter. Early in 1878 Bernoulli decided to return to Switzerland to regain his health. He took a boat at San José for San Francisco, contracted fever at sea, and died soon after arriving in California. His heirs gave the lintel to the ethnographic museum of Berne, where it is still carefully preserved.

About the time Maler decided to devote himself to Maya research, he left Middle America and was gone for six years. His father had died late in 1875, and Teobert was the only direct heir, his older sister having died a few years earlier. As a result of Baden's defeat in 1866 in the Austro-Prussian War, his father's estate had been confiscated. Teobert attempted to recover his inheritance through the services of a lawyer in Mexico City, but this was an unsatisfactory arrangement. So Maler left for Europe in the spring of 1878 to press his case in Baden. While the legal proceedings encountered the usual delays, he spent much time in Paris, where a small, enthusiastic group of Americanists welcomed him. He gave lectures on Mexico, illustrated with slides made from his excellent photographs, and published a half-dozen articles in scholarly journals. He also worked in Parisian libraries, perusing the standard publications on the Maya. Lengthy notes from those works testify to his interest in the subject. Equally important were his introductions to the Americanists E.T. Hamy, Count Charancey, and the Marquis de Nadaillac, and to the anthropologists Paul Tropinard and Jean L.A. de Quatrefages de Bréau. Although there is no record of his conversations with those men, he was undoubtedly stimulated by his association with fellow scholars. During the long wait for a favorable outcome of his legal case, he fulfilled his earlier desire for eastern travel by spending some months in Turkey, Armenia, and the Caucasus. After six years he won the suit against Prussia and received his inheritance. In 1884 he returned to Mexico and settled in Yucatán to pursue Maya studies.

With Mérida and Ticul his bases of operations, Maler made trip after trip to the ruins. Not only did he examine the well-known sites like Uxmal and Chichén Itzá, but, following every lead and suggestion, he sought out unknown and smaller sites. Accompanied by a few Indians as guides and handymen, he traveled light, accepted the hospitality of hacienda owners, and sometimes lived off the land. For him, the work was serious business; with the camera he recorded stelae and structures, and extensive notes and measurements provided the facts for later plans and reports. He was forty-two years old when he embarked on this career, an age when other men consider themselves near the height of their accomplishments; and he continued the arduous labor of travel and examination for two decades. After covering northern Yucatán, he moved south into the Petén and the Usumacinta River Valley, regions rich in archaeological fare.

Two important ingredients affecting the success of every expedition were the natives who accompanied him and the living quarters he occupied while at a site. Although he traveled alone in search of archaeological data, he hired Indian laborers to load and unload the mules, guide the animals along the trail, erect overnight shelters, and clear away vegetation at a site so that he could study the ruins. Maler himself usually laid out the route, after inquiring among all kinds of people for information. If he remained at a site for some time, as was the case at Chichén Itzá, he hired local natives to prepare the place for his scientific work. Generally, he had a low opinion of the constancy and intelligence of the Indians he employed; sometimes he found them lazy, incompetent, or superstitious, and he thought they complained too often about the conditions of their work.

The nature of his living quarters on expeditions varied, depending on the length of time he expected to remain at one place. For an overnight stay he might be forced to sleep in the open in a hammock swung between two trees; if it rained, he covered himself as best he could, apparently with no ill effect from the exposure. When time permitted, his men might throw up a temporary hut to give protection against inclement weather. At sites with ancient buildings still in good condition, he lived in one or more rooms of a structure, and under the circumstances fared satisfactorily.

When traveling in the forest, his men prepared a temporary shelter called a *champa.* Maler described the construction of the roof of such a hut during an expedition on the Usumacinta River. The party landed on the riverbank and under the threat of rain contrived the makeshift structure in short order. "It took barely two hours to build the champa," he explained, "owing to the great ease with which a roof can be made of corrozo leaves. The leaves of the young palms are fully 8 meters long. Each leaf is chopped off a little at either end, and then, beginning at the small end, the rib is split down the whole length. When these half-leaves are bound horizontally upon the frame of the roof with the grooved sides turned upward, one half-leaf well overlapping the other and slanted at an angle of 45°, not a drop of rain can penetrate even during a violent downpour."[3]

At Chichén Itzá he chose a room on the second level of the Nunnery, thirty feet above the ground. It provided reasonable protection against marauding animals, commanded a magnificent view of the countryside, and caught the evening breeze. Altogether, it was a wise choice; archaeologists before and after him took advantage of the same location.

When he stayed at Tikal, he also took up quarters in one of the old Maya buildings, but this time his room was almost at ground level. Sometimes, he wrote, "I found myself surrounded by so many panthers with whom other night creatures, perhaps more harmless, mingled their cries, that I was forced to maintain a great fire at the entrance of my chamber, even occasionally to barricade it with timber."[4] At this place he slept with a loaded rifle by his side.

Although he lived in a cave at Naranjo, mainly because it provided a good darkroom for developing negatives, he found that it had advantages as a dwelling place. As he worked at his photographs at night, he heard his men in their huts "continuing their carousals often after midnight, singing and screeching. . . ." By carefully sweeping the floor, he kept vermin out of the cave. He had obstructing trees at the open end cut down to admit air and light. Even in the daytime the place remained cool and pleasant. "At night, however, there was often life stirring in the trees; it was only the round-headed apes . . . called sloths. As a rule, tigers were heard roaring at a distance, and only occasionally uncomfortably near. Owls often perched in the neighboring trees, breaking the silence of the night with ominous cries and answering again and again when they were imitated. . . ."[5]

An account of one expedition illustrates the routine, surprises, and disappointments he experienced in his work. For a trip to Cobá in 1891 he assembled a dozen natives to accompany him, including several hunters to provide daily food for the party. The trip has particular interest, because thirty-five years later a younger generation of explorers thought they were the first to discover Cobá and the old Maya road which led to it.[6] Maler's report reveals his interest in everything from the spirit of his men to the details of the ruins he found. Within four miles of Cobá, he came upon the Maya road. It was destroyed in the settled areas, but in solitary regions he found it almost intact, though covered with trees. It was five to six meters wide and had been built up about three-quarters of a meter from the ground; on both sides the embankments showed good stone construction. During the quarter of an hour the party traversed the road, with generous use of machetes to clear a path, they came upon a way station, apparently designed for the rest of ancient pilgrims.

As the party traveled through the rainy wilderness near the end of the day, they sighted Lake Cobá and the ruins beyond. The water reflected the sunset, and the declining light outlined the gray and white herons seeking perches in the trees. The men entered a thicket and cleared ground for camp. After placing the baggage on stones and covering it, they tied hammocks from tree to tree, and cut ramon branches for fodder for the animals. The rain had soaked everything so thoroughly that they gave up the attempt to kindle a fire.

They spent an unfortunate night in the camp. As darkness approached, the insects became silent, the men's conversation gradually ceased, the last cigarette was finished, and everyone fell asleep. In the middle of the night a heavy downpour disturbed their rest. Two or three of the men had lodged under a palm shelter left by earlier hunters, and they invited Maler to join them. He refused, however, saying that he had slept in the rain before and did not mind small discomforts. Long ago he had determined to share all inconveniences with his men. When the party had nothing to eat, he did not eat; when there was no water, he did not drink; and if there was no shelter for the others, he also slept in the open, wrapped in a serape. Following that rule, he maintained morale among those accompanying him.

The rain ended at dawn. Dense fog rose from the hills. The hunters, without waiting for breakfast, went into the woods in search of animals. Other men helped to gather poles and palm branches to throw up a rough shelter. Then the hunters returned with game for lunch. Maler and the natives walked to the ruins, gathering fruit from the trees on the way. He found a pyramid eighteen meters high, piles of stone from collapsed structures, and an occasional stela with glyphs too weathered to be copied. They came to another body of water, Lake Macanxox. After they returned to camp, Maler swam in Lake Cobá, noted the alligators, turtles, and snails, and caught a half-dozen fish.

The following day he found the center of the site, with remains of palaces, patios, stairways, and traces of stone walls. He followed the old Maya road again, hoping that it would lead to temples. The party ascended the steps of a pyramid; loose stones endangered the ascent, and one man had a bad fall; at the top they found a temple. In the frieze of the structure three niches held stucco figures of human beings with raised arms. Vegetation covered everything, but Maler cleared a small space to photograph an altar. In constant fear of the untamed *sublevado* Indians in the neighborhood of Tulum, the men fell on their guns upon hearing a commotion at the rear of the pyramid. It was a pack of monkeys playing in the trees, gesturing, crying out, and tasting the fruit. The incident moved Maler to remark that men, dissatisfied with their descent from monkeys, pretended that they descended in direct line from the gods. He surveyed the surrounding area and noticed two other large pyramids at a distance, but fear of the *sublevados* cut short the visit. Early the next morning he reluctantly left Cobá.

When he examined Chichén Itzá in 1891 and 1892, the tenor of his work changed. Instead of traveling and exploring as he had done at Cobá, he remained at the site for three months to make a thorough investigation and photographic record and to excavate some buildings. Living in the Nunnery as described above, he led a simple existence, and devoted himself to the self-imposed task of examining the site. Even though a Lieutenant Ramírez and his wife in nearby Pisté invited him to spend Sundays with them, Maler said nothing about social diversions in his report. Each morning native workers wearing serapes appeared from Pisté and tramped through the dew-covered vegetation to their jobs. About five in the afternoon they left for their homes. When it rained for several days, no one appeared, not even Maler's faithful Sánchez, who brought his daily food supplies.

Maler was busy throughout his stay at Chichén. During the first month he had the Indians clear the structures of heavy overgrowth; he devoted the second month to making photographs and maps; and in the final month he carried on small excavations and looked into unusual aspects of the site. The murals in the Temple of the Tigers on the ball court provided the most tantalizing record of Chichén; although the pictures had been badly damaged, there was always the hope that they might reveal valuable information about the early inhabitants. In some places the stucco had fallen; bat droppings defaced other areas of the wall; ignorant and superstitious natives had hacked at portions of the pictures with machetes; and "cultured" visitors, Maler complained, had generously scrawled their names all over parts of the mural. Patiently he set to work to retrieve as much as possible from the battered pictures. He covered the wall with transparent silk paper, and tediously managed to trace the most important scenes. Unfortunately his copy never became easily available to scholars. In the Nunnery, where he lived, there were also some murals, though they did not yield as much information as those in the Temple of the Tigers.

Each expedition provided peculiar conditions and revealed new information. When he went to Tikal in 1895, he took with him a cast-iron corn grinder to insure a constant supply of tortillas for the native laborers. It is well that he made that provision, because his employees refused to cut down the vegetation and were too superstitious to dig carved stones from the ground. He noticed that the half-breeds in the party became demoralized with fear as night approached; the full-blooded Indians retained their composure day and night, but they never cared to be alone. Maler, in contrast, even though he barricaded himself in his room at night, claimed "perfect tranquility of mind." The darkness did not disturb him, for he was "convinced that the same amount of good and evil" exists in the world by day and by night.[7] AT Tikal, too, he discovered an interesting fact. Many explorers had found it impossible to work there in the dry season because of the lack of water, but Maler found that by digging several feet into the dark ground of a dry water hole he could reach water.

Other problems came up on the Usumacinta River expedition in 1897, but they did not impede progress. "There had been heavy rains during the last nights," he explained. "For almost the entire journey we had to wade laboriously through water and mire. Worn out and drenched, we finally reached El Chicozapote, and took up our quarters in one of the huts, where we were at least sheltered from the rain."[8]

Then he fell sick. "To my great sorrow I had in the last days contracted a bad fever, which now broke forth with great violence. Abstaining from food for three days and taking heavy doses of quinine in coffee, I succeeded in breaking it up completely. In such desperate conditions—surrounded by people who are constantly dissatisfied and grumbling—it is necessary to lose no time in curing one's self, otherwise the case lasts for months and the system is much reduced. In spite of the fact I was very weak I undertook the exploration of the ruined city, . . . where many remnants of buildings covered the extremely hilly tract of land. All, of course, hidden in the dark forest of high trees." A short time later, he noted, "Having reduced my rather severe attack of fever, my appetite returned, but I was obliged to rest a few days in this camp to recover my strength."[9]

On this expedition the ascent of the Usumacinta from

Anaïte to Yaxchilán, a distance of thirteen kilometers, exhausted the men navigating the cayuco. They could make progress against the current only by pulling with all their might on the branches of trees that overhung the river.

Unlike later archaeologists who explored the Petén, Maler did not use chicleros, those men who ranged through the forest to collect the sap of the chicle tree, to guide him to unknown ruins. Chicleros were introduced into the region in the 1890s, though only on a small scale at that time. Maler, however, saw enough of them in his last long expedition of 1905 to condemn the deplorable effect they had on industrious Indians. When he visited Benque Viejo at the entrance of the Petén, he saw the stable village life of the natives disintegrating. The chicleros, accustomed to the free life of the forest, returned to the village to spend their earnings in reckless dissipation; then they fell into poverty and debt until it was time to go into the forest again. They set an evil example for the industrious Indian villagers, who stopped planting their cornfields and neglected their families. The irresponsible Indians would chant, "*I* am a chiclero; it is not necessary to work for anyone." Maler concluded sadly, that chicle "hastens the downfall of the population of the Petén, ruins agriculture and increases the demoralization of the lower classes, naturally inclined as they are to all vices."[10] The deterioration was gradual but pervasive, for later explorers testified to the same evil effect on the chicleros on villages adjacent to the Petén.

Far worse than the chicleros, in Maler's estimation, were the people who did thoughtless and malicious damage to the ancient ruins. He witnessed such vandalism at almost every site he visited, and it made his anger rise to the boiling point. When he worked at Chichén Itzá, he denounced Augustus Le Plongeon, perhaps with good reason, for having opened mounds in search of statues some twenty years earlier without making any effort to restore the damage, and for having left debris scattered about; he also accused Le Plongeon of driving holes in the Nunnery. When Maler found the atlantes Le Plongeon had uncovered in the Temple of the Tigers, he sent them to the Mexican national museum. He indignantly called Le Plongeon and people like him exploiters, not explorers, of the ruins. Did the Mexican government, he asked, permit anyone to attack the temples and palaces of a glorious past, tumbling down parts that struck their fancy, piercing every thick wall in search of mummies, implements, and treasure which did not exist? Did it allow those reckless adventurers to make molds which pulled stucco and stones from the walls, or wrench off finely carved pieces to take out of the country?

During his investigations of Tikal, Maler noted every instance of damage to the ruins. Calistro Barreo, a businessman fallen into debt, and Bernoulli had hacked carved beams out of doorways and sent them abroad. Colonel Méndez, an early explorer of the site, had cut gashes into structures in search of treasure. One Señor Fredrico had made casts of carvings, then built fires in front of the altars. One Emilio Vásquez had led a group of chicleros to the site, where the ignorant men had toppled over every stela but one on the main plaza; this, too, was done in the search for treasure. Maler protested this last act of vandalism to the governor of the Petén. If carrying off decorated panels amounted to looting, he considered unpardonable the damage perpetrated by malicious, greedy chicleros who had no reasonable expectation of finding riches.

In exploring the Usumacinta River Valley, he had grounds to record more cases of vandalism. At Chinkihá woodcutters had removed a stone lintel, found it too heavy to carry, and abandoned it, and Maler could not determine where it originally belonged. Treasure seekers at Xupé broke up a fine, carved mural plaque and deliberately smashed the face of the major figure. One of the most senseless cases occurred at Reforma, where a native worker broke up two stelae, when other stones were easily available, to make an oven to bake a small amount of bread.

Examining site after site, poring over each carved stone, Maler gained a remarkable knowledge of the ancient

Maya. He surmised, for example, that wooden stairs originally provided access to the upper stories of the buildings at Tikal. He also imagined that "thousands of houses or huts built of perishable material, and covered with roofs of palm leaves" surrounded the great center.[11] Decades passed before archaeologists gave attention to house mounds, and their research proved that his speculation was correct. He mastered the general principles of the distribution of structures and stelae at the various sites so well that he could shrewdly guess which items were missing from a site. At Tikal he had the intuition to excavate in front of a certain stela, and he found a fine altar, picturing two deities, buried in the ground. After he examined the ruins on Topoxté Island in Lake Yaxhá, and his boat began to move toward the shore, he carefully scrutinized every part of the land around the lake. One spot appeared to be a natural place for an ancient settlement; he excavated there and found undiscovered ruins.

He understood every line in the carved figures he found at site after site. Years of examination taught him the meaning of much detail at first hand. In his reports the lengthy descriptions of the major figures on stelae help the reader to understand what he sees in the photographs; in addition, Maler interjected his broad knowledge in interpreting the details. Some of his predecessors had fondly believed that the Maya had been a peaceful society, innocent of cruelty; Maler knew better, and he explained how they tore hearts from sacrificial victims and sometimes ate their bodies. In fact, the reader feels that he imagined bloody sacrifices having occurred on every altar. That knowledge, however, did not diminish his amazement at the superb art and the majestic temples of those ancient inhabitants of Middle America.

The artistic achievement of the Maya impelled him to make a complete photographic record of each significant site. He set out to picture all structures, stelae, carved figures, and glyphs. The task required infinite patience; it increased his work and lengthened the time of his stay at each group of ruins worthy of attention. When he chose a site to study, he ordered the Indians to cut down and clear away all vegetation and trees which obstructed a clear view of the pyramids, temples, and carved stones. That was but the preliminary stage of preparation. Sometimes, when he wished to take pictures of decorations on the walls of buildings, the natives had to lash saplings and vines together to form a scaffold sturdy enough to hold him and his camera.

Carved stelae required additional preparation. When he found them lying face down, he had them turned over—not always an easy task—to reveal the sculptures. Workers raised important stelae upright to expose the carving to the full light of the sun. At Piedras Negras, Maler's Indians labored a week at that task. With the aid of a windlass, borrowed in the neighborhood, they raised every stela on the main plaza to its original position. Then Maler removed the moss and washed down the carved surfaces. He learned from experience that a wet surface emphasized the lines in low-relief carving.

Finally, he studied the sun at different hours of the day to determine the time the subject would show up in sharpest relief. After he set up his camera and had everything in readiness, he often had to wait until a slight breeze died down, so that no moving weed or shaking leaf would leave a blur on the negative.

At Chichén Itzá he encountered a unique problem, for during the winter months when he visited that site, the sun did not shine directly on sculptures facing north. So one night he camped on top of a pyramid and photographed carvings with magnesium light. It was a delicate process to secure correct focus and to arrange the light properly. The sudden brightness attracted nocturnal butterflies, and he spent a few moments capturing rare species. After he had completed the pictures, he sat by a fire he had kindled, ate an egg, a piece of venison, tortillas, and two small oranges. The man who seeks few material things, he mused, can be satisfied with little.

He made it a rule to develop all negatives at the site. If

any pictures turned out badly, he could photograph the subject again before he left. This practice required him to bring photographic supplies with him and to rig up a darkroom. At sites like Tikal and Chichén Itzá, where he took up quarters in a "palace," he could easily curtain off one of the rooms for the purpose. At Naranjo, as we have noted, he chose to live in a cave because of the excellent darkroom it provided. "From time to time at night, by the light of the red lamp," he explained, "the negatives made between times with great care on celluloid plates, were carefully developed, washed off in water that had to be brought to the cave, and then hung up to dry."[12] When he eventually completed prints, he carefully identified the subject of the photograph, sometimes adding the location of the object at the site.

Maler led a lonely existence. He never married, had no children, lived in a foreign land, and as far as is known enjoyed no long-term close friendships. Only on a few occasions did he refer to his personal life. Perhaps the most interesting bit of self-revelation appears in the report on the expedition to Chichén Itzá in the early 1890s. Among the crew of laborers who came daily to work for him was José Sánchez, a man whom Maler respected and pitied because of the hard life he led. Any other Indian with a peso in his pocket preferred to drink rather than work; only when the native was reduced to his last centavo was he willing to labor for a day or so. Not so the faithful Sánchez. Industrious and expert with the machete, he worked every day except when it rained. He had married at the age of twenty-two and had a wife to support. At the end of each day at Chichén, he trudged home carrying a bundle of firewood on his shoulder, uncomplainingly he ate his meal, and gazed upon his beautiful wife, Marcelina.

In describing Sánchez, Maler confessed his own feelings. He feared women, and he could not bear contemplating an imitation of Sánchez's daily sacrifice in order to have a wife. The archaeologist bitterly compared beautiful women to roses among thorns. The prudent man, he declared, will look upon them and enjoy their fragrance from a distance, but never touch them. In the case of love, he added, the rule is that what the gods deny us is more for our own good than that which the gods grant us. With the fatalism of the Turks, he accepted the fact that in his firmament there was no star of love. He was fifty years old when he made this confession. Had he had an unfortunate affair in his youth? Exactly what he meant is anyone's conjecture, but his words appear to be an attempted justification of the bachelor existence he maintained throughout his life.

Some years later he made a stronger remark about his life. In a forsaken place on the Usumacinta River in 1905, he happened to read a novel about a heroine who offered herself to the gods to save her country. The tale made him think about himself, and in a moment of self-pity he exclaimed: "Wandering about from one year's end to another in these inaccessible wildernesses in search of remnants of bygone civilizations, denying myself all joys of life, subjected to strenuous labor, many dangers, and the daily annoyances resulting from the perpetual discontent of my men—all this constitutes a kind of immolation."[13] The passage actually says less than it appears to say. He complained about the undesirable aspects of his work; and anyone would sympathize with his complaint, considering that he was sixty-three years old at the time. Only those words "denying myself all joys of life" could apply to other facets of his life, and he left the meaning tantalizingly vague and undefined.

Other revelations by the man suggest that he not only made the best of his singular way of life but also found compensations which made his existence bearable and satisfying, if not completely happy according to conventional standards. At Chichén Itzá, after the day's work was finished, he went to his room in the Nunnery, washed, and changed his clothes. Then he sat on the platform outside his door, ate a simple meal, and watched the shifting clouds in the sky and the sun throwing its last rays over the green expanse on all sides. Dusk came, and the evening star appeared. He returned to his room, where an oil lamp provided light; he read or wrote a little, and then fell asleep. He listened to the familiar chirping of nocturnal insects, the howling of an animal in the distance, and the screech of the owls; all night long some birds, perched on the corner of the building, called to their companions in melancholy tones. Those creatures did not frighten him, he explained; they sympathized with him.

He found satisfaction in the work he completed. After he ended the tasks at Chichén and packed his belongings one morning for departure, he felt a touch of sadness. Man has an affection, he believed, for the place where he has labored and suffered, not for the place of enjoyment and pleasure. He climbed to the top of the building and surveyed all of Chichén. Some buildings stood out clearly in the tropical sunlight; others lay hidden under green growth. Those witnesses of a past civilization—what a picture to remember! Three months of labor at the site had given him a deep affection for the place.

In the course of his travels he also gained the satisfaction of witnessing the beauties of nature in the brush and forest of the tropics. Throughout the reports he mentioned various birds, fish, and trees, sometimes describing their unusual traits. Although he was never rhapsodic, he went out of his way to note the perfect diamond pattern on the body of a snake, the ever-changing tints of the sky at sunset, or the distant silvery chirping of an unknown insect. Never would he have admitted that he felt himself in touch with one of the fundamentals of life, but the reader senses that appreciation behind the literal meaning of his words.

In the upper Usumacinta region in 1898, as he traveled toward Chāncala, he came upon a waterfall in a stream near the trail. He could not move on without photographing the majestic sight, and so he and his workers spent the whole day on the project. They tied lianas to trees to facilitate his descent, with his valuable camera, down the steep ravine; at the bottom he had to find a proper spot in the stream from which to photograph the waterfall, and he made two exposures. Although the natural display had no bearing on archaeology, he valued it so much that he included a picture of it among the photographs accompanying his report on Maya sites.

A few years earlier, on another expedition down the Usumacinta, he paused between El Cayo and Sayaxché to contrast "the lavish beauty of nature" with the "degraded remnants of humanity" that he encountered in the same area. "Luxuriant vegetation of emerald hue bends in flower-laden branches to the water's edge, overreached by a sky of perfect azure," he wrote; "brilliant-hued butterflies and humming birds with metallic sheen fly from flower to flower; gorgeous birds build their nests in every tree; even the snakes and iguanodons are graceful and beautiful. . . ."[14] All of this fairyland beauty! he exclaimed; what a contrast to the sloth and filth of the miserable people who inhabited the land.

One night a decade later, when Indians paddled him across Lake Petén in a cayuco, the beauty of the nocturnal sight again turned his thoughts to the natives of the region. "The trip is especially romantic and beautiful by moonlight or by soft starlight in the stillness and coolness of the night," he wrote. "While the weather-hardened, taciturn Indians of San José or San Andrés bend to their paddles and the cool water ripples and the stars in the dark firmament twinkle full of mystery, an indescribable feeling of melancholy comes over one while pondering on the often hard and thankless life of those representatives of a once great race now rapidly disappearing."[15]

During his last years of exploration he found only one major patron, the Peabody Museum of Harvard University. The reports of his Peabody Museum-sponsored expedition through the Petén and the Usumacinta Valley from 1898 to 1905 appeared in the Peabody Memoirs between 1901 and 1911. The early reports caused no problems; they provide good descriptions of the sites, which often contained little-known or unknown remains. But trouble came with the last reports, because Maler refused to read proof and failed to supply the sketches and maps he had promised to supplement the reports. At last,

Peabody officials broke relations with him. The specific cause of the trouble is not entirely clear. A friendly biographer suggests that explorations kept the man away from Mérida for long periods of time and thus delayed communication with the museum. This reason is scarcely convincing, for during the years of the trouble he undertook no major exploration and was in Europe only briefly. It is more likely, as another commentator explains, that Maler believed that the Peabody Museum was making a profit from the sale of his reports. At this time he had apparently exhausted his paternal inheritance and appeared miserly to some visitors; so it is possible that he believed the absurd idea that the museum was reaping money from his reports.

Whatever the reason for the break with the Peabody Museum, it was unfortunate for Maler. He had on hand piles of manuscripts and a collection of splendid photographs and drawings, none of which appeared in print during his lifetime. In 1910 and again in 1912 he made short trips to Europe to attend meetings of the International Congress of Americanists, undoubtedly in search of a patron. He succeeded only in receiving 750 francs for the sale of 152 photographs to the Bibliothèque Nationale.

In the later years, when Maler was living in retirement in Mérida, Sylvanus Morley and T.A. Willard both met him. Morley, a young archaeologist on his first trip to Yucatán, visited the German at his home on 59 Calle several times in 1907. Maler's English came slowly, and he was at times cantankerous; when he was not drinking beer in a nearby cantina, he ''devil-upped'' (developed) negatives and sold photographs of the ruins to archaeologically inclined tourists. Morley bought photographs from him a number of times—not always the ones he wanted—apparently as a subtle way of helping the aging man. When Maler sold him a Lacandón incense burner for fifty cents—that is, practically gave it to him—the German did not appear to be interested in money.

T.A. Willard, the battery manufacturer who made Maya

studies a major hobby, claimed to have known the explorer over a number of years. He found him suspicious of strangers, and had to call on him four times before he would talk of archaeology. Willard described him as an eccentric misanthrope but also as a man with a kind heart and a lovable personality if one had the patience to cultivate his trust. He had lost faith in mankind because some purchasers of his photographs had failed to pay him. Willard claimed that Maler allowed him to examine the artifacts he possessed and to make a copy of the mural from the Temple of the Tigers.

Maler's hatred of the archaeologist Edward Thompson increased with the years. Morley and Willard listened to his tirades against the man. After Thompson carried on his early project of making molds of the facade of Labná for the World's Fair of 1893, Maler accused him of weakening the foundations of a temple at that site and of damaging the facade with his molding process. Some years later Thompson bought the ruins of Chichén Itzá, and from 1904 to 1907 he dredged many artifacts from the Sacred Cenote there. Maler learned of the activity and wrote a letter to the Mexican government, accusing Thompson of damaging the ancient objects in his dredging operation. A little later he wrote an essay on "The Thompson Case," which was never published. In 1926, however, the Mexican government retrieved Maler's letter from its files as one piece of evidence to justify the confiscation of Thompson's estate.

Willard told another story about the artifacts from the Sacred Cenote. For some unexplained reason Maler believed that he had a claim to that treasure, and so he bribed Thompson's native workers to smuggle as many of the objects as possible from Thompson's hacienda house at Chichén and sell them to him in Mérida. Willard claimed that he was allowed to examine and photograph the objects and to draw up a list of them. After Maler's death, to continue Willard's story, no artifacts were found in his home by Juan Clausing, the Austrian consul who took charge of his effects. Willard concluded that the old man had melted them down and sold the metal for money.

This is an intriguing anecdote, and Willard supported it by publishing photographs of some of the objects. But can we accept the story? Willard liked to write entertaining narratives, had a romantic streak in his makeup, and admitted that he could, and at times did, doctor photographs. There is no doubt that Maler hated Thompson, but Willard gives no convincing explanation of why the German went to the trouble of acquiring the artifacts. More important, the Willard tale contradicts what we know about Maler's character. It is difficult to believe that this man, who loved Maya ruins, devoted decades to recording them, and castigated anyone who moved even a stone at the sites, would have resorted to the destruction of artifacts. Nor is it certain that Maler was as penniless as Willard suggests.

One of the last incidents we know of the man occurred a year before his death. The fine arts school in Mérida asked Maler to teach a course on Maya civilization, because he was the only qualified person available in the city. He agreed on condition that the class should meet at his home. Alfred Barrera Vásquez, who related the story, was the only student to appear; unfortunately, he tells us no more about Maler the pedagogue.

When Maler died in 1917, the First World War was in progress, and Germans received little sympathy. Only one American journal noted his death, devoting only five lines to it; Joseph-Louis Capitan contributed an appreciative obituary of a little over a page in a French journal; and that was the end of it. Later a bust of the man was placed in the patio of the museum in Mérida, a road was named for him at the ruins of Tikal, and someone gave his name to a group of buildings at Yaxhá.

His manuscripts, photographs, and plans remained in storage for years before they found resting places in public institutions. Some photographs went to the Mérida museum and the negatives to the National Museum of Anthropology in Mexico City. The manuscripts and sketches were divided between the Ibero-American Institute of Berlin and the Ethnographic Museum in

Hamburg. Even his short personal narrative of the expedition to Cobá and Chichén Itzá, an interesting work which throws light on the man's personality, did not appear in print until 1932. Finally, in 1971, Gerdt Kutscher published forty of Maler's plans of sites and structures, with an excellent biographical account and some of his photographs. But Maler's three-volume study, the "Yucatán Peninsula," remains in manuscript.

Maler suffered from inadequate recognition. In his last years, a time of life when former animosities usually soften or disappear, he embittered his soul with an incomprehensible hatred of Edward Thompson and a distrust of mankind in general. That quirk of old age, however, was of small moment compared with his undeserved neglect from fellow Americanists. Perhaps his unattractive personality had something to do with it; more likely his residence in far-off Mérida made it easy for them to ignore him. It is possible that the young professional archaeologists considered the man too old and out of date to be worthy of notice. In addition, he was a German and had the misfortune to die during World War I, when, as we have pointed out, anti-German sentiment infected the arts and sciences.

We misplace our sympathy if we pity Maler for the lonely life he led. His existence was neither forlorn nor tragic. He lived in a foreign land by his own choice. Regardless of what we think of the reasons for his never having married, this was his own decision. After all, he had considerable compensations—complete freedom to wander where he pleased, the pleasure of working on what he most enjoyed, and the appreciation of nature in its luxuriant, tropical exuberance.

Fate was unkind to Maler because it denied him the greatest satisfaction he had a right to expect. For decades he devoted his energy and ability, suffering a good deal of inconvenience and hardship, to the accumulation of a valuable factual and pictorial record of the remains of Maya civilization. His photographs were superb, his maps and plans excellent, his reports informative. He knew he had made a valuable contribution to Maya archaeology; and what is more, he performed the task at the time when it was needed. The learned world had grown tired of unsupported theories and fruitless debates about the Maya, which had marked much of the "research" of the nineteenth century. Now a new age was opening; facts were replacing theories, and a young group of archaeologists was ready to advance knowledge of the Maya to broad, new horizons. Maler was a founder, a harbinger, of that new movement, but he failed to receive adequate credit for his achievement during his lifetime. Only a portion of his researches appeared in print; despite the publication of some of his plans as late as 1971, his three-volume work and other maps and plans remain in manuscript.

Did Maler perhaps sacrifice too much for the sake of wholehearted devotion to the cause of Maya archaeology?

2

Alfred P. Maudslay

The work of Alfred Maudslay represented a new attitude that began to transform archaeology toward the end of the nineteenth century. Earlier explorers had searched Middle America for decades to uncover new sites that might explain the mystery surrounding the ancient Maya. Those pioneers revealed the monuments; an advance in knowledge, however, could come only from more concentrated study of the ruins at individual sites. Maudslay aimed to provide that information, and he succeeded brilliantly.

Fortunately, he possessed a good education and the right temperament and financial resources to carry out his ambition. Born in 1850, he was reared in London, where his invalid father, James, lived in Hyde Park Square. Two generations of Maudslays had been naval engineers and shipbuilders who provided vessels for the Admiralty. James Maudslay had a reputation for scientific ingenuity, with several patents to his credit. Although he died when Alfred was eleven years old, it is clear that he left more than adequate resources for his family.

As an adult, Alfred looked back on his education with mixed emotions. His early schooling at Tunbridge Wells and Harrow taught him little; he was not particularly happy, suffered from frail health, and failed to learn to read the Greek and Latin authors. After a period with a tutor, he entered Trinity Hall, Cambridge, and studied botany and comparative anatomy in preparation for a career in medicine. In 1872 he received the A.B. with second-class honors in natural science.

After completing his formal education at the age of twenty-two, he considered becoming a physician, but how serious he was is open to doubt, because he first indulged a youthful desire to travel. With his brother Charles he toured Panama, Guatemala, Mexico, and parts of the United States. His academic training in natural science explains his visit to Yosemite Park, one of the first wilderness areas in the United States to be set aside by federal law for perpetual preservation. At Yosemite he met Anne Cary Morris, a tourist from New Jersey, who later became his wife. The following year he made a journey to Iceland and abruptly changed his professional plans. Believing that his health was not strong enough to permit him to pursue the arduous study of medicine, he gave up that ambition in favor of some other career.

In 1874 he decided to become a planter in the West Indies, but accident caused him to abandon this scheme and move in yet another direction. On arriving at Jamaica to set up a tobacco plantation, a quarantine forced him to transfer to Trinidad. On the boat, however, he fell in with William Cairns, who was on his way to assume the governorship of that island, and Cairns induced Maudslay to become his private secretary. When Cairns was assigned to Queensland, Australia, Maudslay again accompanied him as secretary. From 1875 to 1880 the young man served on the staff of Sir Arthur Gordon, governor of the Fiji Islands, and he gradually assumed diplomatic and administrative duties in various British possessions in the southwestern Pacific, where he achieved noteworthy success in dealing with the natives.

Not until Maudslay reached the age of thirty-one did chance introduce him to Americanist studies, which he had known only from reading John Lloyd Stephens's volumes on the subject. With a view to improving his health, he moved to the warm climate of Guatemala, and planned to amuse himself with visits to some of the ruins described by Stephens. From Lívingston he followed a tedious route by steam launch and muleback to Quiriguá. The first view of the site left him crestfallen, for all he could see on arrival "was what appeared to be three moss-grown stumps of dead trees covered over with a tangle of creepers and parasitic plants, around which the undergrowth had been cleared away for the space of a few feet." Could these be the curious stones Catherwood had sketched over forty years ago? "However, a closer inspection showed that these were no tree-stumps but undoubtedly stone monuments. . . . We soon pulled off the creepers, and with rough brushes, made by tying together the midribs of the leaflets of the corosa palm, we set to work to clear away the coating of moss." What he saw excited his imagination. "As the curious outlines of the carved ornament gathered shape," he explained, "it began to dawn upon me how more important were these monuments, upon which I had stumbled almost by chance, than any account I had heard of them led me to expect."[1] The experience in the forest underbrush made him an Americanist.

The brief stay at Quiriguá gave him a taste of what to expect. He examined and photographed five standing stelae and two altars. How much more did the dense tropical growth hide? On the third and last day, he wrote, "I caught sight of monument B, which lay within a few feet of my camp-cot buried beneath the decaying trunk of a huge tree, and wrapped round with a tangle of creepers and lianas."[2]

Devoted to the cause of Maya archaeology, he spent eight seasons between 1881 and 1894 in Central America, where he examined most of the major sites and a few minor ones for the purpose of providing scholars with the necessary sources of study. He photographed structures and stelae, took measurements, and prepared molds of the important remains. Except for one season at Copán, when the Peabody Museum of Harvard University asked him to supervise its expedition there, he worked entirely for himself and paid all expenses of exploration from his own pocket. And when it came time to make the results known, the sponsors of the *Biologia Centrali-Americana* met the cost of publication.

Season after season he struggled with the trials of fieldwork. Baggage, often cumbersome with bulky materials for making molds, failed to keep up with him. After he reached Mérida on December 24, 1888, in preparation for an examination of Chichén Itzá, he had to cool his heels for a month before the luggage arrived. ". . . I was heartily tired of Mérida . . . ," he exclaimed later, when he recollected the disappointing start of that season.[3] On several occasions he had arranged in advance with government officials for the passage of his impedimenta through customs without examination. But on the way to Palenque, local customs officers at the port of Laguna insisted on opening every package, weighing its contents, and listing each item, more, he believed, "to satisfy their own curiosity than . . . to ensure the unquestioned passage of my baggage into the neighbouring State of Chiapas."[4]

He found native labor the most unpredictable factor in his work. Indians had little freedom; most of them were tied to landowners in a form of serfdom or were required to work four days a week for the state. With small opportunity to recruit free labor, Maudslay had to rely on local officials, whom he paid for the Indians' services, to divert natives from public works to his own needs. On the way to Palenque he stopped at Monte Cristo to find Indian carriers or mules to deliver his equipment to its destination. No native carriers were available and he had to settle for five "wretched-looking beasts of burden with old rotten pack-saddles"; it required two thirty-mile trips with those animals to deliver the baggage to Palenque.

When he retraced the route five years later, conditions had not improved, for he left Monte Cristo "with bad mules, sulky muleteers, and half-drunken Indians" and "had a hard day of it."[5]

At each site he needed workers to clear the thick growth in preparation for measuring and photographing the ruins, but despite firm arrangements with local officials he could not predict how many natives would show up from one day to the next. He began operations at Chichén Itzá with twenty to thirty men; after several weeks the number dropped to two or three, and finally no Indians appeared for a whole week. When he camped at Copán in 1885, many of his workers were suddenly drafted into military service. At Palenque, after the Indians had made some progress in clearing the brush, they suddenly deserted him to participate in a fiesta. Then fifty men appeared and worked for several days; but after that spurt of activity they too disappeared for unknown reasons. So depleted was the labor force that he had to rely on two boys to bring food for the party every day from the village six miles away.

At important sites he planned to make molds of the monuments, especially those with hieroglyphs, in order to preserve the original records for serious study. In this costly and troublesome work he suffered frustrations and sometimes complete disappointment. First, he had to transport the materials—paper, plaster, waterproof wrapping, and cord—from England to the isolated site in Central America. The stela he wished to reproduce had to be cleaned. The actual molding required a skill beyond that of the native laborers, and Maudslay brought a Mr. Guitini from England and three helpers from a Guatemala family named López to supervise the work. At Chichén Itzá he had the services of Henry N. Sweet of Boston and Edward H. Thompson, United States consul in Yucatán, to carry out the task. After the molds were removed from a stela, they were dried and stored until time for shipment. So as to facilitate transportation, each mold was small, covering only a portion of a monument. At Copán

Maudslay used four tons of plaster[6] to make fourteen hundred molds; at Quiriguá the Great Turtle required over six hundred molds using two tons of plaster. To ensure safe shipment, each mold was wrapped in a number of coverings, and several molds were packed in a box, with two boxes to a mule for the overland journey. At the port city the molds were repacked in strong wooden containers for the ocean voyage to England.

After the trouble of producing and transporting the molds, there was also the danger that they might suffer damage or loss at sea. The paper molds which had been improperly repacked at Izabal for shipment abroad "were nearly all destroyed by moisture during the voyage to England."[7] The fourteen hundred molds from Copán had a singular adventure in 1894. Maudslay and his wife left Lívingston on board the ship in which the cargo was stowed. Ninety miles out, the vessel lost its shaft and drifted helplessly for a week. After a small steamer rescued the passengers, tugs brought the boat to port in New Orleans. Then Maudslay had the cargo transferred to another vessel for England. A few days out, the steamer grounded on the reefs near Florida. The cargo had to be removed, but eventually the Maudslays and the casts reached their destination with no more harm than some damage to Alfred's personal baggage.

He entered on the long season of 1891 at Palenque under unfavorable conditions. When he took up quarters at the Palace, "The great forest around us hung heavy with wet, the roof above us was dripping water like a slow and heavy rainfall, and the walls were glistening and running with moisture. . . . " For a month it rained; during that time a monument could be molded only if it were protected by a waterproof covering. With the advent of dry weather, the work progressed satisfactorily for three weeks. Molds which had been dried and completed were stacked on shelves in a temple. One night, however, a "storm burst on us" and spread disaster. The driving rain, continuing through the next day, soaked the temple, and water ran down the interior walls and dripped from the roof. The molds that had been tied to sculptured stelae were "almost washed away."[8] Most of the work of molding had to be repeated. At Chichén Itzá, in contrast, the hot weather almost defeated Maudslay's attempt to make replicas of the low-relief carvings at the base of the Temple of the Jaguars. The heat was so intense that he could not begin work until three in the afternoon; even then the stone carvings were too hot to hold the damp paper in the molds. He managed to reproduce only a few of those figures.

At Palenque he also attempted to clear the stucco plaques of heavy incrustations. Over the years, rain and dripping water had covered those carvings, for which the site is distinguished, with a coat of lime. Maudslay could not rest until he photographed them. So he used screwdrivers, mallets, bradawls, and physical force to remove the lime, which was sometimes six inches thick. After exposing the original surface, he washed the stucco with a chemical solution to make the most effective photographic record.

He took some original stone panels from Yaxchilán and sent them to England. In 1882, as he explained later, "In one of the half-ruined buildings we found a beautifully carved lintel fallen from its place and resting side downwards against the side of a doorway. This excellent example of Maya art I determined to carry home with me, and at once set my men to work to reduce the weight of the stone, which must have exceeded half a ton, by cutting off the undecorated ends of the slab and reducing its thickness." Lacking proper tools for the task, he resorted to a pickax and carpenter's chisels. "By keeping mozos at work at it three at a time in continued rotation, by the end of a week the weight of the stone had been reduced by half. . . ."[9] He managed to transport the carving by canoe, mules, Indian carriers, and oxcart to Belize, where it was shipped to England.

Some years later he received permission from the government of Guatemala to remove more carved lintels from Yaxchilán. Again, he was careful to take stones only from ruined structures. All of the originals went to the British Museum, where they can be seen today.

Although Maudslay described his adventures in a serious, businesslike tone with a minimum of humor, he admitted that there were times of enjoyment, pleasure, and gratification. Able lieutenants lightened the details of his work. In addition to the supervisors mentioned earlier, he employed one Charles Blockley and a Mr. Price for surveying. When another volunteer, Adela Breton, a talented watercolorist, asked what she could do at Chichén Itzá, Maudslay suggested that she copy the murals, considerably defaced at that time, in the Temple of the Jaguars. With care and patience, she completed the task, so successfully that her copy is the one usually reproduced in books.[10]

Maudslay generally enjoyed comfortable living quarters, often at the site. At Palenque, rooms in the Palace housed members of his party very satisfactorily after the rains had passed. In the evening he found "some spot where there was a cool breeze and we could avoid" the mosquitoes; in later years he recalled "the beauty of the moonlight nights when we sat smoking and chatting on the western terrace looking on to the illuminated face of the Temple of Inscriptions and the dark forest behind it."[11] At Copán he lived in the village in one of the primitive public buildings known as the *cabildo;* attached to it was the local jail, a cell seven feet by four, which became his photographic laboratory. During the long season of 1889 at Chichén Itzá, at first he selected the Red House for his quarters, but later transferred to the Nunnery. The latter building proved ideal as it had for Maler; the seven rooms on the second range were thirty feet above the ground; they faced a wide promenade on the roof of the first range and provided an admirable view of the entire site. During most of his stay at Chichén the weather was delightful, and he enjoyed, among other things, hearing the birds singing in the trees. When the rainy season began in May, "we never tired of watching the storm-clouds, three or four at a time in different directions, travelling across the country."[12] The nights were cool, and few insects annoyed the visitors.

He had mixed emotions about Chichén, however. The spaciousness, the broad horizon, and the endless expanse of its ruins exhilarated his spirits. On the other hand, the place had a haunting quality which he admitted he could not convey, "the sensation of a ghostly grandeur and magnificence which becomes almost oppressive to one who wanders day after day amongst the ruined buildings."[13]

The only illness serious enough to interrupt his work in the field occurred during the long season of 1889 at Chichén. He and Sweet caught the fever, but because they suffered attacks on alternate days, they were able to care for each other. At that time they had no native labor available, and they had to bring their own water from the cenote, normally a simple task, but one which the sick men found extremely difficult in their weakened condition. Despite this experience, Maudslay recollected his stay at Chichén "with considerable pleasure and satisfaction."[14]

It should be added, however, that three members of his party suffered illness after he left Izabal in 1884. Price and Gorgonio López returned to Quiriguá to continue surveying and making molds, but the fever attacked them so violently that they quickly gave up the work. When the Maudslays arrived in New Orleans, Anne came down with the fever, but she was able to secure immediate medical attention in the city.

The season of 1885 at Copán began with an unexpected flourish. When Maudslay arrived at the village on February 26, he was received with triumphal arches and an honor guard of soldiers and greeted by a former minister of state of Honduras and a college faculty member. The two hosts, who had waited a week for the visitor, explained that the president of the country had designated them to aid him in his work. Actually, Honduras had just decided to mend its relations with England, and Maudslay, the first citizen of that nation to appear in the country after the new policy was adopted, received the honors.

The reception did not modify the initial coolness between Maudslay and the villagers. For some unexplained reason, the natives "looked upon me anything but favorably when I first came amongst them," he explained. In turn, the archaeologist considered the people dirty and lazy, although he granted that they were "truthful, good tempered, and remarkably honest." The lack of *simpatía* is puzzling; Sylvanus Morley and Gustav Stromsvik in a later generation got along famously with the natives. It is possible that Maudslay was too reserved and perhaps too aloof to appeal to the emotional nature of the villagers. In time, however, the citizens of the town learned to appreciate the sterling qualities of *el sabio*. While he worked there, armies came within thirty miles of Copán, but he refused to flee. Many of his laborers were commandeered for military service, and his regular supply of money from Guatemala City was cut off by the disorders. "When I was reduced to my last dollar, not only did the men left in Copán and the neighbourhood volunteer to go on working for me, saying that they knew I would pay them when I could receive the money to do so, but they actually scraped together the few dollars which could be found in the village and lent them to me, so that I could pay off some workmen who came from distant villages, and were obliged to return to their homes." Don Alfredo, as the locals called him, was deeply touched by this show of "confidence and support."[15]

He was not reserved or aloof when he encountered a fellow archaeologist in the backcountry of Guatemala in March 1882. At that time Désiré Charnay was carrying on his much-publicized exploration of Mexico and Central America. He had ascended the Usumacinta River from Frontera to Tenosique, then went overland almost up to Yaxchilán. He did not know that Maudslay had already camped at those ruins and was short of food. When Maudslay sent some men in a canoe down the river to secure provisions from the Lacandón Indians, the men returned with a message from Charnay. At once the Englishman dispatched a canoe to bring Charnay to Yaxchilán, and quartered him in one of the ancient houses, which had been prepared for his use. In his account of the episode, Maudslay observed that Charnay "very kindly added his ample supply of provisions to my somewhat meagre stock."[16]

But Maudslay failed to tell the whole story. Charnay, who was eager to gain credit for the discovery of the ruins of Yaxchilán, later explained how Maudslay, already on the site, graciously deferred to him. "We shook hands," said Charnay; "he knew my name, he told me his: Alfred Maudslay, Esq., from London; and as my looks betrayed the inward annoyance I felt: 'It's all right,' he said, 'there is no reason why you should look so distressed. My having had the start of you was a mere chance, as it would have been mere chance had it been the other way. You need have no fear on my account, for I am only an amateur, travelling for pleasure. With you the case of course is different. But I do not intend to publish anything. Come, I have had a place got ready for you; and as for the ruins I make them over to you. You can name the town, claim to have discovered it, in fact do what you please. I shall not interfere with you in any way, and you may even dispense with mentioning my name if you please.' I was deeply touched with his kind manner," added Charnay, "and am only too charmed to share with him the glory of having explored this city. We lived and worked together like two brothers, and we parted the best of friends in the world."[17]

In the 1894-95 season Maudslay made his last major expedition into the Maya country. This time his wife accompanied him. The itinerary included the Guatemalan highlands, with stops at Lake Atitlán, Panajachel, and Chichicastenango. In addition to examining the major sites thoroughly, he also took the opportunity to investigate the remains in the vicinity of Rabinal, which Brasseur de Bourbourg had inadequately described a generation earlier, and to measure the sparse ruins at Iximché and Utatlán in order to correct the exaggerations of the earlier writers Juarros and Fuentes. His wife agreed to keep a diary. Their joint experiences appear in *A Glimpse at Guatemala,* which combines accounts of personal adventure with a report of fieldwork, supplemented by accounts of earlier visits Maudslay had made to the sites. The Maudslays wrote and designed the volume over a period of years; it is printed on handmade paper and illustrated with pictures and maps from Alfred's scholarly publications. It remains the most attractive personal and professional narrative of Maya archaeology at the end of the nineteenth century.

In the decades following the last journey to Central America, Maudslay engaged in various activities. For a dozen years he spent some months annually in Mexico, hoping to make something from a gold mine he owned in Zavaleta. Incidentally, he praised the government of Porfirio Díaz because under it foreigners could travel safely through the country. After 1907 he made extended visits to countries in the Mediterranean area. His only major publication during this period was the elaborately annotated and illustrated translation of Bernal Díaz del Castillo's classic work on the Spanish conquest of Mexico, which the Hakluyt Society issued in five volumes; the third volume, consisting entirely of maps, was published to coincide with the meeting of the International Congress of Americanists in Mexico City in 1910.

With ample resources at hand, Maudslay could do much as he pleased. When he sought a pleasant country residence, his chauffeur drove him and his wife around England in search of a suitable spot. He settled at Morney Cross on the Wye River, a few miles from Hereford. There he enlarged a house to suit his needs, and installed his library of valuable books, maps, and manuscripts. He spent much time gardening and fishing, and studied old furniture and embroideries. In 1925 he was annoyed when the doctor required him to give up his hobby of cutting down trees. The following year his wife died, and in 1927 he married a Mrs. Purdon. At this time he wrote *Life in the Pacific Fifty Years Ago,* a memoir of his early adventures, which appeared in 1930. Active almost until the end, he died in January 1931.

Maudslay's great work, *Archaeology,* appears in strange company as part of the multivolume *Biologia*

Centrali-Americana. The reader who peruses the titles in that vast work encounters treatments of arachnida and lepidoptera, diptera and orthoptera, before coming to the archaeology of Middle America, appended to the set as volumes 55-59. Maudslay had the good fortune to know the editors, Frederick Du Cane Godman, a trustee of the British Museum, and Osbert Salvin, a curator at Cambridge University, who invited him to add his contribution. The volumes are attractively printed and were certainly expensive to produce; it is doubtful that a commercial publisher would have risked the cost of issuing the work on Maya ruins as a separate title.

The *Archaeology* is a commanding opus. One volume of text introduces the four volumes of photographs, plans, and colored drawings.[18] Remarkable accuracy and attention to detail made the publication a model of archaeological reporting and a standard reference work on the subject for years to come. The photographs bear compass directions, which are matched by similar directions on the maps. Maudslay employed Anne Hunter to make the drawings, based on the photographs and the molds, which present the inscriptions "restored, as far as with our present knowledge they safely can be, to their original condition."[19] He appreciated the danger of this procedure, but few criticisms of his work have appeared since it came from the press in the 1890s.

The purposes of his labors were several. At first glance, it would appear that he attempted no more than mere description, though his descriptions were more precise and detailed, it is true, than those that had been offered before. But this is only part of the story. Maudslay also planned to make a "careful comparison of the monuments and the inscriptions of the same locality, one with the other, and then the further comparison of the different groups of monuments. . . ."[20] In time, he realized that he could never accomplish that impossible task. Furthermore, he had specific reasons for the production of the molds. He wanted to preserve a record of the original materials; by depositing copies in museums, he believed, he was giving the molds a good chance of surviving after the originals had disappeared. Moreover, the molds preserved an exact record of the inscriptions for the use of scholars, who had so far restricted their study of glyphs to the codices. Once he observed that, for serious work, photographs, no matter how good they are, must be supplemented by examination of the casts.

From the earliest days he gave great attention to the hieroglyphs. He learned that they were to be read from left to right and from top to bottom; he recognized the Initial Series glyph, identified a figure in the Secondary Series, and discovered that the rosette represented the number twenty. Unfortunately for claims of priority, Cyrus Thomas had already announced the reading order of glyphs and Ernst Förstermann had recognized details of the Initial Series from a study of the codices.

When Maudslay learned that Joseph T. Goodman of San Francisco was also working on hieroglyphs, he sought him out in 1892. Goodman, fifty-four years old at the time, had already had a curious career. Born in New York state, he accompanied his father to California in 1856, became a typesetter and then owner of the *Territorial Enterprise,* a newspaper in Virginia City, Nevada. He is always remembered for having given Mark Twain, a reporter on the *Enterprise,* his start in writing. Goodman edited a literary periodical, made a fortune in mining, and settled down to raising grapes. After poring over the inscriptions in Maudslay's *Archaeology,* he identified most of the face numerals up to twenty and some other figures of significance. In time, he concluded that all of the glyphs dealt only with mathematics and the calendar, a view some other Americanists considered too narrow. Maudslay had a conversation with him in San Francisco in 1892, and three years later convinced him to go to England to study the molds. Goodman drew up a table of Maya dates which served scholars for many years. When the California Academy of Sciences showed no interest in publishing the table, Maudslay induced Godman and Salvin to add it to his *Archaeology.* Goodman was never able to support exclusive claims for his discoveries, because friends of

Förstermann maintained that the German had preceded the American in the identification of some of the glyphs. Later on, J. Eric Thompson believed that he found evidence that Goodman had made use of Förstermann's publications.

Deciphering dates raised the question of correlating the Maya calendar with the Christian calendar. In 1905 Goodman put forth a scheme of correlation, which was not taken seriously until it was confirmed by Martínez Hernández two decades later; after J. Eric Thompson amended it, it gained wide acceptance.

In writing about his explorations, Maudslay made occasional suggestions and comments about the sites and the civilization of the early Maya. The Palace at Palenque he considered a collection of buildings erected at various times and designed for religious purposes. He believed that archaeologists had given too little attention to Palenque's tombs and burial mounds, "which I know to be very numerous and believe will prove most interesting."[21] Excavations by later investigators supported his prediction, but he never dreamed that the finest tomb of all rested under the Temple of the Inscriptions. At Copán he found no houses or temples until 1885. He correctly assumed that the pyramids provided foundations for sanctuaries, so he dug on the top of the mound on the north side of the east court and uncovered an elaborate carved doorframe. As for Maya culture, he believed that it had evolved over many years and that it had attained artistic culmination at Palenque and Copán. On the broader subject of the origin of Maya civilization, he held that it was indigenous, and assumed that if any influences had come from Asia they were too few to have had marked effect. He attributed to the Maya a broader geographical range than is now accepted, holding that they "formerly inhabited a considerable portion of Central and South America," and were responsible for Tula, Cholula, and perhaps Teotihuacán.[22]

In later years Maudslay cultivated his interests in a quiet, unobtrusive way. He devoted attention to the Valley of Mexico, and produced the elaborate edition of Bernal Díaz. When stratification attracted attention in Americanist studies, he strongly embraced the value of that new tool for establishing historical sequences.

He exhibited his usual modesty in delivering the presidential address before the Royal Anthropological Institute in 1912. In many professional societies, the speaker uses such an occasion to express some grand philosophical commitment. Not so Maudslay. He chose the title "Some American Problems" to present riddles in Middle American archaeology which called for solution. Showing slides to clarify his statements, he pointed to the appearance of two different races on a stela from Ixkún, called for an explanation of the distinctive decorative style in the structures at Mitla, identified the serpent motif and the water plant or lotus motif and noted the ground plans of Teotihuacán and Kaminaljuyú. Specific and informative, the address posed questions in comparative archaeology.

On those rare occasions when he dealt with unpleasant topics, he controlled his temper, and expressed his views in forceful, though not exaggerated, language. In reviewing the papers of the International Congress of Americanists of 1912, he had to deal with Batres's vindication of his removal of the outer layer of the Pyramid of the Sun at Teotihuacán. In what was perhaps the strongest judgment he made in public, he called Batres's work "a stupendous monument of self assertion and incompetence."[23] Only once did he engage in a public controversy. In 1927 the ardent diffusionist G. Elliott Smith, in an attempt to prove transoceanic contact between Central America and the Old World, revived Jean Frédéric Waldeck's theory that the long-nosed figures seen in decorations at Palenque and Uxmal were elephants. At the time Maudslay was traveling in Egypt, but he was so strongly moved that he sent a note to the editor of the London *Times,* condemning "Waldeck's inaccuracy and the worthlessness of his drawings."[24]

Americanists regarded Maudslay as the dean of Maya studies. When he attended scientific meetings, he made a point of talking to young archaeologists in a kindly, though not condescending, way, and occasionally he reminisced on the trials of exploration in the 1880s and 1890s. At one of those meetings, Sylvanus Morley, already recognized as an authority on Maya epigraphy, counted it an unusual honor when Maudslay invited him to visit Morney Cross.

Official recognition of his services to archaeology came in his later years. Surely his reticence delayed the honors, for the public knew nothing about him, and he made no effort to gain notice. But fellow archaeologists appreciated his contributions. One can be certain that his honorary degrees from Oxford and Cambridge gratified him; the honorary professorship at the national museum of Mexico, however, gave him a special thrill. In the long run, it was T.A. Joyce who arranged the first permanent tribute to the man. During his years in Central America, Maudslay sent many molds and some original pieces to England. Those items were given a brief exhibition at the Victoria and Albert Museum in the 1890s, and then were stored away and forgotten. Three decades later, after considerable prodding by Joyce, the British Museum acquired the molds,[25] added the original panels which that institution already owned, and set up a permanent exhibit in a hall bearing Maudslay's name. Since then the public has been able to see the works, including the Yaxchilán panels which are among the finest examples of Maya art.

Always the scholar, Maudslay bequeathed his holdings to institutions where they would be most useful. Some of his paintings and a sum of money went to the Royal Geographical Society, in which he had long been active. The manuscripts of Gouverneur Morris, inherited from his first wife, who was a granddaughter of the New York statesman, went to the Library of Congress. Cambridge received the objects from his early years in the Pacific. And to the British Museum he gape his library of Middle American manuscripts, books, and maps.

The favorable estimate of Maudslay's contribution remains undiminished. The controversy over priority in decipherment of glyphs recedes with the passage of time, because the understanding of all of the glyphs, the entire problem, remains the vital issue. Maudslay, it seems, realized this, for he never came forth to reassert claims of priority. He brought to Maya studies a new attitude, which was basic to the future development of the field: he believed that the source materials, especially inscriptions, must be made available to scholars and that those materials must be presented with utmost accuracy and detail. Those qualities prompted H.E.D. Pollock, writing less than a decade after Maudslay's death, to characterize him as the first modern archaeologist in the Maya field.

3

Sylvanus G. Morley

In many ways Morley stands out as the most colorful figure among Maya archaeologists of the earlier part of the twentieth century. He possessed a natural social charm, which made friends for him everywhere he went. Closely related to his ability to get along easily with people was his exuberant personality. He enjoyed everything he did, from the simplest chores to the solution of intricate problems with glyphs, and he radiated tremendous enthusiasm for the Maya. His infectious excitement, sometimes amusing in detail, created an aura of liveliness and vitality. A master raconteur, he enjoyed the humor and goodwill his anecdotes produced. He displayed enthusiasm and social charm in the most natural, sincere way, for they were basic to his personality.

Although he exhibited great zest in his everyday activities, he also had his problems. There were unfulfilled ambitions, disappointments, and the trials of poor health. Those misfortunes he considered as incidental interruptions to the full enjoyment of life. The failures and the disappointments he quickly forgot, and when sickness was not overpowering, he indulged in quips and jokes. A lively personality and a driving passion to do things made him a remarkable man as well as an outstanding archaeologist.

Morley enjoyed good luck in his early environment, or to put it another way, he grew up with advantages. He was born in 1883 in a middle-class family in West Chester, Pennsylvania. His father taught science and held an administrative post at Pennsylvania Military Academy, and his mother was the daughter of a Belgian teacher of languages at the same institution. When Vay, as Sylvanus was always known to his friends, entered his teens, the family moved to Colorado, where his father became manager and part owner of a mine. After eleven years in the West, the father died in an accident, and Vay's mother moved back to Pennsylvania.

When Vay attended high school in Colorado, he showed the first signs of interest in prehistoric America. At the age of fifteen he was reading Lew Wallace's *The Fair God* and Prescott's *Conquest of Mexico.* At the suggestion of a friend, he wrote to Frederick W. Putnam, curator of the Peabody Museum at Harvard University, and asked many questions about the pre-Columbian Indians. Putnam, far from ignoring the juvenile letter, advised him to read H.H. Bancroft's *The Native Races,* which was a stiff assignment. Vay located the large set in the local penitentiary and borrowed volume after volume, though he never indicated how much he got out of the weighty reading. On completing high school, he wanted to become an archaeologist. His father vetoed the idea because of the scarcity of jobs in that profession and insisted that he attend Pennsylvania Military Academy.

By the time he completed the three-year course at the academy, his father had died, and Vay, now twenty-one, made another attempt to follow his own wishes. By this time he had discovered how to exert his personal charm to convince people of the utter reasonableness of his desires.

So he easily gained his mother's consent to study archaeology at Harvard and induced his aunt to provide ample funds for his education.

Four years at Harvard prepared him for a professional career and also allowed him the enjoyment of a carefree existence. He spent money on clothes, the theater, dinner parties with a few companions, and dates with girls. Eventually he settled down to courting the young woman who was to become his wife, and he gave increasing attention to the courses in anthropology and archaeology. Alfred M. Tozzer, who had field experience in the Maya country, encouraged him, and Professor Charles Bowditch saw to it that he received several small financial grants. When Morley completed the graduate program, he married; seven years later, however, his wife received a divorce in Reno.

By the time Vay received the M.A. in 1908, he had also gained valuable field experience. Early in 1907 he made his first visit to Mexico and examined the major Maya sites in preparation for future exploration there. He extended the tour to central Mexico for sightseeing, thanks to a generous sum advanced by his aunt. Then, in the summer of the same year, he engaged in excavation in the Southwest under the direction of Edgar L. Hewett, head of the School of American Research in Santa Fe. In company with Alfred M. Kidder, later to become a distinguished archaeologist, and John Gould Fletcher, who had not yet begun his career as a poet, Morley spent two months exploring and excavating Pueblo sites in Colorado and New Mexico. Hewett was so impressed by Vay's ability that he hired him as his assistant.

The six years under Hewett gave Vay valuable experience of various kinds. He made an expedition to Yucatán, carried on more fieldwork in the Southwest, began to give lectures on the Maya, published some articles, and spent several seasons at Quiriguá, Guatemala deciphering hieroglyphs, and during one season managed the entire project at that site. In addition, he learned to get along with Hewett, a man who could stimulate and also exasperate subordinates by being encouraging one minute and callous the next.

During his work under Hewett, Morley threw himself into the only non-Maya cause of his career. Some residents of Santa Fe launched a crusade to retain the old Mexican-Indian style of architecture instead of succumbing to contemporary forms. Vay lived in an old house which he had modernized without changing its lines, and he strongly believed in the crusade. In the end, he led the entire movement. He used the services of specialists in architecture and city planning, learned the value of public relations, and was largely responsible for the ultimate success of the campaign. Visitors to Santa Fe today rarely realize that the Maya archaeologist helped to create the present unique atmosphere of the city.

At the age of thirty, Morley decided he was ready for bigger game. There appeared to be no future in continuing to work under Hewett, and an important, ambitious plan filled the man's mind. With only a few years of experience to his credit, he submitted to the prestigious Carnegie Institution of Washington a plan to excavate the elaborate site of Chichén Itzá in Yucatán. Any outsider would have considered his action presumptious if not foolhardy; by this time, however, Morley knew what he could do, he had confidence in the wisdom of his plans, and he also had a network of friends who could use their influence on his behalf.

For a year and a half he suffered agonies of uncertainty over the outcome of his plan. The complicated story involved sharp differences of opinion among officials of the Carnegie Institution and the indirect influence of friends and enemies of Morley on the decisions of those officials. At one stage the C.I.W. invited W.H.R. Rivers of Cambridge University and Albert E. Jenks of the University of Minnesota to submit their respective plans for research in ethnology so that the most worthy program might be selected. The three plans were printed for final consideration by the board of trustees. Just before that meeting a committee of the board made the crucial decision.

Morley, the youngest and most inexperienced of the three scholars, had his plan accepted. He presented a logical and persuasive account of what he wanted to do at Chichén, complete with excellent photographs. The committee voted two to one for his project, and the trustees ratified that decision.

Some time later the committee selected Morley to head the project, and after six months' delay in notifying him of the appointment, he was hired as a member of the institution's staff. At that time strained relations between the United States and Mexico caused the project to be shelved indefinitely. So by the middle of 1914 Vay had the job he wanted, but he also had nothing in particular to do.

Through good luck or persuasive conversation, he managed to turn the hollow appointment into an opportunity for research which eventually made him a respected scholar in Maya archaeology. During an interview with President Robert Woodward of the C.I.W., Vay spoke excitedly about his last expedition to Central America, explained that he had collected many unknown hieroglyphs, and outlined his plan to assemble all the glyphs he could find in order to establish a chronology of the Maya sites. Woodward listened and thought fast. As a stopgap until the project at Chichén could be launched, he had decided to put Morley to work compiling a bibliography on Yucatán. But Morley's enthusiasm for Maya chronology moved Woodward to act with common sense, and so he told him to continue work on the hieroglyphs. A fortunate decision! No one dreamed that ten years would pass before Mexico would be ready for the project at Chichén; during that decade Morley made annual expeditions to the Maya country and completed a significant part of the work on Maya chronology.

In his travels in Middle America Morley demonstrated a remarkable ability to get along amicably with the natives. Incidents that occurred on numerous visits to Copán, in northwestern Honduras, illustrate his methods. Always sensitive to the feelings of others, he carefully avoided actions that might humiliate a native or cause him to lose face; conscious also of the importance of group thought, he made every effort to observe local customs. Although he had visited Copán several times since 1910 and had made many friends, including the alcalde, when he came from the ruins on the first day of his visit in 1915, he received an order to appear at the town hall to show his passport. Without changing clothes, he hurried to the hall, where a petty official immediately fined him five dollars for entering the place with a weapon—namely, the machete which was part of his field gear. Most North Americans would have been indignant; Morley knew better. Without protest, he went to his room to leave the machete and to get the money, and when he appeared to pay the fine, he encountered Juan Ramón Cueva, his old friend the alcalde, who refused the money even after Morley offered it as a gift to the town. Then several natives invited him to drink, and at once he proposed a toast to the town officials. Next came an invitation to a ball that night, and he appeared in his best clothes, danced with each señorita, as was the custom, and never mentioned the fine.

On later visits to Copán he cemented his friendship with the villagers. Natives informed him of newly found hieroglyphs, serenaded him with a band concert on the first night of his arrival, and in 1919 elected him a citizen of Copán, an honor which touched him deeply. On the publication of his *The Inscriptions of Copan,* he presented a specially bound copy to the village, though he realized that no one could read it. As the years passed, local officials pointed to the book with pride, remarking that it weighed over four pounds. At the end of each season at Copán, Vay carefully paid his bills, including a sum for the privilege of working at the ruins, and then he added a gift of money for the local church. Once he had set up a rudimentary museum in one of the municipal rooms; on a later visit, when he found the items in disarray, he was careful to utter no complaint.

He had equal success in turning hostile natives into friends on a visit to eastern Yucatán in 1922. The independent *sublevado* Indians, who refused to recognize the sovereignty of Mexico and distrusted all white men, lived near the site of Tulum, a walled Maya settlement on the coast. Tulum contained archaeological data that required examination. So Morley hired a rickety motorboat and took Samuel K. Lothrop and Oliver Ricketson, archaeologists, and Muddy Esquivel, a native servant who could speak Maya, to Tulum and boldly camped in the Castillo, the major structure. Candle stubs and decorations indicated that natives worshipped in the upper room of the building. Soon a delegation of Indians appeared and sought the protection of England! It seems that a visitor many years earlier had promised to bring them under the rule of Queen Victoria. Vay greeted his guests with handshakes and a round of wine, and Muddy skirted the confusion of nationalities by explaining that a man now ruled England and perhaps he would soon pay attention to the Indians' wishes.

After a week passed, another delegation appeared; this time each man carried a gun. Why were the visitors cutting down so many trees at Tulum? Were the Mexicans planning to settle there? Morley carefully identified the chiefs and greeted them. He explained that he wished only to photograph the ruins. Realizing that the Indians were not convinced, he placed the decision in their hands: Would they give him permission to cut trees and take pictures? A tense period followed while the natives conferred on the proposition. Finally they announced that they would consider the outsiders as friends. At that, Morley distributed cigarettes and cognac to seal the decision, turned on the phonograph to entertain them, took their pictures, and dispatched a gift of quinine for the sick wife of one of the chiefs. He also left Tulum with the first extensive archaeological report on that site.

Vay enjoyed adventure, especially if it sometimes required resourcefulness, as was the case in 1917 when he served as an intelligence agent for the United States Navy in Central America. Like Herbert Spinden, Morley also became an ensign to carry out secret service. Although he never explained fully what he did, it is clear that he examined the coastal waters of Honduras and eastern Yucatán to determine where enemy submarines might be able to land. The adventures he related about this expedition, however, were not connected with intelligence work. He chartered a boat and crew to take him and John Held, Jr., the cartoonist, who was also on secret service, drawing maps for Vay, down the Mosquito Coast. At one place he encountered several men seeking old Spanish treasure and boldly approached them, hoping that they would not resent his curiosity. Everyone was amiable, even to explaining the trouble they had in interpreting an old map which indicated the location of the treasure. After Vay took a dory to return to his boat, he heard a violent explosion and was sure that they had shot at him. No; they just happened to touch off some dynamite to tear up the beach in search of the elusive treasure. At the town of Princapolka, where a traveling circus was performing for several days, though not on the day of Morley's visit, he paid for a special performance to entertain his party. At Cape Gracias he encountered a man with a revolver who advanced toward him, declaring he was about to kill him. With admirable self-control, Morley talked and talked to the man as he backed away from him, inviting him to have a drink and proposing other diversions before he committed the deed. After tense minutes of parlaying, he convinced his assailant not to shoot. Having settled the matter, Morley turned to leave and then heard the revolver go off. Someone happened to jostle the man, and the accidental shot hurt no one.

Near the end of the expedition he had still other adventures. For nineteen days he and Held were marooned on the Hog Islands off the coast of Honduras. A few people lived on the place, and the two men had the use of a room in an inhabitant's house, though their meals consisted almost entirely of canned beans. Vay contented himself with putting his records into shape and watching

Held draw intriguing sketches. Weeks later Morley visited friends in Guatemala City, enjoyed a Christmas dinner, and on the way back to the hotel that night he experienced earthquakes. They continued day after day until the city was almost completely destroyed. His hotel was demolished. One night he slept in the patio of a friend's house, then for some nights in the United States legation, and finally with friends in a private railroad coach. Walls crumbled at every quake, and the railroad car proved to be the safest place. He experienced his usual good luck. Despite narrow escapes, he suffered no injury, took many photographs of ruined buildings, and continued to make a lengthy record of daily experiences in his diary.

The most dramatic and tragic experience of all of his expeditions occurred during this early period of his professional career. In 1916 he teamed up with Arthur Carpenter from the Peabody Museum to explore parts of the Petén. The season had both successful and disappointing moments, and near the end of the expedition Morley scored a triumph in the discovery of Uaxactún in the northern Petén. Following the lead of a fever-ridden chiclero, the party moved north and west, and above Tikal the chiclero led them to the vast assemblage of ruins, which Vay named Uaxactún. Members of the party hastily examined the area, and Vay found a hieroglyphic inscription, which he read as A.D. 50 (Spinden correlation), the oldest Maya date discovered to that time. Later on, he sent annual expeditions to excavate Uaxactún, with valuable archaeological results.

Feeling happy over the discovery, Vay and his party headed south and east for British Honduras. Just before they reached the boundary, members of the party rode single file through the brush and approached a growth of trees at the side of the trail. Shots rang out and killed Romero, a native guide, and Moise Lafleur, physician of the expedition. At the time Morley believed the attack came from revolutionists, but he later learned that his men had been killed by soldiers from the Guatemalan army. Eventually, he reached British Honduras and was reunited with Carpenter. Morley claimed Lafleur's body and buried it, and received some of his friend's personal belongings. After a harrowing day and a half of these details, during which the Guatemalan authorities failed to give a reasonable explanation for the attack, he wrote a lengthy explanation of the whole affair to President Woodward. Although Vay was naturally an emotional man, he displayed exemplary self-control during the entire crisis. In the weeks that followed, however, he was troubled by nightmares of the tragedy. When he returned to the States, he sought out Lafleur's brother in Louisiana to express his sympathy. Despite numerous protests, the C.I.W. never received apology or satisfaction for the tragic mistake of the Guatemalan soldiers.

In 1923 Morley finally received the long-awaited instructions to arrange for the signing of a contract between the C.I.W. and the Mexican government to launch the project at Chichén Itzá. Carnegie officials, however, did not act hastily; they wanted to inspect Chichén at first hand and also to create goodwill in Yucatán for the work. John C. Merriam, the paleontologist who had become president of the C.I.W. in 1920, had never seen the site. Barclay Parsons, a civil engineer and C.I.W. trustee, had always strongly supported the project. So Merriam and Parsons visited Mérida in February 1923, accompanied by a number of scholars from archaeological institutions in the United States to add prestige to the occasion.

Morley played the role of advance man and general agent for the entertainment of the distinguished guests. He knew the leading families of the city; he was an eligible man of forty, divorced and unattached, who attracted the young women of the old families; and he adapted himself perfectly to Latin American customs and attitudes. A virtuoso in social activities, he moved from one event to another, always fresh and affable, adding a light, humorous touch to conversations. The round of activities extended over three weeks, day and night every day of the week, while the foreign guests were present. Morley was on the go at least sixteen hours a day, all for the purpose of cementing good relations between the Yucatecans and the visitors. Thanks to his physical stamina, his good humor never failed him, and he enjoyed every bit of the strenuous schedule.

The Yucatecans certainly knew how to display friendship and hospitality; they all but overwhelmed their guests with social attention. A band, playing North American college tunes, greeted Merriam as he descended from the train; high officials of Yucatán welcomed him; and then Morley rushed him and Parsons off to a dinner in Centenario Park. One event crowded upon another—the governor's banquet followed by dancing, a meeting of the local archaeological society to confer membership on visiting scholars, all-day excursions to Uxmal and Chichén, a journey to the Cave of Loltún with a banquet served in the governor's private railroad coach, balls of all kinds, and an endless round of formal dinners. Merriam and Parsons began to weary of the festivities, but like gentlemen who realized their social obligations, they steeled themselves for more dinners and long trips to the ruins. During the rigid schedule of activities, Morley found ways to relax. He carried on simultaneous flirtations with several belles of the city, joined a few friends on the rooftop of a restaurant after midnight for conversation, and prepared notes for lengthy entries in his diary. Although somewhat weary after the foreign guests left, he gave an illustrated lecture on Maya civilization to a large and distinguished audience in the Peón Contreras Theater in Mérida.

In the end, he knew that the weeks of social activity had been successful. Merriam and Parsons, especially after the visit to Chichén, were more enthusiastic than ever about the project. Then Vay made a quick trip to Guatemala to secure renewal of the concession to excavate Uaxactún, and managed to circumvent the troublesome Gates, then in charge of archaeology in Guatemala, by gaining the renewal through another official. By April Morley was in Mexico City preparing for the last act of the negotiations.

With friends posted everywhere, he learned of potential threats to the contract and tried to counteract them. In June Merriam came from the States, was entertained quietly to avoid arousing anti-United States sentiment, made a trip to Teotihuacán, where the last details were settled, and paid a courtesy call on President Obregón. The contract was signed.

Morley felt immense satisfaction. He had had the first vision of the excavation of Chichén when he visited the site in 1907; he had gained the prospect of carrying out that vision in 1914 with his appointment to the C.I.W. But a decade had had to pass before he could be sure that the vision would become a reality. In later years, he liked to tell impulsive people the story as an example of the need for endless patience. He was too modest to suggest that his unique personality also had much to do with making the vision a reality.

Nor would Morley admit that, during those active weeks of February 1923 when he had come to know and admire Felipe Carrillo, governor of Yucatán, he had encountered a problem—a problem which he never resolved. Emotional rather than analytical, Vay responded to stimulating people, regardless of their social or political philosophies. Such was the curious friendship between Morley and Carrillo, for the two men represented opposite ends of the political spectrum. Vay was a middle-class conservative whose views had been formed in the years before the First World War. Carrillo, from humble Maya origins, headed a socialist government which aimed to improve the conditions of the native Indians. Vay bridled at the workers' leagues of resistance and the red flags in every village; to him, they represented the Red, or Bolshevist, atmosphere of the country. He had, however, adopted the rule that he must have friendly relations with the highest state officials in the land where he wished to work; and so with some misgiving he arranged an early meeting with the governor.

If Morley usually captivated anyone he interviewed, this time the tables were turned, and Carrillo completely captivated Vay. The governor was a large man, radiating self-confidence, leadership, and geniality. His knowledge of the Maya language and the Maya past and his immediate support of the C.I.W. project won Morley over to him at once.

In the ensuing weeks Vay learned more about this unusual man. Carrillo avoided use of the official palace and carried on business in a makeshift office in modest quarters, where any Indian, no matter how humble, could personally lay his troubles before him. He introduced baseball into many towns of the state to provide a healthy sport for young boys and teenagers. Under his regime the peon gained independence from his overlord, the wealthy were taxed to support social reform, and divorce laws were relaxed. A few years earlier Carrillo had translated the Mexican Constitution into Maya so that the natives might understand their rights. If the governor championed the common people, he was also at home in the best social circles of Mérida; he lived in a fine house on a fashionable avenue, was the perfect gentleman at social affairs, and spoke felicitously on ceremonial occasions.

Carrillo, of course, found a kindred spirit in Vay. The governor wined and dined him, enjoyed Morley's conversation and his deep interest in all things Maya, and never intruded his political philosophy on the archaeologist. Vay marveled at the man's leadership; when the party of visitors became lost in the Cave of Loltún, it was Carrillo who took command, issued stern orders, and extricated the frightened tourists. As the weeks passed, the governor confided in Vay more and more and on one occasion asked him for advice on his love life, which involved three women at the same time. Vay never revealed how he replied to that problem.

Although Morley retained his own political views, he admired the socialist governor. Once, perhaps as a favor to Carrillo, he even addressed a workers' group on archaeology. If the red flags and the socialist philosophy chilled him, he could see sense in baseball for youth and could understand the natives' need for personal dignity.

After attending a dinner of local aristocrats who hated the governor and made snide remarks about him, Morley noted that that class refused to realize that a new age had dawned. A year later, when the military, supported by the aristocrats, overthrew the regime and shot Carrillo, Morley considered it a dastardly deed. He never recognized that he was caught in a paradox, that he respected and liked Carrillo and applauded some of his reforms, and at the same time despised the socialist rule. For Morley, there was no paradox. He recognized only that Carrillo was a fascinating and engaging man and that he liked him.

At this time in the 1920s Vay realized that his attitudes had changed, though he never probed his own thought. In the early years he had been an Episcopalian, attending services irregularly and enjoying the drama of the High Church service. But even before the First World War he deserted formal religion and belief in a future life. He was not, however, as immune to the appeal of religion as he believed. In his hotel room in Mérida he heard strains of music from the nearby church of Tercera Orden, and he wandered in to enjoy the service and the procession. Sometimes he referred to his godlessness, and once he admitted to a Yucatecan friend that he wished he could regain his faith, but that it was impossible. It is interesting that he never attacked religion; he simply remained indifferent to it until he embraced Catholicism on his death bed.

He also responded to the emotional appeal of the Maya ruins. If repeated visits to Uxmal or Copán or Quiriguá dulled the responses of some persons, not so for Morley. Every visit renewed and increased his appreciation of the artistic attainments of the ancient builders. He considered the Governor's Palace at Uxmal the finest building in prehistoric America, a view shared by many other people. From the earliest years he developed the habit of paying a farewell call on the major ruins before leaving a site, remarking that they were old friends who did not wither or die. When amoebic dysentery laid him low one season at Chichén, he refused to depart for a hospital in New

Orleans until natives drove him to the new Temple of the Warriors and carried him on a cot up the steep stairway to see the progress of excavation on the platform of the pyramid. On a visit to Uxmal, some of his associates dug a few feet beneath the surface of the ground and brought up a little clay figure of the Formative, or Archaic, Period. While his friends gasped at the implications of that crude object, Vay turned away unimpressed; any day he preferred the beauty of E-sub VII or the majesty of the Castillo at Chichén. He did not disparage the powers of the mind, for he had deciphered too many hieroglyphic dates to go that far. But when he had the choice, he preferred the visual creations that moved the emotions.

On setting up headquarters in 1924 at Chichén, where he continued to spend half of each year until 1940, he determined to enjoy life as much as possible. Despite many seasons in the bush, he valued the amenities of civilization. At Chichén good food, prepared by an excellent Chinese cook, turned the evening dinner into the social event of the day. All staff members and visitors gathered at one table. Sometimes exotic dishes appeared, and for celebrations like birthdays the cook always prepared a decorated cake. Morley presided at the head of the table, carefully steering the conversation into pleasant or humorous channels, and encouraged the relation of anecdotes or reminiscences. After dinner he might play a worn-out record of "Tiger Rag" on the phonograph or insist on playing bridge.

He married Frances, his second wife, in 1927, and brought her to Chichén. To provide private living quarters, he had a comfortable house with modern conveniences built on the grounds. Frances took over management of the meals for the staff, became interested in the welfare of the children of the local natives, and added a feminine touch to the place.

As director of the archaeological project, Vay relied on able staff members to carry out the daily work of excavation and restoration. His intuition probably helped him to assemble an excellent group of assistants. Jerry O.

Kilmartin, of the U.S. Geological Survey, went ahead in 1924 to prepare quarters for the staff and to survey the ruins. Earl Morris and his wife Anne were in the first party; later on, Karl Ruppert, H.E.D. Pollock, John Bolles, the artist Jean Charlot, and others joined the staff. J. Eric Thompson came from England as a specialist in hieroglyphs. Gustav Stromsvik, who appeared seemingly from nowhere and became a valuable handyman, revealed a variety of unsuspected talents; not only was he expert at contriving mechanical devices, but he also wrote learned papers on metates. Paul Martin put in his first fieldwork under Morley at Chichén, and was grateful for the encouragement he received. These men liked their director, and Morley in turn allowed them considerable latitude and judgment in carrying out assigned tasks. He was always tactful, usually making suggestions rather than giving direct orders, and on the completion of a task, he lavished complimentary remarks on the fortunate man. In the annual reports he meticulously mentioned every staff member by name and cited the work each had done during the season.

Although the men liked Morley for his friendly disposition, they were amused by his foibles, and sometimes played jokes on him. At times he could be naïve or too trustful of his companions. Occasionally he thought up a harebrained idea that his associates found difficult to dispel. He worshipped the Maya past and present, saw only noble virtues in them, and always excused their faults. He could praise the "beauty" of some execrable object, simply because it was Maya. The pranks the staff played on him had no lasting ill effects, because his anger was brief and his forgiveness complete. Despite his foibles, everyone appreciated the good humor he spread among the group.

A stream of visitors, increasing in number as the years passed, came to Chichén. Although many accounts of the excavation appeared in magazines and newspapers, Morley himself was perhaps the most effective public relations representative for the project. He gave each visitor a personally conducted tour of the ruins, explained the significance of the major structures, and injected humorous remarks into the recital. After some years, when the visitors became too numerous, he gave up the tours except for distinguished guests, who were also generally invited to the evening dinner.

As a special entertainment, he sometimes gave a phonograph concert in the ball court. The rectangular structure, 545 feet long and 225 feet wide, open at the top, with walls 30 feet high on two sides, had amazing acoustical properties. Servants placed the phonograph at the north end of the court, and other servants strewed pillows for the guests at the south end. On a moonlight night, with a slight breeze, and the dark shapes of the walls outlined against the sky, the strains of Beethoven or Brahms created an eerie effect. Determined not to desecrate the venerable ruins, he restricted the selections to classical music.

The concerts emphasized the uncanny secret of the ball court. Not only did sound carry perfectly over its length, but in some places the human voice produced a perfect echo. When Vay learned that Leopold Stokowski, famous conductor of the Philadelphia Symphony Orchestra, was studying acoustics for outdoor concerts, he invited him to examine the structure in order to discover the cause of its unique acoustical properties. Stokowski came for several days; he played phonograph records at every conceivable spot in the court, and staff members incidentally enjoyed the orchestral music as it floated over the ruins. Vay and Stokowski became great friends, but the conductor left without learning the secret of the ball court.

Morley relished the life at Chichén. He enjoyed the comradeship of the staff. The stream of visitors seemed to support his conviction that the public wanted to know and appreciate the ruins of the ancient civilization. He continued to work on his own research, compiling glyphs, tracing the generations of the Xiu family, and investigating the Leyden Plate.

He continued to make expeditions during the twenties

and thirties, though not as frequently as formerly. When he could not credit the reports of two groups of assistants who examined Cobá in 1926, he made the trip himself. Several years later he went to Uaxactún to see the progress of the C.I.W. team at that site; the workers did not tell him about the discovery of mound E-sub VII until they brought him face to face with it for the sheer pleasure of seeing his amazement over the flowing beauty of that monument. After C.L. Lundell, cruising the area for oil, reported impressive ruins in southwestern Yucatán, Morley made an elaborate expedition to Calakmul in 1932. In addition to two trips on the Usumacinta River, he made a curious journey to see a group of *sublevado* Indians in Quintana Roo in 1935, and incidentally used his influence to quiet their fears of Mexican authority.

Excitement over his work and a sensitive regard for the natives marked many of his actions in Middle America. He put enthusiasm into everything he did, especially when dealing with Maya archaeology. At a new site he was everywhere at once, striding heedlessly through the vegetation to examine a stela, climbing over ruined structures to see what he could find, and sometimes lying under a stela as the workmen raised it, so that he could read the glyphs at the first moment, while onlookers gasped at the possibility of serious accident or even death. On his first visit to Yucatán in 1907, his feverish interest kept him working on a ruin from six in the morning until six at night without a break, until Adelberto, his native assistant, reminded him that normal men take food at regular intervals. In the museum of the University of Pennsylvania one day in the late 1930s Vay happened to look over the shoulder of a young woman at a drawing board. He became so excited at her work that he went out and collected money from wealthy friends to send her to Middle America to make drawings of the ruins as they looked in their prime. Tatiana Proskouriakoff emerged as a Maya scholar of high repute.

During his many years in Mexico and Guatemala, Vay showed a tender regard for the feelings of the natives. At one site two Indian laborers whom he had never seen before greeted him like an old friend; he replied in the same way, realizing that they only wanted to show their fellows that they knew the archaeologist. When native domestics failed to appear for work because they had been overcelebrating, he ignored the absence and never referred to it. On a trip to Uxmal his chauffeur Jirón, accustomed to driving on flat roads, had to try three times before he could bring the car to the summit of a hill. During the ordeal, Vay kept repeating to his guests that Jirón could do it; and on arriving at the top he boasted that he knew Jirón could do it. At Chichén, Petuch, a native handyman, misunderstood Vay's orders and drove a truck away from the office when he should have waited for Morley. Furiously angry, Vay fired him on the spot. Some hours later, when Morley learned that it had been a misunderstanding and that Petuch was crying his heart out, he rushed to the natives' quarters, consoled Petuch, and restored him to his job. Thomas Gann, fellow archaeologist, had good reason to call Morley the little friend of all the world.

Despite occasional periods of illness, Vay retained his vigor and enthusiasm as he grew older. On various occasions he revealed different facets of his personality and character. When he got caught in internal Mexican politics, he showed astute judgment in extricating himself without damage. Ever grateful to the C.I.W. for the opportunities it gave him, he remained faithful to the institution even after suffering something of a demotion. And perpetual excitement over the Maya moved him to produce books for scholars and to popularize the same subject for the public at large.

When the Mexican Historical Congress met in Mérida in 1935, Morley suddenly found himself in the midst of a hornet's nest. He had invited the delegates to visit Chichén on a Sunday which fell in the middle of the scheduled meetings. Shortly after the sessions began in Mérida, however, a leftist group of delegates, supported by the government of Yucatán, physically took over the meetings and changed the name to the Revolutionary Congress of Mexican History. The fact that Vay detested the leftists was of little importance; more significant was the principle that the C.I.W. must not become involved in the internal politics of Mexico.

On two occasions he had to decide whether to lean toward the leftists or the conservatives. He resolved to follow the example of Alfonso Toro, chief of the department of monuments of the Mexican government, as the wisest course. So one day Morley cancelled an address he was scheduled to give because Toro had done the same thing, and later he refused to sign a complaint of the conservatives against the leftist takeover, despite his personal views, because Toro also withheld his signature.

That Sunday entertainment scheduled for Chichén worried Vay. As a man who valued goodwill and avoided rancor at any cost, he wanted to keep political controversy off the site of Chichén, where the C.I.W. carried on its work. At 9:30 in the morning five buses and twenty automobiles discharged the delegates on the grounds. Morley was in top form as he greeted the guests and then led them from structure to structure, explaining Maya civilization and making humorous remarks. At 12:30, when everyone was weary, he assembled the guests at the main house, where servants distributed sandwiches, tamales, deviled eggs, tinned pineapple, crackers, and cold beer. He read messages of greeting from Merriam and Kidder. When he added felicitous remarks of his own, he committed a grammatical blunder in Spanish, which produced a roar of laughter. Then he led the delegates out to see more structures and hear his explanations. At 3:30 he bade the visitors goodby.

With satisfaction, he realized that he had accomplished his aim. Everyone had been so busy with ruins, a refreshing lunch, happy remarks, and then more ruins that politics never cropped up during the entertainment. If Vay was weary—he had climbed ten pyramids during the tour—he was also happy, for the C.I.W. remained untouched by the events of the congress.

The C.I.W., dedicated to scholarly research, had formulated high standards for its archaeological program. From the beginning, two important policies guided its actions. It refused to ask for artifacts, and it promised to restore many ancient structures. Morley faithfully supported both policies.

The refusal to ask for artifacts which might be found in the course of excavation originated accidentally in 1913, when President Woodward, who disliked the archaeological project, insisted that the C.I.W. must not assume the functions of a museum, but must restrict its work to excavation and scholarly reports of the results. Fortunately, the policy coincided with the rising nationalistic fervor in Mexico, and thus gave the C.I.W. a strong bargaining point over institutions that sought to remove the finest specimens for their museums, a practice which had been widespread in the past.

The other policy of the C.I.W. required faithful restoration of the ancient structures so that the public could enjoy them as a part of the nation's heritage. Mexico insisted on this idea, and Morley supported it, because he wanted to spread knowledge of the Maya to the layman. In order to ensure faithful restoration, the C.I.W. followed the rigid policy of utilizing only stones which had fallen from a structure and adding no others. If modern materials like steel supports were used to preserve a building, they were hidden from view. Restoration, of course, vastly increased the expense and often the problems of excavation. Fortunately, the C.I.W. was able to bear the cost, and it did so willingly, realizing that careful restoration achieved the most acceptable scientific result.

Both policies were illustrated in the spectacular discovery during the early years of the project at Chichén. Earl Morris uncovered a rubble-strewn mound and disclosed the Temple of the Warriors. On finding an inner temple, which he wished to leave open to the public, he solved the engineering problem by inserting steel beams to support the superstructure. Also the two giant stone serpents at the top of the stairs were pierced with steel rods in order to hold them in the original upright position. Today the visitor is not aware of these modern supports. On the other hand, no restoration of the roof of the temple or of the colonnade was attempted, because the materials had disappeared.

During the excavation of the Temple of the Warriors, staff members found a fine mosaic turquoise disk with a fascinating design. But the original wooden base of the disk had decomposed. To preserve the form of the mosaic, the C.I.W. sent Siochi Ichikawa from New York to Chichén, where he spent six weeks tediously transferring the tesserae to a new wooden base. When the restoration was complete, Morley handed the disk over to the Mexican Government in accordance with the agreement that the C.I.W. would retain no objects.

Morley was happy to support policies which benefited both parties. Mexico eventually had restored Maya buildings available for public enjoyment, as well as smaller objects like the disk in its National Museum in Mexico City. The C.I.W. issued many publications, embodying results of excavation and research, and thus made the scientific data available to scholars everywhere. As Morley fully realized, no other policy could have been more successful in establishing good relations between the United States and Mexico.

After a few years as director of the project at Chichén, Vay failed to satisfy his employers in regard to the larger aims of the study of Maya civilization. In the original proposal of 1913, he had presented as the project's goal the elucidation of all aspects of ancient Maya civilization, or, in other words, the contribution of the Maya to the history of civilization. By the late 1920s, after the project had been under way for five or six years, C.I.W. officials considered Morley's aim too narrow, and they placed Alfred V. Kidder over him to develop more meaningful objectives. Certainly this action hurt Vay, though he never indicated it.

By this time Kidder was one of the most respected archaeologists in the country. Two years younger than

Morley, he had been educated in private schools in New England and Switzerland and had completed the A.B. at Harvard in 1908. The work in the West with Morley, in the summer of 1907, caused him to desert medicine for archaeology. He firmly established his reputation with the publication of *An Introduction to the Study of Southwestern Archaeology* in 1924. As Carnegie officials became disillusioned with Morley's objectives, they found Kidder's broad scope and interdisciplinary approach increasingly attractive. Moreover, he possessed unusual gifts as an administrator, for he was amiable, used suggestion and persuasion in place of command, and had a relaxed, casual air which put everyone at ease. And so the Carnegie officials created the Historical Division, and made Kidder head of it. The Middle American project, of course, was the most significant part of the new division. If Morley had to have a supervisor, he could not have been more fortunate.

The story has a curious sequel. In line with advanced thought of the 1920s, Kidder inaugurated a vast interdisciplinary program to produce a grand synthesis, which would answer the "big" questions: how did the Maya rise from savagery to civilization, what factors explain their achievements, why did their civilization fall, and what forces brought the contemporary Maya to their present condition? Kidder conceived environment as the logical beginning of the problem, and broadened the program by bringing in specialists to investigate, among other things, the flora, fauna, vegetation, hydrography, disease, and folklore of Yucatán. Each subject received detailed examination by first-rate scholars in the respective fields.

Kidder's plan, excellent in conception and practical in the anticipated results, ran into trouble. Each specialist could not or would not go beyond his narrow field, and insisted on the need for more detailed study of his area, while Kidder counseled the coordination of the numerous monographs in an attempt to find relationships among them and ultimate generalizations. The synthesis was never accomplished, and the answers to the "big" questions failed to appear. In 1940 Clyde Kluckholn publicly questioned the validity of the program for that reason, and eight years later W.W. Taylor issued a stinging attack along similar lines.

By 1940 the C.I.W. itself began to lose interest in the project; it closed down work at Chichén, and Morley bought a private residence in Mérida. Moreover, a new president of the C.I.W. and the demands of World War II directed the attention of the institution to immediate scientific problems. Then military service depleted the staff of the Chichén project. Finally, in 1952, the archaeological material and many of the remaining staff members were transferred to the Peabody Museum at Harvard University.

These developments had no effect on Morley's activity in writing and speaking about the Maya. He produced numerous scholarly books and articles which commanded wide respect. In this category, he is generally remembered for two compilations resulting from many seasons of fieldwork. *The Inscriptions of Copan,* issued in 1920, and *The Inscriptions of the Peten,* which appeared in 1937-38 in five volumes, were published by the C.I.W. Morley had no regard, however, for printing costs; he made so many deletions, additions, and changes in the proofs of the *Peten* that, even after the most generous interpretation of its rules, the C.I.W. had to charge him $1,240, to be deducted from his salary over a period of three years.

Morley displayed unusual flair for popularizing the story of the Maya from the public platform and on the printed page. He spoke to any audience willing to listen to his recital of the history of the ancient people and the secrets of the hieroglyphs. Delivering his remarks informally and spontaneously, he used slides or motion pictures of the latest expedition as the basis for comments. He spoke in simple language, avoiding scientific jargon and qualifying details, with the result that the audience felt that it understood the intricacies of the subject. His enthusiasm created excitement, and anecdotes provided the light, humorous touch. In Mexico and Guatemala he gave the same presentation, but honored Latin American custom by beginning with flattering remarks about dignitaries in the audience. His failure to master accurate Spanish and his complete disregard for the rules of grammar proved to be a valuable asset, because the audience responded to his humorous blunders with delight. The performance appeared to be extemporaneous; even his friends did not realize that he prepared every detail in advance. He ended one talk with a short happy statement in Maya, which he had carefully memorized for the occasion. Sometimes he would draw a large sketch of a glyph representing the birth date of an attending dignitary, which the audience appreciated as a graceful compliment.

He also had the gift of writing stimulating accounts for the general public. From the earliest days he produced magazine articles extolling the wonders of the ancient Maya. Perhaps he was at his best in several articles in the *National Geographic Magazine,* in which he combined attractive photographs with clear, informative text. The article that gained the widest circulation appeared in *Life* magazine in 1947, accompanied with superb photographs by Dmitri Kessel.

The Ancient Maya, his triumph in popularization, is still found in public libraries all over the country. In it he gave a comprehensive picture of all aspects of Maya life; ninety-six plates and fifty-seven line drawings, carefully selected and integrated with the text, provided rich visual material. His enthusiasm emerged in the numerous superlative claims he made for his beloved Maya. Before the book appeared in print, Kidder made one of his rare unfortunate judgments when he advised Morley to shelve it. Two reputable commercial publishing houses refused to take it. Finally, Morley placed it with Stanford University Press, and arranged for a Spanish edition to be published in Mexico as a way to cut the cost of the illustrations. After *The Ancient Maya* was published, scholars offered criticisms, a few of which were justified. Only two or three specialists recognized the work for what it was: a personal evocation of the ancient Maya through the eyes and emotions of an enthusiastic man who could carry his exciting message to the general public. Morley made his contribution both to scholarship and to popularization; what more can one ask of a professional archaeologist?

If Vay enjoyed considerable freedom to do what he pleased in his later years, he also suffered disappointments. The project in Yucatán had dwindled, and he knew it was slated for termination. Two manuscripts, a history of the Xiu family and a guide book to Chichén Itzá, the C.I.W. refused to publish, perhaps for justifiable reasons. Morley did not even prepare his remaining notes on hieroglyphs, because he knew that the C.I.W. was no longer interested. Most distressing was a misunderstanding over *The Ancient Maya.* Soon after the volume gained favorable notice, the president of the C.I.W. expressed irritation that the author would draw royalties from a book which represented years of work he had done at the expense of the institution. Morley had good reason to believe that the C.I.W. was not interested in his book and did not care to publish it; he had kept Kidder informed of the progress of the manuscript. When the trouble arose, Kidder gallantly shouldered the blame for any misunderstanding, and that was the end of it. Despite the disappointments, Morley never blamed anyone. Following his own philosophy of enjoying the pleasant things of life, he took satisfaction in the reception of his book, its translation into Spanish, and the widely circulated article in *Life.*

Then in 1947 a new career beckoned, when he was named director of the School of American Research in Santa Fe. The C.I.W. continued to pay his salary, but loaned him to the school. He went to work with vigor, merging a museum and an archaeological laboratory with the school, and launching two publishing projects for the school. But little more than a year after taking the post, he died of a heart attack. If he had been lucky in many ways during his career, he was also spared the knowledge of the end of the C.I.W.'s archaeological program in 1952.

Morley was the most lively character in the roster of early twentieth-century Maya archaeologists. To estimate him solely on the basis of his contributions to scholarship, the usual criterion for recalling a leader of a past generation in a scholarly discipline, ignores the fundamental quality of the man. His rich, warm personality added a new dimension, an admirable human touch, to the search for the secrets of the Maya. For him, each day had its interests, either in what he did or in the people he met. He found everything exciting in the human drama taking place around him. Furthermore, he strove to create and perpetuate goodwill among people. If a friendship went sour, he remained uneasy until he could reestablish the old relations.

He also possessed sufficient self-confidence and emotional balance to avoid extremes of feeling. The disappointments of life he accepted as part of human experience. The failure to receive the Angrand Prize or an ambassadorship to Guatemala, which he had reason to believe might be offered, he mentioned only once in his diary and then put out of mind; and he never complained when Kidder was placed over him or when his manuscripts failed to be accepted for publication. Like any man, of course, he enjoyed success, but he never betrayed egoism.

His ebullient nature made him an appealing popularizer of the Maya. In writing and speaking about the wonders of the ancient civilization, he conveyed the excitement of discovery. The specialist who can translate esoteric facts into popular information builds a bridge from the scholarly world to the public mind.

4

Frederick A. Mitchell-Hedges

In the history of twentieth-century archaeology there is no precise category to accommodate Mitchell-Hedges. A self-proclaimed adventurer, he boasted of his contributions to the knowledge of pre-Hispanic civilizations of Central America. He took advantage of the superstitions of the Chucunaque Indians of Panama, sought to establish a record in deep-sea fishing, displayed shrunken human heads to astonished audiences, made money in unknown ways, and berated contemporary civilization for its lack of courage and manliness. As a puzzling heritage to those professional archaeologists who ignored him, he left a macabre object, a magnificently carved crystal skull, which still has specialists guessing. At least, he led a colorful life in what he considered a weak and pallid culture.

He declared that he sought only one major experience in life—adventure. Whether it was strange, exhilarating, exotic, or daring, he did not care, so long as he could savor novelty beyond the drab routine of contemporary urban civilization. According to his estimate, he succeeded brilliantly, for he found excitement in everything he did.

Adventure can be an aimless thing, as Mitchell-Hedges

discovered during the first forty years of his life. He was born in 1882 in a comfortable middle-class family in England. At some time in his early life he joined the family names of his mother and father to form the hyphenated name of Mitchell-Hedges. The boy did not take to schooling, but buried himself in books of adventure and became attracted to life in the remote past. He rebelled against the restrictions of the Victorian world, and resisted his father's plea to prepare himself for a modest, respectable job. Under the guidance of an older friend, he had a brief fling at adventure at the age of sixteen on the northern tip of Scandinavia. That experience, however, failed to satisfy his wanderlust, much to his father's disgust. For some time he worked in a stockbroker's office, and he did not hesitate to display his discontent with the boring job. At the age of eighteen he set off on his own and eventually arrived in New York City. According to his version of the story, he displayed an unusual gift for gambling, attracted the attention of men who played for high stakes in the stock market, and also became acquainted with J.P. Morgan, Belle da Costa Green, Morgan's adviser, and Joseph Duveen, the famous art dealer. It is obvious that Mitchell-Hedges liked to drop names. He managed to make money in the stock market and to associate with wealthy speculators; on accumulating £4,000 he decided he had sufficient funds for his purpose. He also concluded that the wealthy became slaves to their own fame and fortune, and so he gave up his association with that group and left the city.

He returned to England to see what he could do with his money. He bought a house in a fashionable part of London and acquired servants and a Daimler car. With two partners, he formed a business enterprise; but after a brief period his partners decided to eliminate him. He took his revenge by ruining them, though he also ruined himself and reduced his fortune to £400.

During this period he married Lillian Clarke. They had a son, who was about the only satisfaction of this union, for apparently Mitchell-Hedges's interests strayed from home.

Later, he admitted that he had been a poor husband, though the faithful Lillian was always waiting for him when he returned from his numerous trips. She quickly disappeared from his story.

He returned to the United States with no particular purpose. Back in New York City, he avoided his former cronies and took a job at a modest wage with a diamond merchant. He is annoyingly vague on the chronology of his story until 1913, when the urge to see Central America took him to Louisiana and Texas. He wandered about, won $500 in a somewhat dubious fashion in a gambling house in New Orleans, moved on to Texas, sold his dilapidated car for $25, and hitchhiked across the border into Mexico. Before he realized what happened, Pancho Villa's band captured him and forced him to participate in their forays for ten months. Villa did not think much of the gringo until Mitchell-Hedges extricated the leader from a tight spot in one of his raids against North Americans. Finally, when England and Germany went to war, Villa allowed him to return to his native land to join the army. Mitchell-Hedges chalked up one lesson from the Mexican experience. He observed later on that heavy drinking caused Villa's death, and so the Englishman became a teetotaler for the rest of his life.

As we follow his autobiography, the story of his activity during World War I remains hazy. In England, a leg injury disqualified him for military service. While living in London, he befriended a Russian, who later turned out to be Leon Trotsky. Then Mitchell-Hedges returned to the United States and engaged in government intelligence work, but he gave no details. On a brief visit to Canada he adopted a ten-year-old French Canadian orphan girl whom he called Sammy. By the time the war ended, he had sufficient money for his purposes, and once more struck out for adventure in Mexico and Central America. Incidentally, from this period through the remainder of his life he no longer mentioned money; he had enough of it to do what he pleased, and did not bother to explain how he made it.

After the war ended, he made a second trip to Mexico and Central America. Sammy accompanied him for some time; then he suddenly decided to send her to the United States for schooling. On the west coast of Mexico he landed at Mazatlán in Sinaloa, found conditions too unsettled by revolution to please him, and struck south to Salina Cruz in the Bay of Tehuantepec. With innocent curiosity, he began taking pictures of soldiers and was promptly arrested; from his baggage he produced a gift of two gallons of whiskey, which quickly changed the local *commandante* into an accommodating friend. Then Mitchell-Hedges went on to Honduras. Near Trujillo he induced Indians to exchange gold dust, gathered from a shallow stream, for tobacco leaves, and found that he could make fifty dollars per leaf. In Tegucigalpa, the capital, he became acquainted with everyone who was anyone. Among these worthies was the colorful Lee Christmas, Louisiana-born soldier of fortune, who sold his services to presidents or rebels. Mitchell-Hedges asserted that he joined Christmas in some fighting, though he gave no details. But Mitchell-Hedges did describe his service as head of the Mule Division of the Federal Army of Honduras. When he camped his soldiers opposite the rebel forces, he found that the leader of the dissidents was General Alvarado, an old friend; so he settled the discontent by inducing the president of Honduras to appoint Alvarado war and marine minister! If we can believe Mitchell-Hedges, he did indeed have curious adventures.

By the time he ended this expedition and returned to England, he had reached the age of thirty-nine and had already spent some two decades pursuing adventure. At this point he experienced a conversion. He would not give up adventure, which he continued to seek for the rest of his life, but he decided to add purpose and meaning to his haphazard wanderings. Henceforth, he would devote foreign travel to the great aim of increasing scientific knowledge. So he determined to discover strange primitive people for the advancement of ethnology; he would find remains of ancient civilizations to expand the horizon of Middle American archaeology; and he would convert his hobby of deep-sea fishing to a search for rare specimens worthy of display in museums.

Acting on the new resolution, he entered the field of ethnology by going to Panama to visit the Chucunaque Indians, a tribe which he declared was unknown to the scientific world. He seems to have made a preliminary visit to them with one Major Fitz-Williams in the early part of 1922, after which he announced that he and his companion were the first white men to penetrate the San Blas and Chucunaque regions. They brought with them ethnological specimens, including woven cloth said to resemble that of ancient Egypt. So Mitchell-Hedges decided to make a more thorough examination of the intriguing region.

On returning to London, he prepared for a full-scale expedition to the unknown tribe in Panama. At first he believed that he had sufficient funds to finance the project, but on recalculating the expenses, he discovered that he needed more money. At that moment he met Lady Richmond Brown, an old friend, in Waterloo Station. They confided their troubles to each other. She was thirty-eight years old and had just recovered from an operation. She was restricted to a quiet, sheltered life on doctor's orders, but she was "fed up," she said, with watching her friends playing tennis and swimming on her estate, while she stood on the sidelines as a semiinvalid. In turn, he told of the great adventure awaiting him in Panama, momentarily delayed because of the lack of money. At that, she impulsively proposed to share the expense and the experiences of the trip with him. When he was convinced that she was serious, the expedition got under way. In spite of her bold disregard for her physical condition, she fell sick only once on the numerous trips with Mitchell-Hedges in the succeeding years.

For the two explorers, the expedition was a grand success, filled with adventure. They stopped at Jamaica for a time, where Mabs, as Mitchell-Hedges called Lady

Richmond Brown, suffered from mosquito bites all over her body, shot an alligator, and caught deep-sea fish. Blessed with many native servants at this place, she wisely decided not to require each one to wear a uniform, as was her custom in England. Her only illness occurred after the couple had moved on to Panama, where she was hospitalized for several weeks; but she enjoyed good health thereafter. First, they visited the San Blas Indians on the islands, then stayed for a time in Allegandee, their major settlement. Mitchell-Hedges used medicines to relieve their varied illnesses. The white couple cruised among more islands, explored the coastline, and then struck inland.

Finally, they reached the Chucunaque Indians in southern Panama. With adolescent delight, Mitchell-Hedges played upon the superstition of the natives. Dressing himself and Mabs in fancy costumes, he put on a performance at night with flares to make the natives believe that the visitors were in communication with the spirits and had received instructions on how to cure their illnesses, especially a severe itch. After these histrionics, he and Mabs examined the village and discovered that they had entered no felicitous primitive paradise. The natives lived at a low cultural level, used bow and arrow, and worshiped a preserved male foetus. Disease infected every member of the tribe, from smallpox and hookworm to chiggers and the ubiquitous itch. Mitchell-Hedges applied generous amounts of sulfur ointment for the itch, though he was unable to relieve the other complaints. Despite the depressing experience, the visitors acquired many artifacts. It happened that the Chucunaques practiced a form of writing on cloth, and Mabs collected sixteen hundred pieces, dating from the time of the Spanish conquest. After leaving these Indians, the couple rounded off the expedition with deep-sea fishing. They cruised among the islands of the San Blas group; Mabs caught a 415-pound shark; their boat crashed among alligators; and they had to fight the itch picked up from the Chucunaques. They returned to England, confident that their collection of specimens would provide a significant contribution to some museum.

Mitchell-Hedges began talking and writing about his adventures. In fact, he became a minor celebrity, according to his own account, and had to hire a secretary, Jane Houlson. She came from a strict Victorian background, but under his tutelage she quickly shed her narrow view of life. Soon she was going on expeditions with him. In the meantime he wrote for newspapers, and in 1923 he published a book, *Battles with Great Fish,* which he dedicated to Lady Richmond Brown.

For his next foray, he decided to enrich archaeology with the discovery of ruins of an unknown Maya city. For years he had heard rumors of such a place in British Honduras. In 1924 he and Mabs took a schooner to Belize, and invited H.S. Tuke, an artist, and Thomas Gann, a physician and archaeologist who had lived for years in British Honduras, to join them. A crew of nine natives managed the boat. They went south to Punta Gorda, visited some of the offshore islands, and then transferred to a motor launch and two dugouts to reach the interior via the Rio Grande. One day and one night on the river led them to change their plans. Intolerable heat, insects, snags and fallen trees in the water, and a group of inept Carib boys as guides brought them to near disaster. When Gann's dugout capsized, his medical chest and surgical instruments were lost. During the night on shore they heard jaguars roaming about, and suffered from rain and vicious insects. Unable to reach the ruins, the party returned to Punta Gorda.

Leaving Mabs and Tuke at Punta Gorda as a place of safety, Mitchell-Hedges and Gann made another attempt to reach the interior by overland travel on horses. This time they were successful, for they approached Indians who knew the ruins they sought, and finally, the explorers were stumbling over walls and altars and gazing upon a great stone stairway. They called the site Lubaantún. For two days they explored the place, and then rushed back to civilization to announce the good news. At Belize the

Legislative Council of British Honduras granted the explorers a concession to excavate in an area of seventy square miles around the ruins.

The first report of Lubaantún to get into the newspapers of the United States came from a secondhand source and was fancifully exaggerated. One Edmund Whitman, stationed in Honduras, wrote that the newly discovered site had a pyramid three hundred feet high and that the structures were covered with glyphs. Both reports were false.

Mitchell-Hedges returned to England, secured financial support from the *Daily Mail,* and planned to return to British Honduras to examine his find. A curious news release from London suggested that Lady Richmond Brown would lead the expedition, accompanied by Mitchell-Hedges and his secretary Jane Houlson. Although Mabs had not seen Lubaantún, she spoke as if she had been there, claiming that no other white woman had visited the site, and that she was "madly anxious" to return. The article identified her as the wife of Sir Melville Richmond Brown, and reported her as a crack shot and a skilled fisherman, with statistics about several of the giant creatures she had caught in the ocean.

Mitchell-Hedges, Mabs, and Gann made the first extensive examination of Lubaantún during the 1924-25 season. At one period when both men were sick, Mabs directed the natives in clearing the large site. After several weeks, the trees and brush had been cut down, and she lighted a giant fire, which consumed the rubbish and cleared the site. Mitchell-Hedges claimed that the ruins covered an area of six square miles. In the center stood a cluster of pyramids, terraces, mounds, walls, and a large amphitheater with two giant stairways. Later on, he liked to boast of the one million pieces of squared stone that covered the place and of the ten thousand persons the amphitheater could hold. The explorers also found many artifacts—figurines, pottery, weapons, obsidian knives, and human teeth displaying signs of good dentistry. Gann determined that there had been three different periods of occupation; but all told, Lubaantún appeared late in Maya history.

For several seasons Mitchell-Hedges explored the site. After his return to England in the fall of 1926, Sir Frederick Kenyon of the British Museum, one of the few persons who retained faith in the work of the explorer, reported that Lubaantún might well be one of the earliest centers of culture in Central America. Mitchell-Hedges brought Jane Houlson on one of the expeditions and Sammy on another. It was on the last visit that Sammy found a crystal skull under a fallen altar; we shall hear more about that object later on. In 1927 Mitchell-Hedges turned the rights to Lubaantún over to the British Museum.

After 1924 Mitchell-Hedges liked to boast of the discovery of Lubaantún, sometimes forgetting to mention Gann as codiscoverer. What Mitchell-Hedges did not know or did not want to know was the fact that the site had been visited three times before he "discovered" it. A group of Americans found it in the late nineteenth century; Gann examined it in 1903; and Raymond E. Merwin removed three small altars from the place in 1914 for the Peabody Museum. It is equally curious that Gann showed little interest in the site in 1903; after the expedition of 1924, however, he became excited about it.

Mitchell-Hedges claimed that Lubaantún was the largest and one of the oldest of Maya ruins. In 1926 Sir Frederick Kenyon was reported to have said that the site dated from the beginnings of Maya civilization. In turn, Mitchell-Hedges, never overly precise about chronology, declared that Lubaantún had been occupied for more than a thousand years. Recently, however, an archaeologist who carefully examined the site concluded that the buildings were constructed in the eighth century A.D. and that the site was abandoned in the first half of the ninth century. Not only did Lubaantún appear late in Maya history, but it also enjoyed no more than a brief existence.

A well-proportioned man, over six feet tall, Mitchell-Hedges was flattered by the attention he received from natives of Central America. He liked to tell how his size, white complexion and blond hair, and his apparent ability as a doctor brought offers from Indians on several occasions to father some children who would become tribal leaders in the next generation. He steadfastly refused the compliments.

A pessimistic outlook on contemporary civilization impelled him to adopt an adventurous life-style. He considered modern urban life dull, drab, and joyless; it condemned the great mass of people to deadening routine and robbed men of their natural instinct for daring and courage. The trouble, as he saw it, came from modern women, who had feminized the whole civilization by cultivating luxury and extravagance and thus undermined the vitality of all society. He condemned the "liberation" of women in the 1920s, he objected to short skirts and short hair, painted faces and cigarette smoking, and the deference men still paid to the whims of women. As a result of this degeneracy, men, especially young men, lost their vitality. Sports had deteriorated, and the loss of virility explained Britain's decline in commerce and the growth of unemployment. He harked back to the glorious days of the British Empire, which had been established and upheld by aggressive leaders and adventurers. So he called on the young men of his own day to revive masculinity, to assert themselves, and to remember the fine traditions of their nation—in short, to become men again. To sting those youths into action, he called them indolent, weak, and puny. This was the theme of his public addresses in England in the 1920s.

Several days after he gave a lecture at the National Liberal Club in London, Mitchell-Hedges experienced an unnerving incident. As he motored through the country, six assailants stopped his car and bound, gagged, and robbed him. He was so upset over the loss of his suitcase that he said he would give £5,000 for its return, explaining that it contained papers relative to a business deal in Honduras and six human heads shrunken by Central American Indians, which he displayed at some of his lectures.[1] The whole affair turned out to be a practical joke by some young men who wanted to prove that British youth still retained spirit and daring. Several days after this revelation, he sued the *Daily Express* for declaring that he had engineered the incident as a publicity stunt. In the ensuing trial, the lawyers for the newspaper managed to divest Mitchell-Hedges of all personal respectability; they made light of his expeditions, presented him as a humbug, and demolished his reputation. Later on, he declared that he never regained his faith in British justice.

Although he made several more expeditions, they did not excite the scientific world. In 1929, the year following the disastrous trial, he publicly admitted his coolness toward English institutions. Without revealing the real reason, he and Mabs simply said that their explorations were not appreciated. Although the couple had donated valuable ethnological collections to museums in England, he asserted that in the future he would present his specimens only to institutions in the United States. That year he and Mabs gave a thousand items to the Museum of the American Indian, Heye Foundation, in New York. In May 1929, he spoke of a proposed expedition, but gave no additional information except to indicate that he was interested in the origin of the American Indian; he made no trip, as far as is known, in 1929. Early in 1930 he and Mabs, accompanied by two assistants, set off for Honduras. Again the news release suggested that Lady Richmond Brown had initiated the venture. By this time the American Museum of Natural History had lost any interest it might have had in the Englishman and refused to sponsor the expedition; the trip was made under the auspices of the Heye Foundation. No report of the venture appeared except Mitchell-Hedges's statement that he suffered from illness, which left him blind for some time and affected the use of his right eye. The journey was a preliminary exploration for a more ambitious project.

The relations between Mabs and Mitchell-Hedges were never clarified. He always referred to her as his "companion" and gallantly coupled her name with his when announcing achievements of expeditions in which she participated; he likewise carefully indicated that she was codonor of the various gifts of artifacts to museums. By 1930 Sir Melville Richmond Brown, apparently considering her leave of absence overextended, sued for divorce, naming Mitchell-Hedges as corespondent.

By the beginning of 1931 Mitchell-Hedges secured the support of the British Museum and the Heye Foundation for a bold expedition to discover the cradle of the human race in Central America. He announced the hope of finding evidence of an unsuspected ancient culture which would revolutionize the conventional interpretation of the American Indian. Coy and mysterious, he refused to reveal the site to be examined, except to say that it was in the region of Mosquitia, which in turn he located with studied vagueness. He admitted, however, that he and Mabs had examined the site the previous year and had found a civilization dating back to 3000 or 4000 B.C. The site included an ancient city, a cenote, and several caves thirty to sixty feet deep. As a final note, he indicated that the expedition would cost $250,000.

Curious details appeared in a news release the following day. The American Museum of Natural History not only refused to support the project, but two of its scientists, Clark Wissler and Clarence Hay, refuted the Englishman's claims. They asserted that there were no indications that the region was the cradle of the human race. On the other hand, Sir Frederick Kenyon, director of the British Museum, upheld Mitchell-Hedges's claim, adding that although he was no professional archaeologist he was an able explorer.

Other news articles added interesting facets to the story. One John Kelly explained that Mosquitia was no mysterious region, for it had been well known for timber and placer mining. In February 1931, when Mitchell-Hedges arrived in New York, he refused to comment on his plans until he had spoken with his cosponsor, George Heye of the Heye Foundation. By early June the explorer had not yet completed arrangements for the trip. When a newsman asked why he planned a costly expedition in the midst of the depression, Mitchell-Hedges explained that such expeditions opened the way for trade with backward countries.

He visited Mosquitia and came away convinced that he had found remains of a very early civilization. Sometimes he made the claim that he had uncovered the cradle of civilization, but he never published a scientific report of his discovery. Curiously, Theodore A. Morde, also working for the Heye Foundation, reported in 1940 that he had found a "City of the Monkey God" in the same Mosquitia area.

By this time Mitchell-Hedges had become an ardent advocate of the idea of Atlantis. As the major evidence to support his claim, he cited a United States survey of Nicaragua, which indicated geological upheavals in the past and pointed to the existence of sharks in Lake Nicaragua. He believed, moreover, that the Bay Islands off the coast of Honduras were remains of Atlantis, and that artifacts on those islands were suggestive of a very old and advanced civilization. That ancient culture, he said, represented the remnants of people who had been saved when Atlantis sank into the ocean, and those people were the forerunners of the Maya.

He also secured the support of the Heye Foundation and the British Museum for the expedition of 1932 to the Bay Islands. On this venture Jane Houlson, his secretary, accompanied him, and eventually she wrote the report of the trip. The ninety-pound woman had herself photographed in field clothes, holding a gun; complacently she watched the prostitutes of Puerto Cortés ply their trade and became accustomed to seeing her "chief" struggle with giant crawfish and sharks.

Mitchell-Hedges ranged over the Bay Islands in a hurried search for artifacts. Jane and native workers turned up a few vases, numerous potsherds, figurines, chisels, and jadeite beads. On Bonaca he discovered a sacred well with many offerings which netted him eleven hundred specimens, in addition to a barricaded semicircular settlement with a mound and monolithic stones. He had his helpers fill sacks with artifacts; if we can rely on Jane's account, he used no scientific methods in his search and prepared no report on the finds except a crude map of the settlement. Apparently his major aim was to collect quantities of artifacts for the museums of his sponsors.

On the death of his father in 1936, Mitchell-Hedges retired to a residence in England. During World War II he entertained a constant stream of U.S. army officers in his home. On a visit to London he suffered internal injuries from a bomb blast, received treatment at the U.S. Government Research Hospital at Salisbury, and recovered after about a year. After the war he complained of the increased restrictions on the individual, the burgeoning governmental bureaucracy, and the public's abject acquiescence in petty regulations.

The war only delayed the overseas trips he longed to take. In 1950, at the age of sixty-eight, he journeyed to the Seychelles Islands in the Indian Ocean and to atolls off the Malabar Coast. The following year he carried on some archaeological work in Tanganyika, where he believed he found evidence of East Africa's earliest civilization. At the invitation of General Jan Smuts, he visited the Union of South Africa, and he ended his journey with still another search for deep-sea monsters in the Indian Ocean.

Continued retirement exasperated him and embittered his spirits. Although he enjoyed comfortable surroundings in a seventeenth-century house in the English countryside, the life was dull and routine. On writing his autobiography at the age of seventy-two, he took the opportunity to air his hatreds. He was disgusted with the armaments race and the cruelty to individuals who could not enjoy a free, happy life. He found England suffocating, because two wars had robbed it of its virility and wealth, and heavy direct taxation eroded men's normal incentive to make money. Everyone followed a senseless struggle for profit, prestige, and power, and then sought useless honors and titles. Mankind showed few signs of upward evolution, because the moral sense failed to improve.

He remained steadfast in his philosophy. In a parting shot, he advised every young man to decide what he wants to do, and then to accomplish his aim regardless of obstacles. Life must be lived with zest and adventure.

In 1959 he died at the age of seventy-seven. One obituary noted that during his life he had received eight bullet wounds and three knife scars, certainly a fitting observation about a man who prized courage and daring as the most worthy traits of an individual.

During his lifetime Mitchell-Hedges received little notice for his exploits in anthropology, archaeology, and ichthyology. Although he wrote books and newspaper articles and lectured about his adventures and discoveries, he aroused no sustained enthusiasm. In his archaeological expeditions only George Heye of New York and Frederick Kenyon and T.A. Joyce of the British Museum supported him, and their testimonials were general to the point of vagueness as to his actual achievements. In his later years Mitchell-Hedges asserted that great discoveries were made only by individuals outside the scientific world, an opinion reflecting faith in his own work, especially in the Bay Islands. It appears that the only person who believed thoroughly in Mitchell-Hedges was Mitchell-Hedges himself, as is evident in the sketch he supplied for the British *Who's Who,* where he presented his claims in bold relief and without qualification.

We cannot know whether he planned a curious form of revenge on all those archaeologists who had ignored him. At any rate, he left an intriguing carved crystal skull, which has so far defied convincing identification. Everything about the gruesome object, including its discovery, remains a mystery. He and his adopted daughter Sammy purportedly found the object under a fallen altar in the ruins of Lubaantún on Sammy's seventeenth birthday in 1927; in his autobiography he refused to reveal how it came into his possession. Expertly carved from quartz and perfect in workmanship, the skull is complete, with a detachable jaw. If it was made under primitive conditions, it is impossible to calculate the amount of human labor required to produce it. Mitchell-Hedges, always quick to supply information, declared that it was 3,600 years old and had involved the labor of natives for 150 years to rub it down.

The skull is credited with mystical powers. Sometimes a faint light surrounds it and a delicate musical sound emanates from it, according to a person who examined the object in his home over an extended period of time. A scientific analysis disclosed only that the skull and the jaw had been carved from the same piece of crystal.

The provenance of the object has not been determined. If it was found in Lubaantún, a Late Classic Maya site, it is difficult to credit it to that period of declining workmanship. If it came from an earlier age, when and where did it originate? Another crystal skull of similar size and execution is in the British Museum; it came from Mexico and has been attributed to the Aztecs or Mixtecs. The Mitchell-Hedges skull and the one in the British Museum are so similar that one specialist believes that both were made from the same model. Scholars have wondered, of course, whether the Mitchell-Hedges skull is the product of the mechanical arts of the twentieth century. Richard Garvin, who published a small book on the subject, makes no attempt to answer the question. In fact, he ends his account on an occult, mysterious note.

Peculiar aspects of Mitchell-Hedges's *Danger My Ally,* his autobiography, prompted Sibley Morrill to elaborate a hypothesis to explain some of the strange aspects of the story. The English edition of the autobiography contains a brief mention of the skull and a photograph of it, but the American edition omits that information. In addition to this unexplained curiosity, which strikes anyone who peruses both editions of the book, Morrill found several obvious errors of fact in Mitchell-Hedges's account of his stay with Pancho Villa. Then there is the interesting coincidence that the writer Ambrose Bierce went to Mexico and was with Villa about the same time that Mitchell-Hedges was there. Morrill looks into the larger background of events at the time and concludes that

England and the United States were alarmed over what was going on in the country south of the Rio Grande. As a result, he assumes that England sent Mitchell-Hedges and that the United States sent Ambrose Bierce to Mexico as secret agents to provide confidential information. Sometime after the two men served with Villa, they went south through Mexico, and on the way Mitchell-Hedges acquired the skull. When the two men arrived in British Honduras, the skull was left there, later to be retrieved by Mitchell-Hedges.

Morrill believes that knowledge of the skull had to be kept secret in order to hide the clandestine activities of the two agents. For that reason Mitchell-Hedges steadfastly refused to reveal the history of the object; and for the same reason, believes Morrill, the F.B.I. as late as 1954 suppressed references to the skull in the American edition of *Danger My Ally*.

Morrill, moreover, believes that the skull is of ancient workmanship. He is sure that it served the ancient Maya priestly class as an oracle. Going further, he assumes that it was the prototype of the Maya symbol for the number ten.

Morrill's strange account raises important questions and points out some errors in the autobiography. In attempting to answer the questions, however, the author constructs an elaborate story which he admits is no more than a hypothesis. Unfortunately, he fails to throw additional light on the history of the skull or to explain where and how it was acquired.

One can take another approach and ask whether Mitchell-Hedges left the crystal skull as a riddle for the archaeologists. Did he expect the object to perpetuate his name among the professionals who had ignored him? Perhaps more significant than his amateur activity in archaeology and ethnology is the element of mystery he injected into his life as the owner of the still-unexplained quartz carving.

An examination of the views and actions of Mitchell-Hedges leads to no satisfactory conclusions.

Through most of his life he struggled to obtain wealth, honor, and recognition, attributes which he condemned in his last years. The advice to young men to set goals and to achieve them regardless of the difficulties sounds suspiciously like a suggestion that youth should imitate Mitchell-Hedges. His pity for the dull lives of city folk would carry more weight if he indicated how the happy life could be achieved in contemporary civilization. His call on young Englishmen to assert the daring, courage, and initiative of their manhood was punctured, at least to some extent, by the mere prank of the half-dozen mischievous young fellows who temporarily scared and embarrassed him by their boldness.

Mitchell-Hedges, it appears, never thought seriously about his ideas. He failed to work out a reasoned philosophy to tie the snatches of opinion into a coherent point of view. The same naïveté appears in his work in archaeology. Untrained and uninformed, he assumed that everyone would accept his claims at face value and consider a bag of artifacts for a museum as evidence of scholarly achievement.

In the end one can agree with his major contention: he wanted adventure from life and he succeeded in obtaining it. Perhaps that is the fairest way to estimate him—as an adventurer.

5

Herbert J. Spinden

Among the Maya scholars of the earlier part of the twentieth century, Spinden enjoyed unique gifts and offered unusual contributions. He was endowed with a keen aesthetic sensitivity, which gave him insight into primitive song and pre-Columbian art. Not only did he possess a prodigious memory for all kinds of facts, but he also had a mind which sought the relation among disparate data and evolved simple generalizations from a complicated subject. In addition, he was aware of what was going on in allied fields and drew upon those disciplines to support the argument at hand.

The broad range of activities in which he engaged also marked the man as unusual. He observed elections in Cuba, gave learned as well as popular lectures, arranged educational projects, devised a plan to give jobs to returning soldiers, championed the Indians, set up two projects for the unemployed in the 1930s, and mounted exhibitions in museums. He pursued these activities in addition to expeditions, writing, research, and attendance at professional meetings.

Perhaps the most unusual quality of the man was his humanistic approach to archaeology. Scholars in that field had always given lip service to the goal of applying what they had learned to life in general, but as more intense specialization invaded the field in the twentieth century, the goal was increasingly overlooked. Not so with Spinden. He boldly fused the results of his study with his high sense of values to examine his own contemporary culture. If the results he offered were not entirely original or especially brilliant, they were refreshing and challenging in a materialistic age. In fact, some of his ideas appear more pertinent today than when they originally appeared in print.

He learned to live with success and disappointment. Three of the profession's honors were awarded to him: the presidency of the American Anthropological Association, the Angrand Prize, and the Loubat Prize. Several universities in Latin America made him an honorary professor, and his own government sent him to lecture in South America in his later years. Modest and unaccustomed to expressions of egotism, he never boasted of the recognition he received. Likewise, he took the disappointments of life with equanimity. Some of his manuscripts remain unpublished today, gathering dust on the shelves of research institutions. Among the contributions he made to archaeology, several failed to interest his colleagues and others were severely challenged or fell into disfavor over the years. If he complained occasionally to his friends, only once did he refer in print to the disregard for his system of correlation. He had learned to accept the disappointments as well as the satisfactions of life.

Spinden's background and early experiences did much to prepare him for a career in archaeology. His paternal grandfather had emigrated from Switzerland and settled in Iowa sometime before 1850. A son, Eugene, became a teacher, married, and moved to Huron, South Dakota, where he became a newspaper man, one of the first in the territory. Herbert was born there in 1879, a decade before the area became a state. He explained in later years that he had started life on the edge of civilization. The building in which he spent his childhood always remained in his memory. It was constructed of sod blocks against the bank of a river; a combination of sod and poles formed the roof, and the windows at the front were covered with oiled paper. After a few years his father managed to move into a larger house, heated by a stove which burned river grass for fuel.

Before attending college, he traveled widely. His family moved to Tacoma, Washington, where he attended public school. As a young man he worked with railroad surveying parties in the Northwest, and in 1900, at the age of twenty-one, the lure of gold took him to Nome, Alaska. Unfortunately, he left no account of those early years, no indication of critical moments in his education or of the adventures he experienced.

He received his academic training at Harvard University, the best institution at the time for an introduction to anthropology and archaeology. Like other college students, he sometimes chose courses for odd reasons; he signed up for Professor Roland Dixon's course on Indians because it gave him free afternoons to canoe on the Charles River. But he also made wise choices, particularly when he took Professor A.M. Tozzer's course on Maya archaeology, which prepared him for his future career in that field. Tozzer, it should be noted, took an interest in Spinden and used his influence in later years on the young man's behalf.

During the period at Harvard Spinden gained valuable experience in fieldwork. In the summer of 1905, Professor Dixon took him and George Will, a fellow student, to North Dakota and spent a few days telling them how to proceed with excavation. For six weeks the two men uncovered a Mandan village, and also studied the culture and language of the tribe. The report they drew up appeared in print in 1906, the year in which Spinden received the A.B. degree.

He stayed on at Harvard from 1906 to 1909 to earn the A.M. and Ph.D. In the summer of 1907 the Peabody Museum sent him to the Northwest to study the Nez Perce Indians. Fortunately, he gained the confidence of Jonas Hayes, a former shaman and tribal chief, who related numerous myths which had come down over the years. In the following summer Spinden continued field study with the same tribe. Eventually, he produced several publications growing out of these expeditions.

All told, he was a busy man at Harvard. As a graduate student he held a teaching fellowship in Dixon's general course in anthropology. But his resources were so meager that he supplemented his income by selling vegetables and other items to make ends meet. He spoke at the club of the anthropology department, and probably made his first acquaintance with his future colleague Vilhjalmur Stefansson while on the campus.

For his doctoral thesis Spinden made full use of two strong qualities he possessed, the appreciation of art and a remarkable memory. When he found little artistic appeal in the primitive remains of European people, he turned to the new field of Maya sculpture and architecture, and made full use of the work of Maler and Maudslay. He produced a brilliant analysis of the evolution of styles in *A Study of Maya Art,* which remains a landmark on the subject.

On completing his training at Harvard, he became a museum curator, and he worked in museums for forty-two years. He was at the American Museum of Natural History until 1921, at the Peabody Museum at Harvard until 1929, served concurrently at the Buffalo Museum (1926-29), and filled his last post at the Brooklyn Museum until 1951, when he retired at the age of seventy-two. For several decades he made numerous expeditions to collect objects and to find data for his hypotheses. In addition, he wrote many books and articles, lectured frequently, and arranged exhibitions. He appeared to enjoy everything he did, displayed good humor, and relished daily living.

He carried out projects on his own initiative.

Fortunately, he had a free hand in this regard; and in the earlier decades of his career he put forth his best ideas. Before describing his ideas, though, it is necessary to learn about his personality.

He looked like a somewhat oversize professional man. He had prematurely white hair, shaggy eyebrows, and wore thick glasses because of nearsightedness. He weighed over two hundred pounds, though he carried his weight well. A friend found him a somewhat comical figure as he rode away from Copán in 1917—a huge man astride a small white horse, with his feet almost reaching the ground.

Associates familiar with his peculiarities considered him pleasant and affable. He talked constantly and he liked to argue. His mind was stored with facts, and he was prepared to support either side of a proposition. He engaged in argument for the fun of it, though that trait made him appear contentious in the eyes of some persons. He talked much, because he took a lively interest in everything from primitive man to contemporary civilization. He enjoyed puns, bons mots, and tall tales. The nature of his humor varied. Writing from Colombia in the fall of 1918, he explained that he had suffered six attacks of fever on the expedition, and that Bogotá had four thousand cases of influenza and four thousand to five thousand cases of typhoid; he called it "a nice healthy place with fine scenery."[1] On the other hand, he is reported to have told a group of young women about an animal in Yucatán that treed human beings and starved them to death; thus, all over the peninsula one saw trees holding cross-legged human skeletons!

A gregarious fellow, he liked many people and particularly enjoyed social gatherings. He got along well with everyone, displayed no personal enmities, at least in his published writings, and rarely reviewed books unfavorably. He had a strong sense of loyalty to certain colleagues and institutions. Harvard, the Brooklyn Museum, the Republican party, and members of the clubs to which he belonged could do no wrong. He enjoyed the presence of attractive women, and paid them gallant compliments.

If people meant much to him, he could be careless or negligent in other matters. He gave little attention to what he wore, except on those unusual occasions when he was happily self-conscious over a new suit of clothes. He smoked Dutch Masters cigars constantly, heedless of where the ashes fell. In daily work he greeted everyone pleasantly, unless he was deep in thought on a problem in archaeology, when he could pass associates in the hallway without noticing them.

Essentially a modest man, he never directed attention toward physical discomforts he suffered on expeditions. He returned from one trip with infected garrapata (tick) bites and was laid up for a month, but he did not parade the inconvenience. As we shall see later, he barely mentioned the hardships of his 1926 expedition, and we know about them only through the stories of his associates.

Like many scholars, he was unconcerned about disorder in his affairs. His desk was piled high with all kinds of papers. No one was allowed to touch the sacred mass, for he declared confidently that he knew exactly where to find any item he wanted. One secretary, however, doubted that he could live up to that claim. With so many things to do, he put off details until the last moment. In the summer of 1924 he got off to Europe hectically as usual because of his failure to carry out details in time. On that occasion he was scheduled to give his paper on "New World Correlations" to the International Congress of Americanists. He hoped to carry printed copies to his colleagues abroad, but he made so many changes that he had to be satisfied with page proofs.

In the latter decades of his life, he found it difficult to adjust to or to accept some of the new developments in archaeology. He became increasingly tenacious of the ideas he had developed, and sometimes refused to acknowledge discoveries that controverted his views. Even after Hermann Beyer proved that the variable of the Initial

Series designated the month of the series, Spinden would not surrender his earlier interpretation that the variable forecast the subject of the inscription. When radiocarbon dating entered the field in the 1950s, he would have nothing to do with it until a C-14 test on a wooden lintel from Tikal produced exactly the date he had advanced on the basis of the style of the carving; then he happily informed his friends of the confirmation of his interpretation.

In later years his view that Quetzalcoatl was a real person and his contention that the hero's father was buried at Holmul received no serious notice from archaeologists, who saw no foundation for his claims. He also talked much about the significance of prime numbers; this subject, too, his hearers completely failed to comprehend. After associates deserted his system of correlation in favor of the Goodman-Martínez-Thompson system, he suspected a plot abroad to discredit him. The repudiation of his system wounded him severely, but he kept his feelings out of print except on one occasion when he referred to it with sadness and disappointment rather than with anger.

In the earlier part of his career he spent much time in expeditions to Central and South America. Details from several of those journeys provide a picture of his experiences. In 1914 he joined Sylvanus Morley to examine sites in the Petén and along the Usumacinta River. Always sensitive to nature, he wrote, on leaving Belize for the interior, "We are on board the Thistle and sailing up the old river on the way to El Cayo. . . . It is early morning and the level sun is stealing into the green shadows of the river bank."[2] After some days, the beauty of the Petén jungle became monotonous as the men sweltered under the high trees and slowly made their way on mules along the tedious trail. The guide and cook accompanying them could do little to relieve the inconveniences of the journey. Bejuco vines, thorns, and insects added minor annoyance to the travelers' fatigue. Upon arriving at a site, the party set up a temporary camp as close to water as possible. At

Naranjo, however, the water hole was a half-mile from the ruins; at night the mosquito bars over the beds kept out sand flies but admitted fleas, which made sleep a miserable experience.

After they settled down to examine a site, each man concentrated on his special interest. Spinden looked for art and architecture, and sometimes copied the carvings on stelae; Morley, as usual, constantly searched for new date glyphs. Both men worried over the success of their photography. Although the pictures they took at Naranjo turned out well, the men feared that the hot, moist climate could damage the film they carried with them. They continued to take pictures, but as a precaution they spent considerable time sketching hieroglyphs and pictorial carvings so that they might bring back a complete record.

The journey down the Usumacinta provided a different experience. Floating along on a large dugout shaded by an awning, the explorers marveled at the strength and endurance of the natives who poled the boat hour after hour in the broiling sun. Just before they reached Yaxchilán, news of revolution forced them to return upstream. At Seibal a full day's work extended from 7:30 in the morning until 4:30 in the afternoon, a strenuous stint for gringos in the tropics.

After Spinden left Morley, he went on to British Honduras and worked out from Punta Gorda among the Caribs. All told, he had covered some fifteen hundred miles by the time he returned to the United States. When he was interviewed by a reporter, Spinden posed the question of whether climatic change accounted for the great decrease of Maya population in the Petén since the days of the ancient populous civilization there. Had he perhaps already read Huntington's book on the climatic factor?

The First World War brought Spinden an unusual assignment for his country. Several years before the United States became involved in the conflict, he already shared general sentiment of the day with his hatred of Germany for its lack of decency and fair play. On the sinking of the *Lusitania* in 1915, he expressed indignation in a letter to a New York newspaper. Hold the German ships in our harbors as hostages, he advised; withdraw our diplomatic representatives from that nation, and "put the brand of renegade upon their people who scorn the laws of God and man."[3]

Before the United States entered the conflict, a number of archaeologists, including Spinden, offered their services to the government. By arrangement, as soon as war was declared, these men were commissioned ensigns in the U.S. Navy and served as intelligence agents in Central America. Spinden's task was to round up mahogany wood for airplane propellers. Details of his secret work have never been made public. He traveled as an employee of the American Museum of Natural History and engaged in scientific research as a cover for his assignment. A museum official ingeniously explained Spinden's mission by saying that he had gone south "to collect material for American manufacturers of textiles who, since the beginning of the war, have been availing themselves of the collections of the American Museum."[4] This statement, which was true as far as it went, was only a small part of the truth.

Spinden had his own explanation of the mission. In the beginning of the expedition he traveled with John Held, Jr., the cartoonist, also on the secret mission but without official status. As they waited for their boat in New Orleans, a local news reporter interviewed them. Spinden blandly explained that he was on a mission "to study primitive experiments of food values still in use among the natives." He added that the Indians made a white liquid from grain mash, "which will be of inestimable value to our soldiers."[5] He had a way of saying impossible things with great earnestness.

Eventually he and Held joined Morley at Copán. There Held became an assistant to Morley and also a secret agent, and later drew maps of the coast for the U.S. Navy. During the overnight stay at Copán the visitors were awakened by explosions and music long before sunrise;

the sounds resulted from the natives' war on a plague of grasshoppers.

Three weeks later Spinden assumed an unexpected role. He was in Honduras when news of the destructive earthquake in San Salvador impelled him to visit the stricken city, where he had his headquarters. "I was in Tegucigalpa, Honduras," he wrote to a friend, "when the first reliable news of the shock came through on Saturday. I set out at once, traveling down the coast, a ride lasting from 7 A.M. to 9 P.M., then by motor boat to Amalpa, where we arrived after dark. A visit to the commandante resulted in special permission to leave before the opening of the port, at 2 P.M. I began the last stretch of water travel at La Unión, arriving in time for the morning train. The railroad is still under construction, but a slow train consumes a tedious day in reaching Zacatecoluca, some thirty miles distant. Here I was fortunate enough to secure immediate passage by auto to the capital, and we pulled into the stricken city at 9:30 P.M. . . . .

"Our entrance into the darkened city was dramatic. When we came to the large church of Candelaria we found that the painted image of Christ had been set up in front of it and a thousand persons were kneeling on a platform and in the muddy street, each with a lighted candle. The automobile lamps showed heaps of debris on either hand as we rode through the streets to my lodging. Fortunately, this house was built of wood and my outfit was intact. . . . "

A few days later Spinden welcomed Morley and Held, who had worried about his safety. The three men pitched in to help Boaz Long, U.S. minister to Salvador, to relieve the distress. Ninety percent of the houses had been destroyed or rendered unsafe. "We quickly hope to set up shelters which will last through the six months of the rainy season, just begun," Spinden explained. "Many of the well-to-do families are camped in the park or on the drill ground near the city. The poorer people have set up miserable shacks of mats, burlap, and sheets of rusty tin."[6]

Spinden saw that the relief could serve to check German

influence in Salvador and Central America. "We are hoping," he explained, "that the United States Government will generously offer aid." "We believe it would be an excellent move, even if all questions of humanity are left out. The German colony has united in a gift of 10,000 pesos. This has been equaled in the single donation of Minor C. Keith, now on a tour of inspection in this country."[7] Keith, an American, was a high official in the United Fruit Company.

According to one story, Spinden unwittingly became involved in local politics and had to leave San Salvador in inglorious flight. Before the earthquake, President Meléndez had Lake Ilopongo dammed to produce electrical power. The natives, believing that when the level of the lake rose the volcano became active, blamed the quakes on the engineering job and hence indirectly on the president. So government officials appealed to Spinden and Morley, who were considered visiting scientists, to write a newspaper article to allay the discontent. The two men prepared an account, most of it innocuous because it dealt largely with myths and traditions of the Indians; but at the end the authors added the idea that the quakes were acts of nature, stating that the lava from the neighboring volcano would fertilize next year's crops. The president, his officials, and Boaz Long considered the article a brilliant stroke until two coffee growers invaded the U.S. legation, determined to kill Spinden and Morley for deluding the poor farmers. Long did some fast talking, and the archaeologists quickly left town.

Months later Spinden encountered Morley and Held again, this time way down the Mosquito Coast at Bluefields, Nicaragua. For eleven days the two archaeologists had a wonderful reunion; they talked together, played bridge, enjoyed a daily oyster cocktail, and lived in a hotel operated by a German. Morley described Spinden as contentious, because he liked to argue for the sheer pleasure of it, but also as a most likeable friend.

We do not know what intelligence assignment took Spinden to out-of-the-way Bluefields. He spent much time examining the old town newspapers, which were certainly of no value to the war effort. He was probably gathering information for a historical article on the Mosquito kings of that region, which appeared in print seven years later. Unfortunately, nothing more about this period of his secret service is known, except that he appeared in such diverse places as the Gulf of Fonseca, Panama, and Cuba.

When Spinden carried on expeditions in Guatemala, Honduras, and Nicaragua from 1919 to 1924, he utilized the usual resources of archaeologists traveling in Central America. The United Fruit Company and its personnel provided helpful assistance. Like other explorers, Spinden enjoyed free passage on United Fruit's boats between the United States and the countries where it operated. In addition, its local representatives gave incidental but important aid to his explorations. In the Trujillo area of Honduras, company workers led him to archaeological remains on land recently cleared for banana plantations. With the vegetation removed for miles around, he could easily locate and study sites of ancient villages that had been hidden for centuries.

When it became popular in the 1920s for some persons to criticize corporations for economic exploitation of Central America, Spinden understandably defended United Fruit. He praised the seaports, railroads, and plantations which that organization had constructed, and then called the company an empire with a new ingredient, sanitation, which was much needed in the region.

In the Petén of northern Guatemala he appreciated the value of the chicleros, those men who wandered through the tropical forest to locate chicle trees, whose sap formed the basis of chewing gum. Although these men were tough, coarse, and despised by many persons as the scum of civilization, they knew the forest and often encountered ruins in their travels. In a town like El Cayo in western British Honduras at the entrance to the Petén, chicleros spent some time each year squandering their money on liquor and women. Following standard practice among archaeologists, Spinden offered a stipulated monetary award to any chiclero who would lead him to an undiscovered Maya site or to stones with carvings and hieroglyphs. Moreover, explorers also had reason to be grateful to chicleros, for many a time their abandoned palm-thatch huts in the depth of the forest offered shelter for the night or during a shower. Spinden paid tribute to the despised chicleros as useful auxiliaries of exploration in the Petén.

Spinden also learned to value the lowly mule as the most dependable mode of transportation for travel through the Petén. Each animal could carry a man or a sizable load of baggage. Although the pack train moved slowly along the dusty trail or mud strip, depending on the weather, and men and animals almost suffocated from the heat, the mules eventually reached the destination. But even mules could not always withstand the dangers of travel, for snake bites and accidents took a toll. Spinden estimated a 20 percent mortality rate among the mules on each expedition.

In the backcountry of Nicaragua and Honduras, he employed local Indian guides, whom he admired for their ingenious adaptation to the natural environment. They knew the trails, excelled in swimming, and were good shots when food was needed. Once he entrusted himself to seven Paya Indians, who conducted him up the Plantain River for six days. The wife of one native, carrying her eighteen-month-old child, acted as cook for the party. The group traveled in two pitpans, mahogany dugouts, each thirty-five feet long and three feet wide. Spinden marveled at the endurance of the Indians. On one occasion the mother carried the child and a seventy-five-pound metate by tumpline for eight miles. When Spinden discovered several carved stones he wanted to take with him, the men suspended them from poles and carried them for eight miles, even through pools of water which at times covered their heads.

On the trip down the Usumacinta River he found local natives helpful. The party traveled in a dugout canoe, meals were prepared on a mud fireplace at one end of the boat, and at night the group camped on the riverbank, attended by fireflies and howler monkeys. At one stopping place Spinden asked a small party of local natives about carved stones; they responded with a blank look of ignorance. At that, their cook volunteered the suggestion that the explorer might be interested in "The Broken King." This proved to be a magnificent low-relief sculpture of an ancient worthy, resplendent with feathered headdress and battle-axe, and bearing a date of the early sixth century A.D.

If Spinden had to choose between professional and social activity, research won the day. When he went to Mérida in 1923 along with other archaeologists to help inaugurate a new program of excavation, he stayed away from the ceremonials—receptions, balls, formal dinners, and everything else the hospitable Yucatecans could devise to entertain guests. One formal meeting, however, he could not in all conscience avoid, for on that occasion the new local archaeological society granted membership to distinguished foreign scholars. He showed up late at the formal affair, in unpressed street clothes, just in time to be escorted to the front of the hall to receive the honor. Where he was during the week of celebrations no one knew, but we may be sure that he was studying the ruins or delving into documents in the library. As soon as the festivities ended, he set off for Nicaragua and Honduras, and returned to the States three months later with news of the Chorotegan civilization he had discovered.

An expedition of several months in 1926 received more public notice than any other venture Spinden undertook. He joined Gregory Mason to explore the eastern coast of Yucatán. Mason, a thirty-six-year-old journalist, tall, lanky, and weighing two hundred pounds, had considerable experience in news reporting. On joining the staff of the *Outlook,* a New York periodical, in 1914, he was sent to Yucatán to investigate the revolution and the state monopoly on sisal. During the assignment he took a week off to visit Uxmal, which kindled his interest in the ancient Maya. Other assignments, however, prevented him from following up the subject at once. He was sent to Russia, Japan, and Central America; the latter assignment included two visits to Mexico. In 1923 he published his first article on the Maya, a description of Chichén Itzá, occasioned by plans of the Carnegie Institution of Washington to begin excavations there. Three years later he wrote a biographical article about Edward H. Thompson, Maya explorer, and prepared a novel, *Green Gold of Yucatán,* which must have been well under way or completed before he joined Spinden, because it was published shortly after he returned to the United States. The novel shows an acquaintance with Yucatán, Quintana Roo, and the ruins. In one episode embattled North Americans fight from the top of the Pyramid of the High Priest and from the Castillo in Chichén Itzá. Romance, action, derring-do, and stereotyped characters fill the pages. If the novel was no more than a run-of-the-mill story, it indicated Mason's deep interest in archaeology. He wanted to lead an expedition of his own.

He met the cost of the venture by exchanging his journalistic skill for the expense of the trip. *The New York Times* paid the bills, and in return he supplied about a dozen articles from the field for publication in the newspaper. Other institutions cooperated. The Peabody Museum loaned Spinden to the venture; the American Museum of Natural History sent Ludlow Griscom to study the fauna of Cozumel; and the U.S. Navy appointed Ogden T. McClurg to map coastal landmarks in eastern Yucatán. Before setting out, Mason had a conference with Tozzer, Morley, and Samuel K. Lothrop at the Peabody Museum, and those men agreed that he would find something interesting on the eastern coast of the peninsula.

The party cruised up and down the coast of Yucatán and visited the island of Cozumel. They examined Tulum, which was well known, and explored other ruins that previous visitors had seen only from the water. Perhaps the most interesting find was Muyil, a Maya ruin which they explored for six days. At Paalmul, another site, they found that the temple had the unusual feature of a round wall in the rear. In addition, they met Indians and their leaders, and they learned not to press investigation too far; one chief refused to show them two inland ruins, probably because the places were used as religious shrines. All told, the expedition provided interesting experiences but actually little of archaeological significance. Mason wrote a book about the trip, featuring dangers, adventures, and the exotic atmosphere of the region. Spinden had little to say about the trip aside from matter-of-fact remarks in several newspaper articles.

Mason, who had good opportunity to observe Spinden, noted that he suffered from constant seasickness; once he took to his bed for two days because of exposure and stomach trouble. Generally, he was in good spirits, took everything in stride, and demonstrated common sense. Spinden explained that he never carried a gun among the natives; lacking any sign of racism, he treated everyone with respect. Associates could not help marvel at his great fund of information, which, Mason claimed, ranged from facts about thermodynamics to barroom ballads.

Spinden's modesty prevented him from complaining about hardships. In one dispatch he reported only that he had a narrow escape from a "norther," a violent wind and rain storm common in Yucatán. Actually, he and Griscom were on shore when the storm broke, though the remainder of the party had managed to return to the schooner. For four hours the two men waded through swamps and thorny bushes, until their friends on the boat sighted them at dusk.

After several men left the party, the others gave up the schooner and made a long overland journey through Quintana Roo to Chichén Itzá. There Mason attempted to determine if a tunnel ran from the High Priest's grave to a pond, as had been rumored by the natives, but he was unable to learn the answer. After Mason left for the States, Spinden traveled to the Bay Islands off Honduras to follow his own researches.

By participating in this expedition, Spinden helped Mason to launch a career as a journalist-ethnologist. By 1928 Mason had carried out an expedition to British Honduras, where the rules on removal of artifacts were relatively lax. In Mexico, he was not allowed to excavate or export any objects; British Honduras permitted him to take out of the country half of his finds, which he turned over to the Heye Museum. Five more expeditions followed, three in Central America and two in Colombia. At least one of these trips was carried on entirely by airplane. Then in 1933 Mason announced an expedition with an unusual slant: he planned to hunt apes in Wyoming and Honduras in order to prove that man originated in the Western Hemisphere. The results of that quest were not published. He was more fortunate in studying the Tairona Indians of Colombia; the report of that work became his doctoral thesis at the University of Southern California. In the late 1930s he entered the teaching profession and eventually headed the Department of Journalism at New York University until 1954.

Two of Mason's nonfiction books appeared in the 1930s. *Columbus Came Late* gave the reader an elementary knowledge of pre-Hispanic Middle America. *South of Yesterday* related the adventures of two expeditions, including the mission to the Taironas. Mason was a popularizer, attempting to make archaeology and ethnology attractive to lay readers, and apparently he hit upon the proper formula, as is evident in two of his articles in the *Saturday Evening Post* in 1929. Perhaps it is unwise to go back and peruse writings which appealed to readers at that time. Our knowledge of archaeology has increased a great deal in recent decades, and styles in popular writing have a way of dating quickly. If Mason helped readers to broaden their knowledge of America's past, he fulfilled his purpose.

After Spinden married in 1928, he and his wife usually traveled together, and the nature of the expeditions gradually changed. Instead of roughing it, as Spinden had done in the earlier years, the couple took advantage of the conveniences of civilization and acted more like informed tourists, poking about the vegetation of sites in Yucatán or in the Veracruz area to find evidences of ancient settlements. Once they made molds of buildings at Hochob for the Brooklyn Museum. In the 1930s Spinden's trips south increasingly became lecture tours, interspersed with sightseeing.

As long as he retained his job, he remained active. Although the pace of production slowed, he continued to turn out papers and arrange exhibitions. After the death of his first wife he married again, in 1948, and had a son. When he was retired from the Brooklyn Museum in 1951, he had reached the age of seventy-two. Then he went to work on the republication of his two major early books, *A Study of Maya Art* and *Ancient Civilizations of Mexico and Central America,* combined them in one volume, added an appendix, and called it *Maya Art and Civilization.* It appeared in 1957 as the last major work of his career. In the ensuing decade his health declined, and he died in 1967 at his home in Croton, N.Y. It is strange that fellow archaeologists failed to mark his passing with the customary tributes in the professional journals.

The archaeological hypotheses which Spinden developed grew out of the interaction of findings on expeditions and an active mind which constantly suggested ideas, sought the interrelation of various data, and achieved broad generalizations. It is likely that the ideas came first, and that the explorations simply provided proof to support the proposition. All told, Spinden offered some half-dozen major hypotheses during his active professional life.

A Study of Maya Art, his major publication on ancient Middle America, provided a striking contribution to a new field of investigation. The detailed examination of carvings and architecture and the comparison of figures and buildings from many sites established an evolutionary pattern of development, ranging from archaic simplicity to classic strength and beauty, followed by exuberance and flamboyance, indicative of decline. He detected the steps of development so thoroughly that he was able to date a monument solely on the basis of its style. When he tested his conclusion with dates from deciphered glyphs, he could point to a precise correlation in almost all instances.

The presentation also showed Spinden to be a master of clarity. He described the meaning of each line in the complicated sculptures and indicated how a natural figure became abbreviated and stylized. He used clear, simple prose, and integrated the 315 illustrations with the text. The layman can still read the volume with complete comprehension.[8]

Spinden had great respect for Maya art, and he fought the diffusionists so that America's pre-Columbian people could retain claim to their achievements. Diffusionists held that a trait, whether it was the building of pyramids or a style of decoration, was devised once and then spread to other countries and continents. Spinden and other scholars of his age condemned diffusionism as one more unproved theory, like those of the nineteenth-century investigators, which diverted scholars' energies from establishing a solidly grounded basis of facts for archaeology.

G. Elliott Smith, the British anthropologist who emerged as a prominent leader of diffusionist thought in the early twentieth century, argued for the worldwide spread of cultural traits. He insisted that some Maya carvings depicted the head of an elephant, thus linking Middle America with Asia and Africa. He seemed to score a point. As early as 1916, however, Spinden insisted that the figure was that of a macaw, a bird native to the Maya region. When Spinden discussed ancient agriculture the following year, he asserted that methods of cultivating the soil in Middle America had also been indigenous, without overseas influence.

In the mid 1920s Spinden issued his longest and strongest attack against the diffusionist school of thought.

He showed that a fundamental difference of opinion about man was at the heart of the argument. The diffusionists, he claimed, believed that most men lacked inventive ability but possessed retentive memories. The champions of indigenous origins, whom Spinden represented, held that all men were similar and had the ability to think; therefore, they were able to solve most problems by induction and deduction. He believed in multiple invention, that is, the idea that men at different times and places had devised similar solutions to similar problems. Thus, the achievements of the ancient Americans had been possible without transoceanic contact. Spinden concluded his argument with a tinge of sarcasm: Norsemen had lived on Greenland for four centuries, which, he pointed out, was the only opportunity Europe had to influence America, but nothing came of it.

On several other occasions he considered it necessary to refute the claim of foreign influences on New World culture. Early in his career he rejected the theory of Stanley Hagar that the zodiac had been introduced to America from Europe before 1492. When Professor Olaf Opsjon announced that a runic inscription had been found in Spokane, Washington, suggesting that Northmen had traveled as far as the Pacific Northwest in A.D. 1010, Spinden came out against the idea and declared that no runic inscription which had been found bore a date. Some years later Dr. Hermann Walde-Waldegg announced that he had found a connection between Maya culture and the culture of Asia by citing syllables of Sanskrit, Chinese, and Japanese in the Codex Borgia. At once Spinden denied any connection between the languages of the two continents.

In 1917, Spinden set forth one of his most seminal ideas—his theory of the origin and spread of agriculture in the Americas. He seized upon three traits—the cultivation of seed crops, early use of pottery, and Archaic culture (known later as Formative or Preclassic)—and declared that they had originated together in the highlands of central Mexico and then had spread up into the present United States and down into South America. Assuming that pottery started with sedentary people who practiced agriculture, he found the spread of agriculture and pottery similar in geographical extent.

New World agriculture in central Mexico developed from particular circumstances, according to Spinden. The hard conditions of a semiarid environment drove a hungry population to invent irrigation, which in turn gave rise to steady cultivation of the soil. Moreover, the wild grass teosinte, from which maize developed, flourished in the Mexican highlands. Later, inhabitants of the humid, heavily forested tropics adopted agriculture to their environment, and that conquest of nature made possible the rise of Maya civilization. Finally, agriculture was adapted to the temperate regions. Spinden assumed that the origin and spread of agriculture provided the great "antecedent condition for all the high cultures of the New World."[9]

The hypothesis illustrated the way his mind worked. He seized upon details, perceived interrelations among those details, exercised a comprehensive grasp over a large subject, and reduced the synthesis to simple conclusions. In this case he contributed an idea which archaeologists continue to use as a frame of reference. Although the findings of the first half of the twentieth century seemed at first to invalidate Spinden's theory, certain discoveries that have occurred since the 1950s have revived an interest in the hypothesis.

Spinden considered his most important contribution to be the correlation of the ancient Maya calendar with the Christian calendar. Until a correlation could be achieved, Maya dates floated in a vacuum. Beginning in 1919, he announced a correlation, which he continued to uphold through the succeeding decades. He fixed the zero date of the Maya calendar at 3373 B.C., which his associates generally accepted. Then he posited the first day of Maya recorded time as 613 B.C., and the formal beginning of the day-to-day calendar as 580 B.C., by which time a symbol for zero and the use of place-value notation for numbers had been devised.

At first, scholars generally accepted his system, which was a contribution at the time it was proposed. But during the mid 1920s a competing system known as the Goodman-Martínez-Thompson correlation, which placed all dates about 260 years later, began to gain favor. Spinden continued to search for additional confirmation of his system. Finally only a few persons, among them the German astronomers Hans Ludendorff and Arnost Dittrich, subscribed to it.

In the 1950s, when radiocarbon dating entered the picture, some dates derived from that technique supported the Spinden correlation, saving it from complete repudiation. As late as 1964 the first volume of the *Handbook of Middle American Indians* provided a table of pre-Columbian history according to both systems. Archaeologists today generally concede that the G-M-T correlation accommodates more of the facts than Spinden's system, but they feel that neither system is completely satisfactory.

Spinden was intrigued by the possibility that the ancient natives of Central America had contact with the inhabitants of South America. His search for mahogany during the First World War took him to Nicaragua, where he examined archaeological remains. After later explorations in that country, and after studying collateral material from history, ethnology, and linguistics, in 1923 he announced the discovery of the ancient Chorotegan culture. It had extended from northern Honduras through much of Nicaragua and Costa Rica. Although the Chorotegans were of Mexican origin, they inherited some of the earlier Maya traits, flourished from the twelfth to the fourteenth centuries A.D., and were then replaced by the present tribes, whose ancestors moved up from South America. The Toltecs and later the Aztecs of Mexico extended their sway over the Chorotegans, and this facilitated active trade between upper South America and central Mexico. Spinden believed that the gold of the Aztecs, so attractive to the Spaniards, originated in Colombia and passed along a trade route running through the Chorotegan area and up through Yucatán to Mexico City.

Spinden had less success in convincing associates of his belief that Quetzalcoatl had been a real person in Mexican history who possessed all the noble virtues attributed to him by legend. After the great man's death, he became a mythical figure and then a god. In different regions his name took various forms. Quetzalcoatl's capital was Tula, which Spinden and other archaeologists of his day identified as Teotihuacán. His empire extended from Durango in Mexico to San Salvador, and from the Pacific north through Yucatán, an area roughly twelve hundred by six hundred miles. The Toltecs under Quetzalcoatl captured Chichén Itzá in A.D. 1181 and made it a secondary capital. Later on, Spinden added more details to the story. He claimed that Quetzalcoatl died on April 4, 1208, when the planet Venus last appeared as the evening star, and that the great man was transformed into the God of Venus. Moreover, the Pyramid of the Dwarf at Uxmal, he asserted, contains an inner temple which was dedicated to Quetzalcoatl and might have been the place where he died; and the Caracol at Chichén Itzá was dedicated on the seventy-second anniversary of the hero's death. Finally, he believed that Quetzalcoatl had buried his father in a structure at Holmul in A.D. 1164. Fellow archaeologists dismissed most of these theories on the grounds that they had grown out of Spinden's imagination rather than being based on substantial facts.

On the question of the age of man in the Western Hemisphere, which had always provoked argument, Spinden again took a position that ran counter to accepted views. As scholars began to push man's existence further back in time, he went to the other extreme and insisted on the relatively recent arrival of man in the New World. In the late 1930s he chided fellow scientists for a romantic attachment to antiquity, and scoffed at the estimates of twelve thousand to twenty thousand years as the age of man in the Americas. The suggestion that Folsom man existed some ten thousand years ago drew his scorn. He claimed that a heterogeneous cultural mass migration from Asia had occurred around 2500 B.C. as the result of a German invasion of northern Europe, which in turn pushed people eastward. Although Aleš Hrdlička and Diamond Jenness supported him, most anthropologists contended that men had arrived in the New World in the more distant past. In line with his theory, Spinden also held that the mound builders of the Mississippi Valley were direct ancestors of the tribes existing there at the time of Columbus. In this instance his views received increasing support.

In the endless debate over the cause of the rise and fall of Maya civilization, Spinden had his opinions, though he devoted relatively little attention to the subject. Ellsworth Huntington's proposal that a climate different from that in the Maya area today could account for the rise of that civilization and the great population of the area in ancient times appeared to Spinden not to fit the facts. He was more positive about the downfall, which he thought was caused by yellow fever.

His work on identifying hieroglyphs failed to produce useful results. To his credit, he went beyond calendrical glyphs and studied the whole range of writing, and he proposed several identifications of signs; in each instance, however, other scholars eventually demonstrated that his solutions were not valid.

He undertook some incidental activities in the cause of archaeology. In his early career he found the Stephens stones on the Cruger estate on the Hudson River and had the American Museum of Natural History acquire those carvings, which John Lloyd Stephens had sent to the United States in the nineteenth century. During the depression of the 1930s he headed a government project for the construction of models of ancient Maya buildings. Later, he and his friend Vilhjalmur Stefansson directed another government project to collect all travel literature relating to the Americas; of the contemplated 250 volumes, at least 8 dealing with South America were completed.

The possibility of the destruction of Indian sites in the

United States alarmed him in the 1930s. Not only did pot hunters destroy mounds in the Mississippi Valley to build up private collections of artifacts, but visitors to the national parks in the Southwest vandalized those primitive sites which were open to the public. In a strong statement he called on the government to close those sites by planting thorn bushes or poison ivy around them; and he added that the public could learn more from lectures, motion pictures, and books than from visits to the sites. In this instance Spinden probably spoke in a moment of passion.

More surprising than his views on archaeology were his ideas on other subjects, especially primitive culture and contemporary civilization. In formulating a theory of society, he naturally drew data from the expeditions and also from the study of Maya art. Then he applied his mind to those materials, formulated his views of civilization, and eventually advanced criticisms of contemporary culture.

He found that the vital strength of primitive society lay in a powerful emotional instrument which he called the "oversoul" or "psyche." The psyche, an embodiment of the beliefs and aspirations of the members of the group, comprised mutual cooperation to advance the general good, justice for all persons, and general moral, ethical, and religious beliefs. A common allegiance to those principles bound the members of society together in a strong spiritual union that made almost any achievement possible. Spinden believed, in fact, that mutual cooperation had brought about "progress," or the advancement of civilization.

Aesthetic expression in the plastic arts and literature formed an important part of every society, because it faithfully reflected the group psyche, and at the same time it comforted the individual with visual reminders or oral recitations of the ideals he shared with fellow members of society.

Two major themes—communal concepts and functionalism—recur in Spinden's discussion of art. If primitive art took the form of illusion, magic, and symbolism, it possessed a rationality of its own; it gave logical expression to beliefs of the group. If art rendered the ideals intelligible, symbols suggested the spiritual world, and decoration became a communal language. Poetry and myth performed the same function as art by expressing the noblest thoughts of the psyche.

All worthy art, moreover, sprang from usefulness, according to Spinden. Nature demonstrated how function produced beauty, and early primitive art automatically gave the useful object good lines and attractive form. But when specialization entered the scene, it led to complicated expression, eventually developed into flamboyance, and lost sight of utility. For this reason, Spinden opposed art for art's sake; when beauty became an end in itself, decadence set in and the vital spirit of art died. He had already developed this idea in his study of Maya art.

Using his definition of civilization as a yardstick, he found many things to criticize in his own culture, ranging from national art and hypocrisy to individualism and the relation of man to nature.

On the assumption that art reflected the essential hopes and ideals of society, he concluded that the United States, or any European nation for that matter, had failed to achieve an aesthetic expression of its people's psyche. No imitation of Greek or Gothic styles would suffice for a modern nation, he pointed out, because the art of those nations differed from that of ancient Greece or medieval Europe. Moreover, a national aesthetic expression must enrich the lives of the people with joy and satisfaction and express their hopes and aspirations.

The United States of the twentieth century, he observed, was an industrial nation, but art in machine-made goods had not embodied the national spirit. The trouble lay not in the machines but in the individuals who supervised them. Flimsy construction and planned obsolescence, encouraged by leaders in politics and government who wanted to create jobs, defeated the ideal of honest craftsmanship. Men took no interest in their work; they labored not for the satisfaction of a well-finished product but solely to make money in order to buy mechanical pleasures, most of them stupid and wasteful. The evil began with the deficient education of youth, who received little knowledge and few ideals in the schools.

Spinden offered only one specific solution in the field of art. He believed that ethnological museums provided important source material for modern applied arts. Those materials, of course, had to be adapted to the needs of contemporary culture. During World War I, he explained, American manufacturers had been cut off from European sources of design, were thrown on their own resources, and began to find help in museums. As a result of that wartime experience, he set up an exhibition of industrial art at the American Museum of Natural History in 1919. At that early period of his career, he expected to see his hopes carried out. The ideals of the people, he said, "demand expression in our clothes, our pots and pans, our railways, steamships and aeroplanes. . . . National art is the embodiment of group consciousness, it crystallizes loyalty, it is the voice of team work."[10] As time passed, however, he realized that aesthetic expression failed to voice the highest spirit of the people.

If the nation had so far failed to produce a meaningful art, it also displayed developments which undermined its spiritual solidarity. The modern insistence on individualism worried Spinden. When a man received praise because his expressions or actions differed from or controverted the ideals and high purposes of the nation, his action began to fracture the national psyche and introduced divisions among the people instead of solidarity. Surely Spinden did not suggest that everyone must be a mere conformist; he believed that creative work in art and literature should reaffirm the ideals of the community as a whole. Great art and literature always voiced the positive hopes of the people at large. As Spinden saw it, the opposite was taking place in his own culture; art and literature as products of individualism were shattering the social psyche. In fact, individualism as an end in itself could lead only to chaos.

1. Teobert Maler. From *Teobert Maler: Die Bauten der Maya*, by Gerdt Kutscher. Courtesy Gebruder Mann Verlag.

2. Lintel 26, Yaxchilán. Photo by Maler, illustrative of his care in recording low-relief sculpture. From Peabody Museum Memoirs

3. Cobá. Note pyramids, upper right. For years the ruins of Cobá were lost in the thick growth. Maler discovered the site near the end of the nineteenth century; in the 1920s several archaeologists, unaware of Maler's find, believed they had discovered the site. Photo by Andrew Dees. Courtesy University of South Alabama.

4. The Nunnery, Chichén Itzá. Maler, Maudslay, and, briefly, Morley used a room on the level above the broad stairway for living quarters. Photo by Andrew Dees. Courtesy University of South Alabama.

5. Alfred P. Maudslay in his room at Chichén Itzá, 1889. From *A Glimpse at Guatemala . . .* (1899), by Alfred P. Maudslay and Anne C. Maudslay. Photo by H. N. Sweet.

6. Maudslay's camp at Copán. From *Archaeology,* by A. P. Maudslay.

7. Doorway, Copán. Maudslay's drawing of his reconstruction of the sculpture. From *Archaeology,* by A. P. Maudslay.

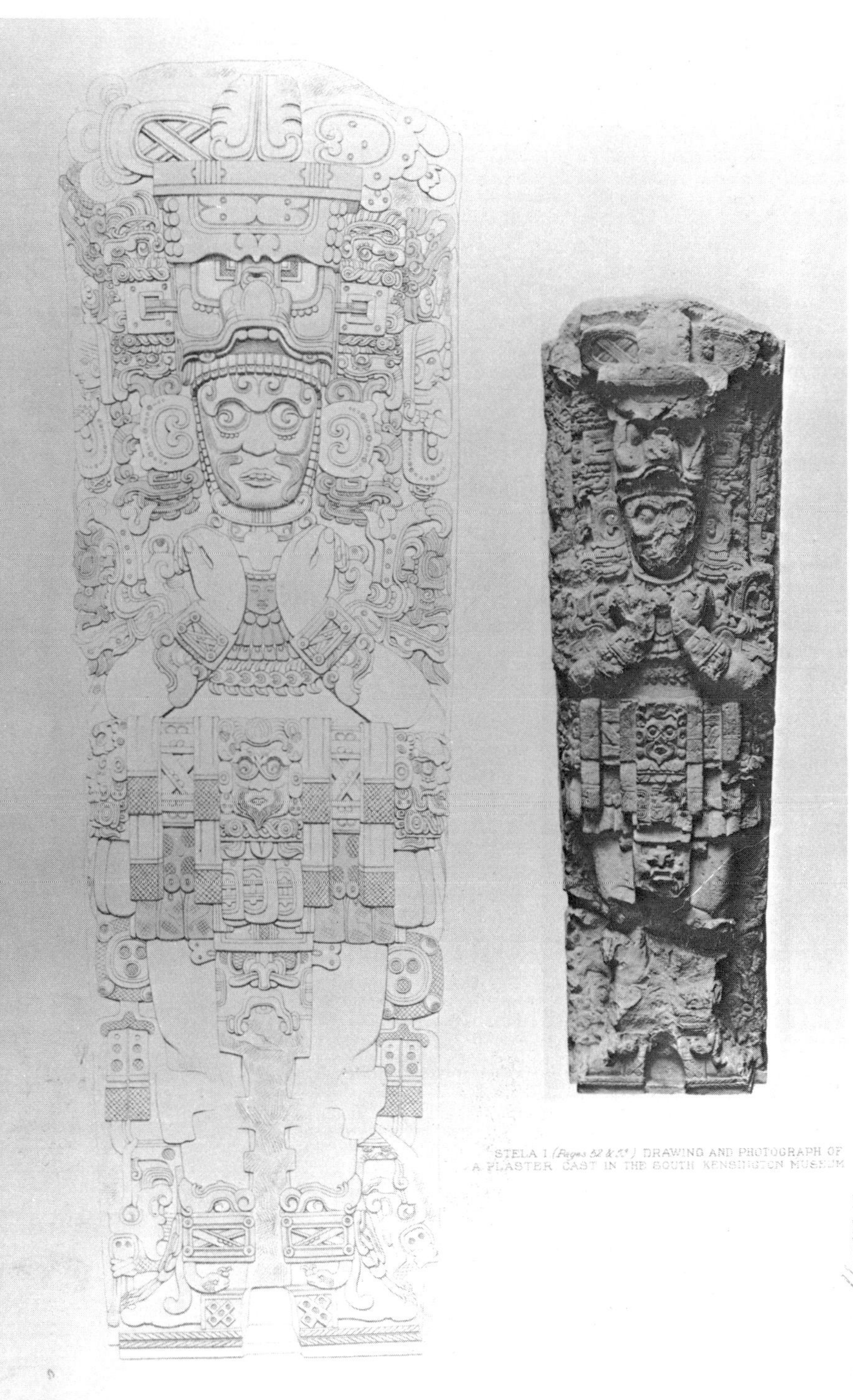

STELA I (Pages 52 & 53) DRAWING AND PHOTOGRAPH OF
A PLASTER CAST IN THE SOUTH KENSINGTON MUSEUM

8. A page from Maudslay's *Archaeology,* showing his method of presenting a photo with an accompanying drawing to bring out the lines.

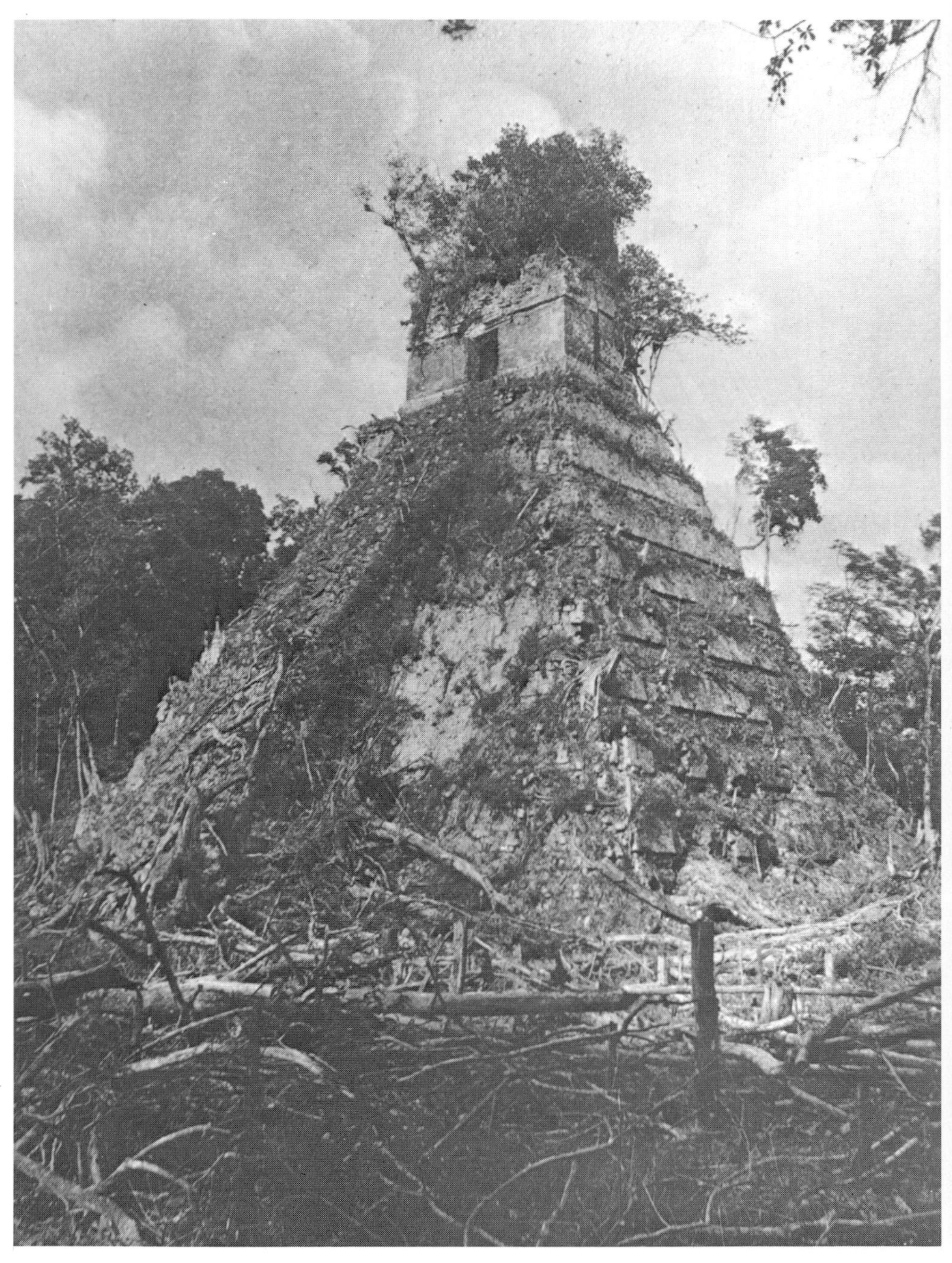

9. Temple I. Tikal. From *A Glimpse at Guatemala . . .* (1899), by Alfred P. Maudslay and Anne C. Maudslay.

10. Temple I, Tikal, after reconstruction by the University of Pennsylvania. Photo by Andrew Dees. Courtesy University of South Alabama.

11. Stela E. Quiriguá. The monuments of this site inspired Alfred P. Maudslay to undertake the study of the Maya. Photo by Andrew Dees. Courtesy University of South Alabama.

12. Sylvanus G. Morley at the Temple of the Initial Series, Chichén Itzá. From *Sylvanus G. Morley and the World of the Ancient Mayas,* by Robert L. Brunhouse. Copyright 1971 by the University of Oklahoma Press.

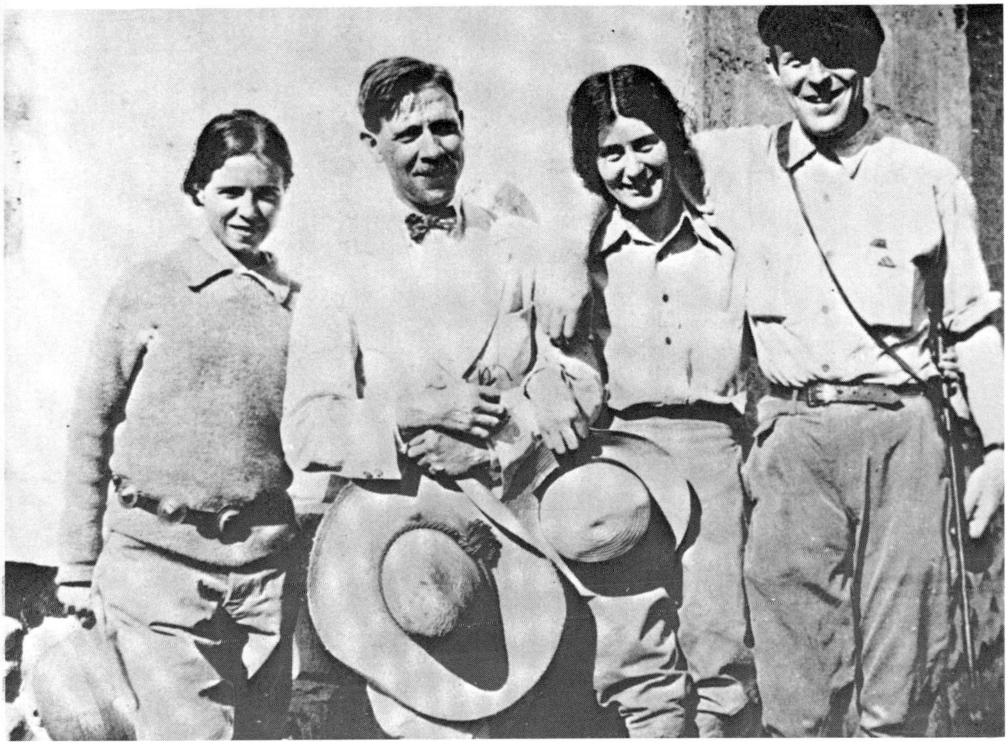

13. Mr. and Mrs. Sylvanus G. Morley (left) with Mr. and Mrs. J. Eric S. Thompson, Chichén Itzá, 1930. From *Sylvanus G. Morley and the World of the Ancient Mayas,* by Robert L. Brunhouse. Copyright 1971 by the University of Oklahoma Press.

14. Part of the Ball Court, Chichén Itzá, with Temple of the Jaguars at upper left. The court has remarkable acoustical properties. Morley used to hold phonograph concerts here at night, with his guests seated in the enclosure in the center of the picture. Photo by Andrew Dees. Courtesy University of South Alabama.

15. House of the Governor, Uxmal. Morley considered this the finest Maya structure. Author photo.

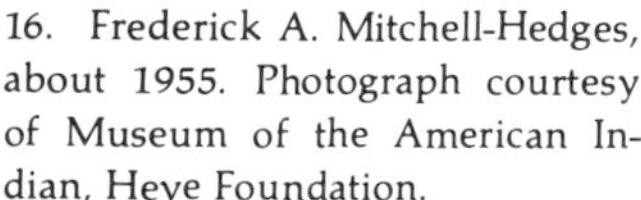

16. Frederick A. Mitchell-Hedges, about 1955. Photograph courtesy of Museum of the American Indian, Heye Foundation.

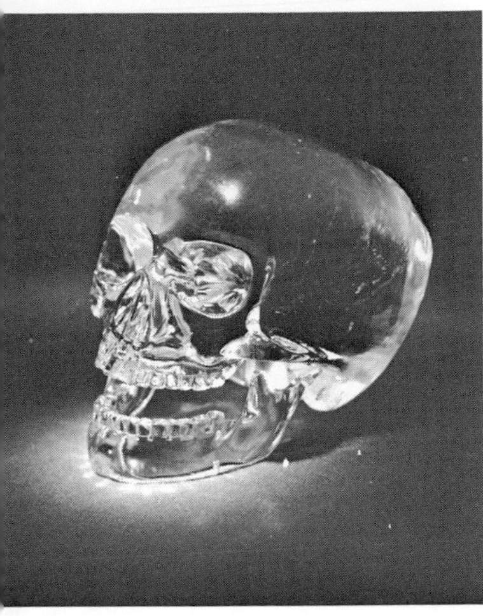

17. The crystal skull originally in the possession of Frederick A. Mitchell-Hedges. Photograph courtesy of Museum of the American Indian, Heye Foundation.

18. Herbert Joseph Spinden leaving for expedition of 1932. Photo courtesy Mrs. Ailes Spinden.

19. Spinden at Uxmal, 1930s. Photo courtesy Mrs. Edwin E. Stretcher.

20. Pyramid of the Dwarf, Uxmal. The temple atop the mound has intrigued many archaeologists. Spinden believed that an inner temple was dedicated to Quetzalcoatl. Photo by Andrew Dees. Courtesy University of South Alabama.

21. View of Tulum, looking toward the Caribbean. A late Maya site, it was surrounded by walls on three sides; these can be seen at left and through center of picture. The Castillo, right, rises above all the other buildings. Morley made several expeditions to Tulum, when intruders still faced the possibility of Indian attacks. Spinden visited the site in 1926. Photo by Andrew Dees. Courtesy University of South Alabama.

22. The Caracol, Chichén Itzá, is a circular structure, believed to have served as an observatory for the ancient Maya. Some restoration was carried out when Morley was in charge of archaeological work at Chichén Itzá. Spinden maintained that the building was dedicated in the thirteenth century A.D. on the seventy-second anniversary of the death of Quetzalcoatl. Photo by Andrew Dees. Courtesy University of South Alabama.

23. William E. Gates in his library, Point Loma, California, 1915. Photo courtesy Gates Collection, Harold B. Lee Library, Brigham Young University.

24. Part of the museum of the Department of Middle American Research, Tulane University, c. 1931. Photo courtesy Latin American Library, Tulane University.

25. Frans Blom, 1937. Photo courtesy Middle American Research Institute, Tulane University.

26. Gertrude Duby Blom, 1960s. Photo courtesy Gertrude Duby Blom.

27. Temple of the Inscriptions, Palenque. The piers of the temple originally held stucco figures. Inside is the floor slab with plugged holes, which intrigued Blom. Years later, Alberto Ruz Lhuillier examined the same stone and brought to light a magnificent tomb in the inner depths of the pyramid. Photo by Linda Schele. Courtesy University of South Alabama.

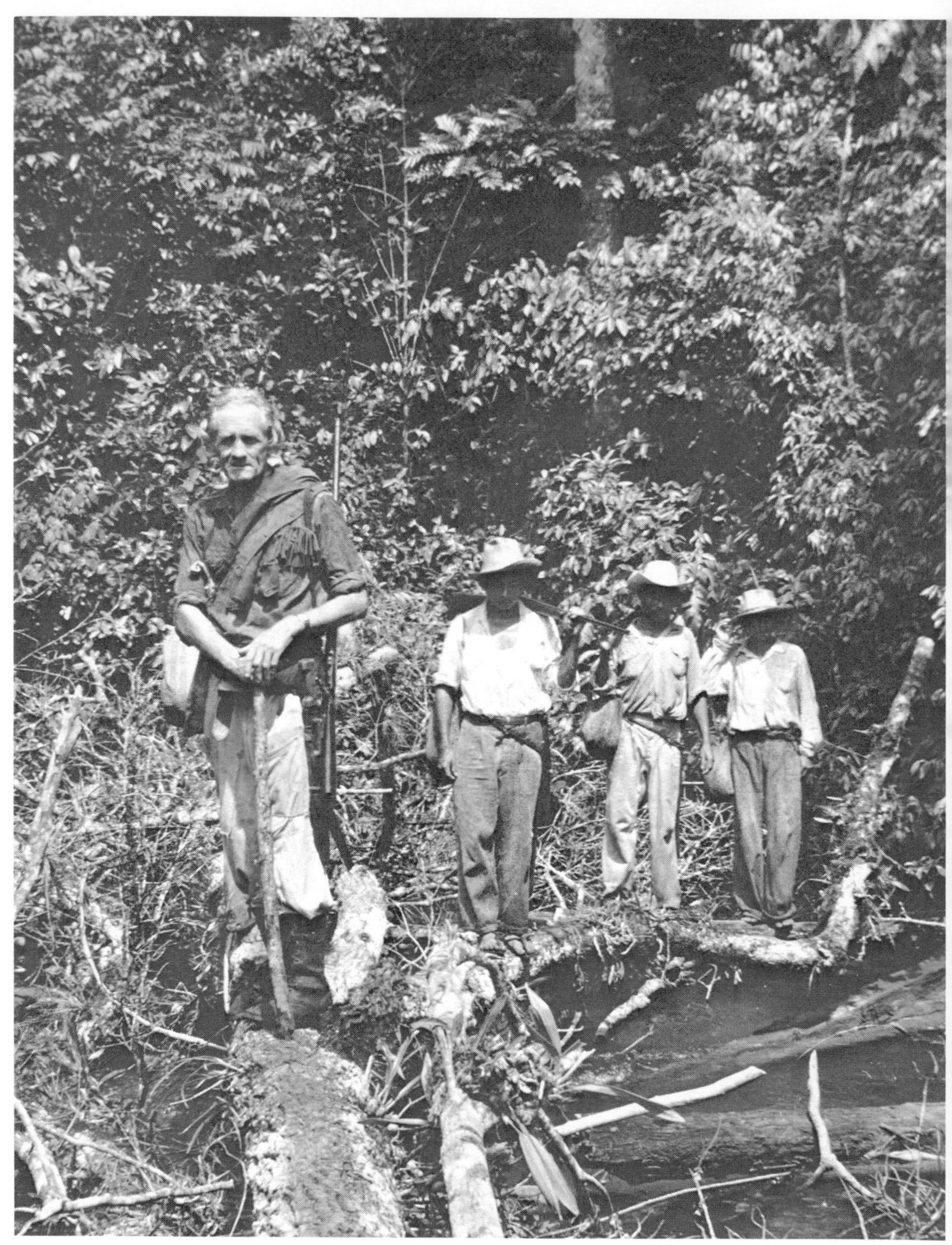

25. Frans Blom, Chiapas, 1948. Photo Courtesy Gertrude Duby Blom.

Equally damaging to the cohesive spirit of the nation were hypocritical actions that betrayed the ideals of the psyche. Although the equality of all human beings was a cherished American belief, the nation went against its own creed when it excluded other nations and races from participation in its ideal. The expansionist urge of the late nineteenth and early twentieth centuries sought to dominate "inferior" people, thereby excluding them from the operation of the teachings of mutual cooperation, sincerity, and aid to fellow human beings. Christian nations acted hypocritically when they elevated their religion, polity, and art to a position superior to "barbarous" cultures; in so doing, they assumed the role of a chosen nation and set aside the principles of mercy and fair play in dealing with outsiders. Such an exclusive attitude negated the moral precepts of the psyche, and could lead only to the destruction of society itself.

Spinden pointed to another facet of the same charge when he claimed that modern man mistakenly considered himself a superior being. Actually, Spinden contended, modern man had achieved no more than a mechanical, not an absolute, advance over uncivilized groups. In other words, the intrinsic mentality of twentieth-century man was perhaps no better than that of his primitive ancestor.

Belief in the equality of all people led Spinden to defend the Indians who had been suppressed by the United States; here was a specific and glaring instance of the way the American people and their government ignored the accepted principles of mercy and justice. Spinden knew the Indians firsthand; he had worked with them season after season for a decade during his collegiate and early professional years. He respected them, found virtues in their culture, and deplored the treatment they had received at the hands of the white man. His basic defense was grounded on the conviction that the aborigine was equal to the white man in racial and physical respects; the fact that the Indian had been retarded by a restrictive policy did not mean that he was an inferior human being.

In 1924 Spinden declared that it was high time for the government to arrange an honorable settlement of the

Indian problem and to provide fair and decent treatment for the red man. The Bureau of Indian Affairs, he asserted, had followed a deliberate policy of destroying tribal bonds. It had taken children from their homes to off-reservation boarding schools like the Carlisle Indian School in Pennsylvania, thereby depriving them of their normal security and emotional sustenance and in the end leaving them human trash. The only sensible plan was to educate the young Indian without separating him from his home. Spinden distrusted the Bureau of Indian Affairs so heartily that he urged Congress and the Secretary of Interior to keep a vigilant eye on that vast bureaucracy. In making these criticisms, he was some years in advance of the Meriam Report of 1928, which detailed all the evils of governmental policy toward the red man.

On at least two occasions Spinden came out against specific white attitudes toward the Indians. In 1922 he publicly opposed the Bursum land bill, which proposed to grant potential legal rights to whites who settled Pueblo Indian lands and to force the Pueblo Indians to prove ownership of their lands. Spinden branded the bill a sheer steal. When the bill finally passed, it was in a modified form.

In the same year he also issued a strong rebuttal to a woman who denounced the evils of Indian native dances. He criticized those churchmen who condemned Indian religious practices out of hand, exaggerated the nature of the Indian ceremonies, and urged highly questionable methods to convert the red man to Christianity.

If Americans ignored the basic human rights of other people, said Spinden, they committed an equally sad mistake in violating the simple operations of nature. The artificiality of modern civilization contributed to the degeneration of man's physical condition, and war killed off the strongest specimens while institutions protected the physically and mentally unfit. In still other ways modern man, who gloried in the mechanical ability he had achieved, ignored nature and paid the price. He farmed the prairies, and the wind carried away the topsoil. He built levees along the rivers to prevent floods and thus drained the rich, dirt-laden waters out to sea, where they could not fertilize the land. He did nothing to prevent erosion of hills and valleys. He used land for the immediate profit he could take from it, not realizing that land is capital for present and future generations, and he put none of his profit into restoring and renewing the earth. Already by the early 1930s Spinden laid the blame for the reckless destruction of natural resources on the pervasive policies of business and industry.

Modern man not only ignored nature, he also ignored common sense. Business operated on the assumption that the demand for gadgets of all kinds would constantly increase. The failure to practice conservation, Spinden predicted, might lead to a struggle for self-preservation, but in turn war and conquest defeated the ideal of mutual cooperation. Within the state itself, dubious political practices pitted class against class. In vain he pleaded for a simpler life, for first-rate craftsmanship, for creative imagination and ideals to guide the people toward a better spiritual standard of living.

In later years his indignation rose to high pitch, as he shuddered over the story of the American past. When he prepared a catalogue to illustrate the westward movement, he cried out against the shameful and thoughtless waste of those earlier years—the waste of the beaver, buffalo, gold, silver, forests, and farming land. One after another the great natural resources of the nation had been wantonly expended.

He pointed out that in primitive society man did not attempt to conquer nature; he considered himself part of nature, and he used nature only to satisfy his basic needs. The Indian, Spinden declared, never presumed to be lord of creation; the aborigine was grateful that he might use the fruits of the earth and enjoy the natural beauty about him. In later years Spinden's pessimism increased. He concluded that man's attempt to control nature was a doubtful proposition in the long run; nature could revolt and in the end have the last word. After all, he believed that all men have limitations; they lack omniscence and omnipotence, and what is worse, they cannot wisely correct errors.

In an ironic twist of phraseology, he advised that contemporary man must retain certain "savage" virtues. Although Spinden admitted that he preferred civilization because it offered greater opportunity for enjoyment and for production of material goods, he maintained that modern man can learn valuable lessons from the savage he despises. He declared that people on New York's Broadway exhibited worse manners, more selfishness, and less intelligence than the inhabitants of a native village in Honduras. What were the "savage" virtues? Primitive people support their fellow creatures in pain and want; they insist on fairness, exhibit good humor, and respect hard work; they possess remarkable memories, demonstrate unusual resourcefulness, and appreciate the changing face of nature. The education of the "savage" child comes from his environment, not from formal schooling. Apparently Spinden believed that environment had more effect than the school on the civilized child. Anticipating the charge that the Aztecs sacrificed a procession of human victims to their gods, he contended that the gods of speed and thrill in his own age also required a hecatomb of human prey.[11]

Whatever one might think of these views, and some of them appear more relevant now than a generation ago, it is evident that Spinden attempted to extract humanistic values from his knowledge of early man. Long before Robert S. Lynd wrote his book *Knowledge for What?* in 1939, Spinden gave the answer to Lynd's question. Sometimes he remarked that only a sensitized mind can make the past of America speak to the present; Spinden possessed that kind of mind.

In addition to offering major contributions to archaeology and a hypothesis about civilization, he put forth other ideas, some of them apparently conceived on the spur of the moment, which touched on so many different topics that they cannot be neatly classified. He proposed that soldiers returning from World War I should seek careers in other nations as representatives of American business. After observing elections in Cuba in 1920, he advocated a policy of nonintervention in the affairs of that island and the creation of an advisory committee to aid the Cubans in solving their own problems. With firsthand knowledge of the tropics, he pointed out that the greatest production of food occurred in that zone, and that industrialized nations should seek to feed their factory populations from that source. He always responded to the need for fairness. Good Republican that he was, Spinden called the whispering campaign against Al Smith's religion in the presidential race of 1928 shameful. And he strongly opposed the importation of seized German art to the United States following World War II. After a visit to Mexico in 1935, he praised that nation's system of rural education. He declared that the conquest of yellow fever could come only through the cooperation of all nations. But when he proposed to demonstrate that language indicated the equality of human minds, fellow scientists were unimpressed.

A high regard for the Indians prompted him to make particular claims for them. He liked to point out that four-sevenths of the agricultural crops of the United States—maize, beans, squash, pumpkins, tobacco, and other native produce—were a heritage from the American Indian, and that the white man in modern America had not cultivated from wild stock a single important staple. The art of the aborigine, he contended, provided another great gift to modern Americans. He liked to describe the pyramids of Middle America as forerunners of the skyscraper. When he declared, however, that the Maya had anticipated Einstein's theory of relativity, he encountered opposition. In 1930 the United States Census Bureau called on Spinden to help in drawing up a correct classification of Indian tribes for the purpose of the census.

Spinden also engaged in the usual professional activities. He attended the regular meetings of archaeologists and anthropologists, served as a member of the Social Science Research Council for several years, conducted seminars in Mexico for the Committee on Cultural Relations in Latin America, and gave lectures in South America under the auspices of the United States government. Gifted with a simple, clear style of writing, he published magazine articles to acquaint the general public with archaeology. He was not satisfied, however, until he could carry his message into the classroom.

The education of the child, he believed, must be enriched and broadened by a knowledge of earlier cultures, especially those of prehistoric peoples of various parts of the world. In 1930 he gave lectures over the radio on subjects like "Indian Children as Artists" and "The Fine Arts"; slides were shown during the broadcast in school auditoriums, correlated with the speaker's voice. A little later he advised teachers to include the ancient Indians in courses on American history in order to offset racial and national propaganda. History should be taught with realism, he said, but at the same time with appreciation of ideals as they emerge in the story.

When he was in charge of the school service at the Brooklyn Museum, he secured a grant from the Carnegie Corporation of New York to devise a course for the schoolchildren of New York City. Entitled "Visual Instruction in Human Geography," it consisted of fourteen units, including the Arctic, the Amazon, Africa, the Pacific area, Roman Britain, and the travels of Marco Polo, and ending with the ancient civilizations of Central and South America. He prepared 244 poster plates with black and white line drawings for use in the classroom, and arranged a syllabus for the teachers. He took this project seriously; on a visit to England he studied Roman ruins at first hand for the preparation of one of the units. Aware of the value of visual presentation of factual information, he later drew up an elaborate chart of Maya chronology.

Spinden always had a commonsense approach to the search for knowledge in his professional field and the proper way to utilize the results. He sounded the alarm that there was too much factual information accumulating in each scholarly field for the individual scholar to master and use effectively. The new, scientific emphasis on factual data in archaeology, he warned, was nurturing the seeds of its own undoing. He identified the villain as specialization.

The first anthropologists, Spinden pointed out, began their study with the aim of explaining man's psychic unity, his beliefs of brotherhood with living beings, and his attachment to the spiritual forces of the universe. Looking back on classes at Harvard, he insisted that Professor Tozzer was one of those early scholars who emphasized unity as opposed to specialization.

Spinden condemned the modern worship of details at the expense of generalization. Unlike other critics of specialization, he did not attack the problem as a case of more and more about less and less, for he valued all sound factual information. He deplored specialization for the way it emphasized the spectacular fringes and directed the investigator away from the great central truths of the subject. On one occasion he went so far as to claim that overspecialization in all fields inevitably led to the destruction of the best elements of civilization.

Sometimes he identified himself as a generalist. Undoubtedly, he used the word to indicate that he treated subjects in a broad, inclusive way rather than from the narrow approach of the specialist. As early as the 1920s he called for "correlations," that is, the reduction of knowledge to simpler terms. In American archaeology, for example, he summarized the state of knowledge on ten subjects, ranging from the age of early man to pottery, textiles, and diseases. His comprehensive approach appears in a number of his studies, which also illustrate his far-reaching grasp of his subject. It must be admitted that he was well equipped for this approach. He had a good general knowledge of the world, past and present. He was well informed on American archaeology and ethnology from Alaska to Patagonia, and his general knowledge also extended to other parts of the world. He knew how to draw upon allied disciplines for significant facts. More important, he could marshal the information for the purpose at hand; his disciplined mind saw the major outlines of a subject and supplied the pertinent details to support the generalizations.

Several of his publications provide excellent examples of effective presentation. *Ancient Civilizations of Mexico and Central America,* designed as a handbook, required a wide grasp of knowledge and clear organization. Although his specialty included only a few parts of the broad area he treated, he was equally at home in discussing northern Mexico or Panama. He presented the major factual data, knew when to generalize and when to resort to specific illustrations, chose pictures effectively, and employed simple language that the layman could understand. This was the first comprehensive book on the subject, and thereafter no informed reader could plead ignorance of the pre-Columbian cultures of Mexico and Central America. He revised the volume twice, and it remained in print for decades.

Two of his articles illustrate his unique ability to make the essential facts stand out, even for the lay reader. In a study of the population of the American Indians before and after the coming of the white man, he gathered statistics from numerous sources, used them carefully, and then summarized his findings in six simple generalizations. His treatise on sun worship followed a similar pattern except that he broadened the investigation to include Europe, Asia, and America. That article also ended with broad, striking conclusions about early religion.

In one of his last books he showed how a monograph on a restricted subject could be presented without the drawbacks of specialization. In 1950 he published the story of tobacco in America before 1492. Although *Tobacco Is American* is a small volume, it covers all aspects of the subject in brief but comprehensive fashion. The simple prose moves along easily, and the pages inform without the ballast of footnotes, yet an inquiring reader can identify the sources the author used. In fact, the interested layman can peruse the account with profit and without painful concentration, and find a neat summary of the major points at the close of the volume. Spinden was able to practice what he preached in the presentation of a specialized subject.

Like other archaeologists, he had his weaknesses. He put forth some ideas which associates could not accept, he sometimes persisted in retaining interpretations after they had been invalidated by other research, and he was reluctant to adopt some of the newer developments in the profession. Generally, these traits appeared in his later years, a phenomenon which can hardly be considered unusual.

It is interesting, however, that some of his contributions to archaeology demonstrated remarkable persistence in a field where new interpretations have a way of quickly antiquating older views. His correlation system and his hypothesis of the origin and spread of agriculture, despite numerous attempts to discard them, are still in the vocabulary of the archaeologist, though no longer as prominently as in the past. The *Study of Maya Art* has withstood the passage of time even better, for it remains the starting point for anyone taking up that subject.

Aside from his work in archaeology, Spinden will remain a significant figure in other activities. His use of professional knowledge to evaluate contemporary culture provides a constant reminder of the nagging problem, Knowledge for what purpose? He boldly applied his learning to his own culture and achieved a bitter, critical result. Whatever the validity of his estimate, he, unlike other professionals, at least made the attempt to use knowledge for humanistic ends.

In still another direction, he demonstrated his strong belief in the importance of knowledge of prehistoric man by striving to introduce that subject to the public at large and to interest schoolchildren by way of special courses.

Perhaps his most valuable contribution, applicable in his profession as well as in other disciplines, appeared in his struggle against the blight of specialization. He realized how the specialist increasingly limits the range of his study and thus increases the problem of narrowness. Spinden provided an answer, whatever its value, by synthesizing large numbers of factual data into simple generalizations. Fellow scholars, however, paid no attention to his warning that specialization restricts the individual's grasp and that overspecialization can eventually smother scholarship under the weight of factual detail.

Those scholars who today look back condescendingly upon Spinden as an old-fashioned man fail to appreciate the full sweep of his ideas, the suggestions he offered in areas beyond archaeology, and the broad insights he attained. Spinden still has something to say to the modern world.

6

William E. Gates

In the story of twentieth-century Maya studies, William Gates is a curious character. He experienced more joy in a rare book than in an archaeological discovery in the field. He strove to decipher the meaning of the hieroglyphs, but he spurned the use of all carved glyphs from the monuments. The documents he published appeared in limited editions and can be found today only in rare book rooms of specialized libraries. Condemning his own culture as too materialistic, he studied Maya language as a path leading back to a golden age in the distant past. He believed in theosophy and Atlantis, as well as in humanistic education. The strangest aspect of the man was his personality, easy to describe but difficult to grasp. On occasion he could convince people of his unusual ability or of great plans he had for a project; at other times he appeared egotistic and self-righteous. He made enemies with ease and imagined plots on every side to deprive him of the acclaim he deserved. How can one explain William Gates?

Gates adopted and deserted several careers before he hit upon Maya linguistics as his major interest. Born in Atlanta, Georgia in 1863, he was the son of a man from New York and a woman from Maryland. Later on, he liked to explain that his forebears included Sir Thomas Gates, second royal governor of Virginia, and General Horatio Gates of American Revolutionary War fame. His strong awareness of lineage was but part of his feeling that he represented the virtues of an old-time southern gentleman. When he was three years old his family moved to Philadelphia, where he attended school. He entered the Johns Hopkins University for his undergraduate training only a few years after its founding. Although he said little in later life about the quality of the instruction he received, he crusaded consistently for a humanist curriculum which President Daniel Coit Gilman sponsored at Hopkins.

In college he took all the courses in political science and Germanics with a view to research in the history of law. After receiving the A.B. degree in 1886, he pursued law courses at the universities of Maryland and Virginia, and planned to draw up a concordance of every word in Anglo-American law. This was the first of his many projects to compile or collect facts, glyphs, or books.

Because of poor eyesight he gave up the history of law for the study of languages. He worked with Saxon and Gothic, perhaps in college, and then studied Sanskrit and Chinese; by the mid 1890s he developed a passion for ancient Egyptian texts. Interest in Chinese prompted him to acquire a collection of the art of that country; and with the study of Egyptian, he began to buy the texts of that language. The collecting drive, already evident in these early years, was later directed toward building the library of Middle American books and documents for which he became best known.

Although the details of his income in this period are not known, he felt the need to acquire sufficient resources so that he might live without physical labor and indulge his personal tastes. About 1890 he moved to Cleveland, Ohio and, perhaps with the aid of family funds, set up an agency to sell typewriters; then he transferred to the printing business, and specialized in producing legal papers. He must have had some knack for business, because he managed to make the money he desired within fifteen years. It seems, however, that he did not enjoy the business world or the cares connected with it, and he deserted mundane affairs for the study of linguistics.

His first encounter with Maya hieroglyphs was undertaken deliberately, but he never explained why those enigmatic characters fascinated him. It seems that in perusing some German magazines he came upon an article which stirred him to look into Maya glyphs. While still in the printing business in 1898, he acquired a copy of the Troano Codex and pondered the strange figures on its leaves. They intrigued his curiosity with the same magnetic pull that the Maya ruins of Palenque and Copán exerted on Guillermo Dupaix, John Lloyd Stephens, and other men of the earlier nineteenth century. When Gates examined his first codex, a few men were beginning to understand the elementary principles of deciphering the date glyphs. Gates decided to interpret the entire range of Maya writing as his life work. He sold the Egyptian documents and later gave his Chinese art collection to a museum. In 1900 he issued his first publication, a compilation of Maya calendar tables, in an edition of ninety-four copies. This is the earliest indication of another of his continuing pursuits, the publishing of books in small editions.

He had amassed sufficient money by 1905 to guarantee the independence he desired. There were apparently no women in his life, and of course no children to care for, so he was free to move about at will. He transferred his residence from Cleveland to Point Loma in California, where he lived for a dozen years in a theosophist community presided over by Madam Katherine Tingley. The community provided a unique atmosphere for serious-minded people like Gates. An experimental school taught several hundred children and offered a variety of educational fare—public lectures and correspondence courses, performances of Greek drama and Shakespeare, and elaborate productions of music and dance. The printing press, for a time managed by Gates, turned out artistic products. Silk culture, a bee farm, and horticulture gave work to some of the members. Two large white buildings, each with a prominent dome, were the visible trademark of the community. Gates enjoyed the place and the people. In later years he looked back with nostalgia on Point Loma, saying that it teemed with youthful spirit in his day.

He agreed with the beliefs of the brotherhood, respected Madam Tingley, and enjoyed freedom to pursue his study. Although a stint of labor was required of many members, those with special attainments were allowed to cultivate their particular talents. By 1910 he acquired the title of Professor in the School of Antiquity connected with the community. During the years at Point Loma he gradually acquired a personal library of fine items on prehistoric Middle America; he published some books and articles; he added to the font of type reproducing Maya hieroglyphic characters which he had begun to make in 1900; and he studied Scandinavian and some languages of Asia, hoping that they might prove helpful in the decipherment of the glyphs. In later years he claimed to have a speaking knowledge of thirteen languages.

In this period he came under the influence of theosophist thought. Apparently he accepted among other things the belief in reincarnation, the idea that man in America is older than in Asia or Africa, and, most important for his studies, the conviction that man in prehistoric times possessed knowledge and insight far exceeding the attainments of modern man. And so Gates hoped that by deciphering the Maya glyphs he could open a way to the great wisdom of the past. It is revealing to know that the School of Antiquity at Point Loma was originally called the School for the Revival of the Lost Mysteries of Antiquity. The writings of Madam Blavatsky strongly influenced him, as is evident in quotations from her writings which he included in his own publications of this period. In "The Spirit of the Hour in Archaeology" he openly admitted his debt; "the views and position" in that paper, he said, "are my own, but they were first hers."[1] Among the lectures he gave during this period were "The Arts of Expression," "Theosophy the Saving Power of the World," and, at the Panama-California Exposition, "H.P. Blavatsky and Archaeology."

It is not clear what part archaeology played in Gates's outlook. When he joined the community, Madam Tingley talked about an archaeological expedition to Central America, a prospect which apparently appealed to him. There was more talk but no money to carry out the project. In his later years he demonstrated no deep interest in archaeological exploration or excavation, and, as we shall see, he did not agree with the aims of contemporary archaeologists.

Gates made his first trip to Mexico after the United States had entered World War I. It is difficult to understand why his study of glyphs had not taken him to the land of the Maya long before that time. During the visit, however, he showed little interest in the ruins. Rather, he sought out old Maya manuscripts, which he believed his agent had failed to uncover in a journey in 1915. Boasting that he traveled fifteen hundred miles by mule and on foot to out-of-the-way places, Gates had to admit that no more manuscripts existed.

More surprising was his role as an unofficial investigator of political and social conditions in Mexico. From July 1917 to April 1918, he wandered about the central part of the country as well as through Yucatán. Claiming only to be an archaeologist and book collector, he moved from state to state and interviewed President Carranza and leaders opposed to him, Zapata, Félix Díaz, and Meixuiero; and in Yucatán he studied the government of Governor Alvarado. Gates went to Mexico favorably disposed toward the Carranza regime, but he soon became highly critical of Carranza because he openly opposed the United States and appeared to be pro-German. After speaking with leaders of the opposition to Carranza, Gates concluded that Zapata proposed the best program for the country. In Yucatán, however, Alvarado's policies appeared to Gates to be a carbon copy of Russian bolshevism, with a whole program of socialistic reforms and numerous workers' leagues of resistance.

As he traveled through Mexico he was warned of great personal danger if he entered areas controlled by the rebels, but he boldly went where he wished. He met with Zapata sympathizers in Mexico City itself; in rural regions he moved into forbidden areas by prearrangement with the rebels and by ignoring government orders. He portrayed those actions as if they were cloak and dagger affairs in which he always accomplished his aim and at the same time kept Carranza officials ignorant of the fact that he "was more than a scientific traveler."[2]

After he returned to the United States, an anonymous author in *The Mexican Review* purported to reveal him as a naïve conspirator. The author charged him with having led six or seven mules, heavily laden with arms and ammunition, destined for the rebels; Carranza soldiers had seized him, according to the article, and only by the friendly intervention of a United States agent was he released, on condition that he must leave the country at once. In addition, the author declared that Carranza officials later obtained documents proving Gates's connivance with the rebels. These anonymous charges, of course, are questionable. It should be noted, however, that later on Gates boasted that the Carranza government denounced him as an agent of the rebels.

In perspective, perhaps Gates's attitude toward Mexico was more indicative of his personality than his activities there. He assumed that he had the task of investigating conditions because Carranza's government censored news of what was actually going on by preventing access to the region of the dissidents. Gates also appeared to believe that he must find a solution for that nation's problems. Porfirio Díaz, he claimed, had been popular, but had made the mistake of opening the nation to foreign business exploiters and of ignoring the Indian peasant. Gates agreed that the United States must not intervene. He seemed to favor Zapata as the man to overthrow Carranza. Gates called for improvement of the conditions of the Indians, a constitutional government, a friendly attitude toward the United States, and the end of socialistic reforms. When he attempted to spell out a coherent program, only a vague formula emerged. A coalition of all liberal elements, enlisting the support of Carranza's opponents, he believed, would create a policy of reconstruction, which could be fostered by money and cooperation from the United States. Within a few years Mexico did achieve political stability, but there is no evidence that Gates played any part in it.

After his return from Mexico he rarely engaged in projects not directly connected with Maya linguistics. He even brusquely refused some invitations to speak to groups with the explanation that he did not care to perform for audiences. One notable exception was his brief activity for the Maryland Academy of Sciences. Although he gave the impression to others that he had been made an adviser on archaeology for that institution, the records show that his connection was more tenuous. In the winter of 1919-20 he addressed the academy on his explorations among the Indians of Middle America and displayed some original documents of the sixteenth and seventeenth centuries. It was reported that he generated considerable interest among the audience. In recognition of his scientific work on the Maya, he was made an "Honorary Associate . . . with the rank of Academician for Life."[3] There is no indication that he performed any service, even of an advisory nature, for the organization.

By this time he had dropped his association with the theosophist movement and was attempting to mingle with recognized scholars. In fact he played a part, perhaps the most active part, in the creation of the Maya Society in 1920. In April about a dozen scholars met at the home of John B. Stetson, Jr., in Philadelphia. Stetson, the hat manufacturer, hovered in the background as an occasional sponsor of Maya projects; in this instance he opened his home to the scholars. They elected Gates president, and set up an executive committee. The full story of the creation of the organization has not come to light, but it seems certain that Gates was the prime mover and that he expected to use the society to gain respect and recognition for the books he planned to publish under its auspices. By 1922 the records listed thirty-two members.

The Maya Society was a curious affair. Its members were outstanding Maya scholars of the day, and many of them represented an approach to anthropology and archaeology at variance with the views of Gates. At the first full meeting of the organization, at the end of 1920, Gates managed to put down all opposition and dominate the group. The fact that he secured legal title to the name of the society without telling its members indicates his determination to control it for his own purposes. We will hear more of this later.

One of the younger members of the Maya Society was Sylvanus Morley, trained at Harvard in Maya studies and fully experienced in exploration in Middle America. Morley was beginning to gain some name for himself when he and Gates first struck up a cordial acquaintance after the First World War. It happened that Morley had an attractive personality, a buoyant spirit, and a talent for making and keeping a large circle of friends. After numerous annual expeditions to Middle America in search of date glyphs, he published the results of his work in 1920 in *The Inscriptions of Copan,* an impressive and useful collection of glyphs. Gates had a hand in the volume. Morley appreciated the fine items in Gates's library and used several of the documents in the volume; moreover, he invited Gates to contribute an essay on Maya linguistics and asked him to prepare the index of the book. Those favors Morley carefully acknowledged, along with the aid of many other persons. Later on, when Gates complained that he had not received sufficient credit for his help, he ignored the time and patience Carl Guthe gave to the preparation of the manuscript for the press. Even when he was on the sidelines of a project, Gates felt that the limelight should fall on him.

In the ensuing years, Gates revealed more unpleasant aspects of his personality. By the beginning of 1921 Morley proposed that Gates might loan some of his important documents to the Carnegie Institution of Washington, and he also invited Gates as a special favor to join his expedition that year. Early in January Gates and Morley conferred with President Woodward of the Carnegie Institution. Morley shuddered on seeing Gates appear at the stately quarters on P Street in high-laced field boots. Eventually Morley realized that that breach of good taste was insignificant compared with Gates's actions on the expedition.

When the exploring party, consisting of Morley, Oliver Ricketson, A.K. Rutherford, and Gates, arrived in Guatemala City, Gates went to work microfilming five hundred pages of documents and studying the sounds of the native language. At the time Morley had just completed writing "Holon Chan," an imaginative story for Elsie Parsons's book *American Indian Life,* and he asked for Gates's opinion of the manuscript. Gates replied that it would do. Although that judgment had no effect on Morley, it revealed Gates's failure to appreciate imaginative, colorful prose. In fact, although he was a linguist, he exhibited a remarkable inability to write clearly or precisely, both in his correspondence and in his scholarly works.

Gates stayed on in Guatemala City for two months and then joined the Morley party at El Cayo, jumping-off place for the Petén. At Naranjo, Ricketson or Rutherford happened to find an inscribed stela; Gates openly expressed his peevishness at not having discovered the glyphs.

A more important incident also occurred at Naranjo. The previous year Thomas Gann had sent a servant to break up some of the stones of the Hieroglyphic Stairway and send them to him in British Honduras. The job was botched; the mule could carry only a few of the stones, the remainder were abandoned, and fragments lay scattered over the ground. Morley deplored this operation by his friend, but in an effort to preserve the glyphic texts complete, he gathered up the fragments and sent them to Gann to be fitted into their proper places. Morley and the Carnegie Institution strongly condemned pillage and smuggling of stones. But Gates overlooked the good intentions of Morley, and later accused him of sending artifacts out of the country.

As the expedition proceeded, Gates had good days and bad days. At Tikal he found the inscribed base of Stela 6 and regained his cheerful spirits. On the journey from that site, however, traveling by mule exhausted him by eleven o'clock in the morning. The fifty-eight-year-old man obviously lacked the stamina for exploration in the Petén. Then tension built up between him and Rutherford, and a verbal explosion erupted between the two men several days later in camp. Morley called it "bush nerves," the result of irritations and inconveniences in traveling through the jungle. The next morning Gates pointedly refused to accompany the party on a visit to the ruins of Ixlú. That night the Americans enjoyed a convivial meeting with an old friend at Flores, and the following morning Gates exploded over what he considered a disgusting social gathering. At a grand picnic a few days later, Gates, to everyone's surprise, was in good form and presented a gracious toast to the local governor. After six weeks with the expedition, Gates left to carry on his own business, to the relief of Morley's party.

Gates had planned to ride a horse to Guatemala City and then go on to Chichicastenango to study the Quiché language for three weeks. It is not known whether he followed the plan, but it is clear that by the time he returned to the United States he had scored a triumph. He secured the post of director general of archaeology and director of the museum in Guatemala. He planned the creation of a national museum, protection of the nation's historical treasures, and a grand exhibition to celebrate the quadricentennial of the Spanish Conquest. He spent some time in Guatemala in 1922, solidifying his power and appointing agents. A law, passed at his behest, vested in him all control over the national ruins. He bought a farm near Chichicastenango for his residence in the Quiché country. In Guatemala City he arranged to remodel the Temple of Minerva, a favorite landmark, for the new museum. He appointed T.T. Waterman, an American archaeologist, to direct the museum and to carry on some excavations at Kaminaljuyú, and P.W. Shufeldt as inspector of the ruins in the Petén. Shufeldt, incidentally, was a wise choice, for he knew the Petén well and took an interest in the ancient ruins. On going to Mexico as a young man, he had collected birds for the American Museum of Natural History. Soon, however, he entered the coffee business and then the chicle business. When working in southern Campeche, he turned in reports on Maya ruins which the archaeologists ignored. Later, in the Petén, he was a progressive chicle manager, building roads and good houses. His company opened the region around Uaxactún and thus indirectly aided later expeditions of the Carnegie Institution in getting to that site. It was Shufeldt who showed Morley endless house mounds and convinced him of their significance.

In the course of 1923, Gates faced more and more trouble in Guatemala. Waterman assumed his post in the capital, but Gates spent only one month in the country. He conducted his business from his farm in Virginia by cable with Waterman and especially with a native, Sinforoso Aguilar, secretary of the museum. As the fall of the year approached, Gates found his plans crumbling one by one. He either lacked administrative ability or suffered from naïveté, and there is no doubt that he failed to understand Latin American politics.

By this time he had become angry with Morley and the Carnegie Institution, charging them with attempting to prevent other archaeological institutions from excavating in Guatemala. In addition, he accused Morley of smuggling those artifacts out of the country and of using Guthe's doctoral thesis as his own research. Assured that the new law gave him complete control over the ruins in Guatemala, Gates determined to make the Carnegie Institution knuckle under to his whims. But he misjudged his enemies. After Morley had secured an important concession in Mexico for a vast project at Chichén Itzá, he went to Guatemala City to renew a concession for excavating Uaxactún. Soon he discovered that he could not work through Gates; so he resorted to his longstanding friendship with top government officials and secured a grant to excavate Uaxactún and several other sites.

When Gates discovered that he had been circumvented, he realized also that his loss of prestige endangered the other projects he had in hand. He blustered and threatened by cable. Guatemalans who had opposed his tampering with the Temple of Minerva in 1922 now became more vocal, and work on remodeling the building for a museum came to a standstill. Organizations in the United States which had offered exhibits to celebrate the quadricentennial in 1924 hesitated or lost interest in the project.

Gates learned that he was no match for the Carnegie Institution. He sent a vitriolic letter to President Merriam, filled with fantastic charges. Then in November he went to Washington for a conference with Morley and Carnegie officials, expecting to browbeat them into recognizing his authority in Guatemala. The brutal truth came out: the Carnegie people had secured their permit from a high Guatemalan official and were responsible only to that man. To make matters worse, Gates failed to supply Waterman with funds for the projected excavation, and the two men quarreled. Gates's threatened resignations did not budge higher-ups in Guatemala, and his "unconditional" resignation late in November 1923 was accepted.

The collapse of the Guatemalan enterprise embittered the proud man, and he determined to "get" Morley the next month at the annual meeting of the Maya Society. Curiously, back in January 1923, some members of the society had been so upset by Gates that they wanted to oust him as president. Morley, however, counseled patience and convinced the dissidents to retain Gates for another year. When the annual meeting took place at the end of 1923, Gates attempted to have Morley expelled from membership, and the society dissolved in bitterness.

For a time the man did not know what to do. The Guatemala enterprise had failed, and then the Maya Society came to an unfortunate end. Early in 1924, when he met a friend in New York, he confessed his quandary: Should he return to raising chickens in Virginia, prepare the Maya material for publication, or continue the struggle to save Guatemala from looting archaeologists? He could not know that he would follow none of the alternatives, for fate was about to confer on him a unique role.

Within a few months Gates moved from the embarrassing debacle in Guatemala to a new post which held out brilliant prospects for the development of Central American studies in the United States. It is ironic that he received the appointment not so much because of his particular ability but because of the collection of books he planned to sell. The story of this coincidence of events involved a newspaper editor, a banana baron, and a university president.

Back in 1921, when Gates resolved to specialize in Maya linguistics, he offered a sizable portion of his library for sale—that is, the non-Maya items pertaining to Mexico north of Oaxaca. He sent the books to New York City for disposal at auction, but various delays prevented the printing of the catalogue until 1924. News of the proposed sale got abroad and collectors over the country looked forward to acquiring rare items.

In New Orleans, Marshall Ballard, editor of the *Item*, learned of the sale before the catalogue had been issued, and had a brainstorm: It would be a capital idea for his city to acquire the collection. After all, New Orleans had a natural interest in Central America, especially by way of commerce. Just how Ballard believed that the esoteric documents would directly help his city was not explained. At any rate, he proposed the idea to his close friend Samuel Zemurray, a tall Bessarabian immigrant who had come to Alabama as a young man, discovered that he liked to eat bananas, then got into the business of selling them, importing them, and finally raising them in Honduras. By 1924 his Cayumel Fruit Company was a flourishing concern. Zemurray lived just off the campus of Tulane University. Somehow, he also considered Ballard's idea good enough to be willing to put up the money—$60,000 for the collection, $300,000 to endow a department of Middle American research at Tulane, and funds for the first archaeological trip sponsored by the new department.

Needless to say, President Dinwiddie of Tulane found the idea entrancing. Perhaps his institution could make a name in the field of scholarship as well as on the gridiron. Events moved fast, because the collection would shortly go on sale in New York. Ballard interviewed Gates on March 12; two weeks later President Dinwiddie and the trustees agreed to pay $60,000 for the collection. By early April the president was in New York arranging the purchase. Everyone was happy except those collectors who hungered for particular titles and, of course, Mr. Parke and Mr. Bernet, the auctioneers, who never had the opportunity to prove that they could have brought in $100,000 by selling the items at auction.

Back in March during the early stages of the negotiations, someone in New Orleans had a bright idea, which was adopted without investigation. Those books and manuscripts, once they were acquired by Tulane, needed a qualified scholar to make intelligent use of them. Gates, of course, was the man for the job. So Dinwiddie, Ballard, and Zemurray agreed that Tulane would acquire the collection only if Gates came with the books as head of the new department. Gates needed no coaxing; he would generously sacrifice his studies in the quiet of his Virginia farm to assume the university post. He did not explain, of course, that he would do anything to obliterate the memory of the fiasco in Guatemala.

News of the double arrangement appeared in New York and New Orleans newspapers on April 3, 1924. Although Dinwiddie was still in New York completing the purchase, it was Gates who made the announcement from his Virginia home. That news release was a strange affair, not because it dealt entirely with Gates, as one might expect, but because of a number of dubious statements it contained. He explained that he was president of the Maya Society, which was technically true, although the society had disintegrated. In addition, he made it clear that he still held his posts in Guatemala, which was entirely false. And his statement that the endowment of the new department was expected to be increased to $500,000 was no more than wishful thinking. It is possible that Gates deliberately anticipated Dinwiddie in making the initial announcement in order to direct all attention to himself; his violation of the usual protocol by which an institution announces its own appointments was a harbinger of trouble to come.

Tulane made the mistake of acting too fast; it acquired a collection and a director before it had adopted a program for the new department. As it turned out, Gates, of all people, formulated the objectives to be pursued. The evolution of these aims tells much about the man. He always maintained that he had been appointed with complete power to develop the department according to his own judgment; and there is reason to believe that that was the case. He also claimed that he gave the name of Middle American Research to the new department. When he announced his appointment in April 1924, he put forth modest aims: The department would study the language and history of Middle America and send out expeditions. A few days later he said that the first task would be the translation of old documents about medical knowledge of the Maya. In addition, Dinwiddie announced the hope that Tulane would publish books with Gates's Maya type font.

Gates arrived in New Orleans in May 1924, and received considerable attention. Of the numerous newspaper articles about him, Lyle Saxon's interview was flattering if a bit conventional. He reported Gates as simple in manners, easy to approach, and irrepressibly enthusiastic about his work; and he concluded that the newcomer was a scholar, a gentleman, a thinker, and a human being. Gates could hardly have done better in describing himself as he wished others to know him. In addition, Tulane formally introduced him to the public. Middle American exhibits were displayed on the fourth floor of the new science building. Townspeople flocked in, and President Dinwiddie presented the new director, who in turn spoke on the relations of Tulane with Caribbean nations; then the audience viewed the exhibits. Gates was at his best on such occasions.

A day or so later he gave a newspaper interview and added several new angles to the objectives of the department. Those expeditions to be sent to Middle America, he explained, would aim to improve the condition of the people, encourage road building, improve public health, and foster better understanding between the United States and Latin America. Thus, he joined social service for the neighbors of the south with Maya scholarship as the objectives of the department.

Gates announced another idea in that interview which must have made President Dinwiddie raise an eyebrow. "We are going to bring back, at Tulane," the director declared, "the study of the humanities; we are going to recreate the philosophies of the peoples; we are going to develop a broad scholarship instead of mere fact-gathering."[4] What did this mean? Did he plan to overhaul the curriculum of the university or did he intend the innovation only for the new department?

After Gates returned from a meeting of the International Congress of Americanists in Europe, he had more to say about the objectives of the department. His imagination went into high gear and he announced a vastly expanded program. In November a local newspaper called it "a scientific dream never before dared,"[5] and so it was. He proposed another collecting project; the department would compile data on all aspects of Middle America, past and present, which would comprise a "library of 100,000 indices." Every subject—commerce, science, botany, mineralogy, archaeology, biology, sanitation, transportation and travel, and Indian education—would be catalogued. The great data bank, said Gates, would suggest remedies for Middle American problems; it would stimulate trade; it would make Tulane one of the great universities of the country. Tulane had the funds to begin the project, he declared, and he was assured that more money would be forthcoming when it was needed. Tulane would become the University of the Caribbean. He ended the interview on a commercial note. The data bank would stimulate prosperity of the Latin American nations, increase their buying power, and in the end expand world commerce. Thus, the accumulated objectives of the department now included scholarship, social service, the creation of a data bank, and stimulation of commerce.

He visited Mexico and Honduras early in 1925 to do spadework for his program. In Mexico City he gave an interview which resulted in a long, flattering article in *Excelsior*. He discussed all of his ideas, ranging from the Maya type font to Tulane's plan to fight disease and poverty in Middle America. There is no indication that Mexican officials showed any interest in his plans. In Honduras, however, he had better luck. There he inspired the government to consider the creation of a national museum; a commission was duly set up to formulate plans, and Gates was named honorary president of the group. As a gesture of goodwill, the government sent books and a silk national flag to the department at Tulane.

Back in the United States, Gates burned with excitement over the novel prospect of combining social service and commerce in an attempt to uplift Honduras and at the same time to increase the trade of New Orleans. Local newspapers announced the good news. He declared that the Crescent City could become the seat of authority and reference for Central America by grasping the vast commerce those republics would soon engage in; it could in fact outstrip New York City. "He spoke quietly, firmly, almost solemnly; yet his body had grown tense with emotion."[6] As for Honduras, he said that his task at Tulane was to develop the agriculture and industry of that nation, advance its social welfare, build a transcontinental railroad, chronicle its history, found libraries and museums, and stabilize its government! Surely this was a unique concept in the history of higher education in the United States, for Gates proposed that his department would do everything short of actual annexation of that Central American country.

When Morley passed through New Orleans several months later, he gave an interview. He wanted to congratulate Frans Blom and Oliver La Farge on their successful expedition through Mexico. But Morley was a kindhearted soul, and he could not snub his enemy Gates in public. So he praised the director's plans for the economic development of the nations to the south, and then, probably with a dubious inflection in his voice, he remarked that it was the first time that anyone had had the vision to combine business with archaeology. Morley had the ability to pay a compliment to an enemy—not so Gates. Earlier that year, when the two men had found themselves in the same breakfast room in Washington, D.C., Gates had pointedly refused to speak to Morley.

Long before Gates had developed his expansive objectives, he assembled a staff to put the department into operation. Alan W. Payne, a journalist, became his assistant. When the director was away—and it seems that he traveled much of the time—Payne was in charge. On at least one occasion Gates sent Payne to Honduras to visit archaeological sites and to collect information for the vast project Gates planned to operate in that nation.

In retrospect it is clear that Gates made a fundamental misjudgment in November 1924, when he told Dinwiddie that the department should shun archaeology and not collect objects for a museum, because other institutions provided too much competition in those fields. He did not explain that he had no sympathy with contemporary professional archaeologists. Instead, the Middle American Research Department should emphasize plant studies, dealing with medicine, botany, dyes, and hardwoods. Despite his own advice, however, Gates went ahead and added an archaeologist to his staff. It came about in a curious way.

Gates realized that he needed professional men to give the department strength and respectability. At first he announced that John P. Harrington of the Smithsonian Institution, who had helped him with language studies a few years earlier, would become his professional assistant. But the man declined. Then Alfred V. Kidder and Thomas A. Joyce were approached, and they too turned down the offer. On the recommendation of Professor Tozzer at Harvard, Gates sounded out Frans Blom, who was desperately seeking a full-time job. In October, Gates had two long sessions with Blom at the Peabody Museum, and several weeks later he invited the man to his home in Virginia for three days, displaying his library and explaining his plans for research and publication. Gates almost won over the young archaeologist. In the end Blom could not resist the salary of $3,000 a year, though he realized the danger of working under the erratic director. Incidentally, Gates's salary was $5,000; the total budget of the department was $15,000 annually, the income from the Zemurray endowment. By 1925 other members of the staff included Ralph Roys in Maya language, Andrew C. Hartenbower and Earl S. Haskell in tropical agronomy, and Oliver La Farge, temporarily taken on to help Blom.

The appointment of Blom pleased Gates immensely for several reasons. He had managed to take that promising young man away from Morley and the Carnegie Institution, whom he had hated since the Guatemala days. If this attempt to even old scores with his enemies prompted Gates to employ this particular archaeologist, he made a serious mistake. At the time, however, he exulted in the choice and crowed over Blom's qualifications: "Old Danish family; five languages; King's messenger in the war. . . . Blom counts his friends in the Legations crowd; also stays with Archie Roosevelt at Oyster Bay. Knows young Frick well, and reports him as getting very keen on our subjects."[7]

Early in 1925 Gates sent off three expeditions: Blom and La Farge spent six months on an important archaeological journey from Veracruz to Guatemala, Hartenbower and

Haskell surveyed the soil and plants of Tabasco, and Payne went to Honduras.

By mid August 1925, however, Gates found events taking an unpleasant turn. When Blom and La Farge returned to New Orleans, they received all the public notice in the newspapers. Gates's name rarely appeared in those accounts, and Hartenbower and Haskell figured so lightly that it is impossible to know what they did accomplish. Surely all of the attention Blom received nettled Gates, because he did not sympathize with archaeology, and he yearned for more notice for tropical plant research and those grandiose ideas for the development of Middle American nations. Was the tail beginning to wag the dog; was Blom overshadowing Gates in the department? On still another account Gates appeared to make no headway. He had held out the bait to businessmen of New Orleans by predicting great stimulation of trade with Middle America, but no businessmen wrote checks to increase the endowment of the department or even to contribute small sums to the Exploration Fund.

By the fall of 1925 the department was in serious financial trouble. Something had gone wrong. Back in March Gates had made it plain to Zemurray that the department needed a total endowment of $2 million; in fact, the budget for the next year should be $50,000. According to Gates, Zemurray told him to carry on his plans and the board of trustees would take care of the need. But the philanthropist himself did not offer to pay the necessary funds. In the months that followed, the trustees failed to add a cent to the departmental budget. Then at the end of September, after Gates had submitted the department's expenses for the past year, he was informed that he had overdrawn the account by some $2,000. Gates resigned and then withdrew the resignation some weeks later. He also noticed that Dinwiddie turned cool toward him. The president explained that hereafter all expenses must be submitted through regular university channels, and that every new person employed in the department must be approved by the president.

To make matters worse, Gates began to detect a change in Blom since the explorer's return from his expedition to Mexico and Guatemala. The young man who had looked so promising back in January—coming from a good family and knowing all the right people—now acted more independently, perhaps even impudently, toward the director. How ungrateful of Blom, whom he had employed when he was down to his last hundred dollars! After Gates had been out of town, he returned and claimed that Blom had carried on the business of his office, even to opening his mail. He suspected, moreover, that the young man had engaged in some financial irregularities in the department. In November Blom went to New York City, ostensibly to visit his mother, who had come to the United States to see him; but he also called on museums there, seeking funds for an expedition in the coming season. Well, who was the director of the department? Gates wired Blom to stop his solicitation, just to show him who was in command; in turn, Blom wired his resignation to Dinwiddie, who took no action on it. Through all of this feuding Gates could not understand why the university president, a fellow Virginian, appeared to support Blom and not him.

From October 1925 to March 1926, Gates felt the pressure closing in on him. Blom dealt only with Dinwiddie, a situation which prevented Gates from accepting the archaeologist's resignation in December. Gates, however, was careful not to resign again, as he had done so frequently in Guatemala. Finally, in February, the president transferred the department's library to the university library, an act which removed Gates's books from his control. The trustees did not act on Blom's resignation, but held it in abeyance pending a reorganization of the department. Gates still hoped to save himself and wrote another long letter to Dinwiddie, detailing the abuses and indignities he had suffered. Early in March the university dismissed Gates, continuing his salary through the academic year. Unwilling to admit the mistake it had made in taking him on less than two years before, the university issued no public statement that it had fired him.

Gates could not let the matter rest. His impulsive nature forced him to air the whole affair in a seventy-page pamphlet he issued in May. That publication provided the first news report of his severance from Tulane; only then did the university release its formal minutes of his dismissal. The pamphlet, entitled *The Development and the Disruption of the Department of Middle American Research . . .*, is a strange document. With apparent impartiality, Gates spread before the world the correspondence between Dinwiddie and himself, which seemed to portray Gates as a virtuous man with high motives, a scholar devoted to organized research, and an administrator with marvelous plans for the future greatness of Tulane, a man beset by unaccountable enemies bent on destroying him and his reputation.

A careful perusal of the pamphlet raises questions which did not occur to Gates. Why did Zemurray withhold additional funds from the department? Why did Dinwiddie gradually cool toward the director? Why did Blom become increasingly independent and even impudent? Gates implied that sheer malice motivated his enemies. His presentation, however, is not convincing. Something is missing from the story as he set it forth, and the missing element was his prickly personality.

One witness to the clash failed to see Gates as a hero. A student who had observed the man at Tulane found him unbearable. "He is all in all, the most colossal egoist of any man we have ever observed who has any claim to distinction." There is a basic "defect in his mental makeup, a neurosis of some sort, that kept him constantly suspicious of others"; there is "his overweening ego—a fear that someone was plotting, under cover, to dim the spotlight that shone upon him, or to shift the beaming rays from himself to another."[8] Somehow Gates had a way of exhibiting his worst traits even to those not closely associated with him.

In the pamphlet of vindication he revealed irrelevancies and misjudgments. He castigated the "one-sided and arrogant Germanized analytic method" dominant in higher education in his day,[9] and deplored the failure of Tulane to return to the humanities as the correct training for college men. Incidently, this became the major reason for his leaving the Johns Hopkins University twelve years later. He also declared wistfully that President Dinwiddie, a member of an old Virginia family, had not kept his word with Gates, a fellow Virginian. Liberal education and the honorable word of a gentleman were southern virtues Gates steadfastly maintained as heritages of his youthful training in the late nineteenth century. His ability to misjudge a situation appears in his claim that he had been appointed to a lifetime endowed chair at Tulane. When he was dismissed, he appealed his case to the American Association of University Professors. But since he had nothing in writing to support his claim and had not even held a teaching position at Tulane, the association refused to grant him a hearing.

During his short stay in New Orleans, Gates did more than display the personal oddities of an eccentric. He created certain unfortunate conditions in the department which the institution had to live with for years to come. He was responsible, first, for a startling incongruity between the staff and the library resources of the department. Three of the members specialized in some aspect of Maya studies, but the Gates collection acquired by Tulane dealt only with the non-Maya region of Mexico north of Oaxaca. When the G.H. Pepper library came to the department, it featured works on the Indians of North America. How a staff of Maya specialists was expected to use a non-Maya collection was never explained. Gates, of course, did not care, because he had his own Maya books in his personal library, which he hoped eventually to sell to Tulane.

Less important than the incongruity was Gates's refusal

to catalogue the department's library. It seems that he had an aversion to taking that necessary step even with his own books. At Tulane, however, this idiosyncracy created serious problems. Some time before Gates was dismissed, Blom appealed to Dinwiddie to hire a cataloguer, but not until months after Gates left did a trained person finally begin to list the holdings. Much later a thorough checking of the 1924 sale catalogue of the Gates collection revealed that Tulane had not received all of the items listed.

The defeat in New Orleans left the sixty-three-year-old man upset and undecided what to do. Two months after his ouster he told a friend that he could not concentrate for more than half an hour at a time; he felt so drained of energy that he contemplated giving up his Maya work, and he even considered spending a year traveling in Asia and the Mediterranean. In the end, however, he retained the things that were dear to him—life at Auburn Hill and scholarly pursuits. In the quiet of rural Virginia he resumed the study of linguistics. Eventually his home proved costly; after improving the farm land and adding a study and library to the house, he ran so deeply into debt that only the help of friends saved him from bankruptcy. After selling the farm and a collection of manuscripts in 1929, he regained financial stability.

He sought affiliation with an academic institution, doubtless as a way to lend respectability to his work. In 1930 he made an arrangement with the Johns Hopkins University. It happened that Joseph Ames, the president of the institution was a former classmate of his. Ames gave the linguist an academic berth with the title of research associate, which involved no teaching duties. Gates moved his library to the campus and arranged with the university press to publish his writings.

At the same time he revived the Maya Society, this time entirely as a one-man affair, to hold his library in trust and to issue publications under its imprint. On one occasion he confided to J. Eric S. Thompson that he contemplated the society as a club for "gentlemen" like himself and a few select friends. When he did restore the organization, it included no social functions for gentlemen; it was a mere front for his publishing activity. During the 1930s, twenty-one books and one volume of the *Maya Society Quarterly* appeared under the society's imprint. Gates was carrying out his cherished aim of issuing his own writings and reproductions of documents, but he was disappointed that so little notice was given to those works. The only other news about him appeared in a few articles in local newspapers.

There is no record of Gates's personal appearance until the mid 1920s and the early 1930s, when he was in his sixties. He seemed to fit the stereotype of the scholar. In New Orleans he was known as "the little gray man out at Tulane" because of his gray hair and gray eyes. Thick-lensed spectacles, a moustache, and a goatee suggested wisdom and authority; slightly stooped shoulders betrayed advancing years. Impulsive movements of his body, biting remarks about his dislikes, and the admission that he devoured crime stories indicated the forceful spirit he still possessed.

For a short period he broke off study and publication to travel to the Southwest and Mexico in 1934-35. Interest in the Indian New Deal prompted him to lend a hand in carrying out the program. At the request of John Collier, Commissioner of Indian Affairs, Gates spent several months in Arizona and southern California, part of the time aiding the Yuma tribe on economic and political problems arising from the new law; unfortunately, he never explained the nature of his services in detail.

Then he proceeded to Mexico, where he spent two months examining the operation of the government's program for education of rural Indians. He found the results gratifying. Mexican peasants, he reported, had transferred their faith from the church to the classroom; six million illiterates were becoming self-supporting and self-confident farmers. By way of contrast, the United States had lagged far behind its neighbor in the concern for its aborigines.

A striking incident occurred on this journey, when he

visited Yucatán. He stopped off at Chichén Itzá, seat of the archaeological project of the Carnegie Institution, and he was upset that Morley and other staff workers were cool toward him. What could he have expected in view of his actions toward Morley and the Carnegie Institution a decade earlier?

By 1935 he realized that his approach to deciphering the Maya glyphs had failed. In a newspaper interview he admitted that he was abandoning the problem and leaving the task to some other person to solve. Five years later, at the time of his death, an obituary suggested that he had interpreted about twenty Maya characters; but the scholar David Kelley later on credited him with only one certain identification.

All things considered, it is surprising that he managed to remain on the Hopkins campus for eight years. Although he did not teach, he saw one student, Elizabeth Stewart, through her graduate studies and a dissertation on Maya history and linguistics. By 1938, however, he had had enough of Hopkins. A few years earlier Isaiah Bowman, distinguished geographer, had become president of the institution, and Gates could not approve the general philosophy of education emerging at Hopkins. He championed the humanistic tradition and charged Bowman with fostering vocational or professional training; the fact that a university might train a young man for a job was too much for Gates to swallow. He left many of his books stored on the campus, moved to Washington, D.C., and planned new quarters, including a printing plant, for the Maya Society. But he was unable to carry out the project, and so he arranged to continue his studies in two rooms at the Library of Congress. Shortly after this move, his health declined, and he died in April 1940, at the age of seventy-seven.

His final defeat occurred after his death. He had hoped that his library would form the nucleus of a research center at some university. Technically, the Maya Society held his books in trust; he appointed his sister, Mrs. Henry C. McComas, vice-president of the organization, and she had the task of disposing of the collection. Four years passed before a sale catalogue was prepared, and eventually the collection was split into three parts and disposed of to different institutions.

Up to this point we have not described Gates's ideas, his collecting activity, his public announcements, or the nature of his publications.

Gates's ideas, broad and sweeping as they were, provided the rationale for his study of Maya linguistics. Discontented with the materialistic civilization of his own day and with Christianity as he saw it practiced, he yearned for a philosophy that would promise a more perfect state for mankind. In the earlier years he encountered mystical beliefs when he studied oriental languages, and they apparently led him to join the theosophical community in California. There he found a view of life congenial with his nature and promising a better future for mankind.

He held that if man were to improve himself he must respond to and cultivate his higher nature. During recorded history, man had acted only on a materialistic, animal plane of existence, impelled by fear and driven to war. Gates complained that contemporary scientists studied man only as a physical creature and advanced his culture only in a materialistic way. On the other hand, if man responded to his higher nature and considered himself "as of divine descent," he could rise above the evils of this world, abolish "self-aggrandizement and war," and pass "through learning to knowledge and Wisdom."[10]

What of the past? Gates predicted that when modern man accomplished the great task of self-improvement, he would discover that the ancients had already attained the higher state. By studying the old civilizations, Gates expected to encounter man in a more felicitous condition.

He believed that civilizations older than those so far discovered would come to light. As early as 1910 he declared that an understanding of the Maya hieroglyphs would produce "a new conception of past history."[11] He repeated the idea a little later when he predicted that Central America would "bring us still more and greater surprises." The Maya "possessed the tradition and history of the existence of Atlantis"; and "when we need and can use that sort of inspiration, the proofs are there to be discovered. . . . "[12] The Maya ruins represent "the very end of that race"; something important preceded that great age.

The study of archaeology and linguistics, he believed, will lead us to that great past. Both disciplines, however, must be considered in the context of the culture they represent. Contemporary archaeologists lacked that comprehensive approach, because each man cultivated his own narrow speciality; also archaeologists, like scientists, considered man an animal, and thus confined themselves in a "thought-cage." Archaeology must include the insights of mythology, symbolism, and astronomy. Gates declared that in the end all knowledge derived from the proper study of archaeology must be applied *"to the betterment of conditions today."*[13]

There is no evidence that he ever engaged in dirt archaeology, though sometimes he gave the impression that he had done so. After returning from Guatemala in 1921, he announced that he had found an inscription dating back to 120 B.C. That would have been interesting news indeed, but he never referred to this date stone again. Several times he sought rights to excavate; he said during the trip of 1917-18 that he received such a concession in Mexico; and as we know, he desperately wanted to control all digging during his regime in Guatemala. Everything points to his personal disinterest in dirt archaeology. Likewise, he gave little or no attention to ruins at the sites in Mexico and Guatemala. Apparently, he looked upon the fruits of archaeological research as so much information to be utilized in speculation.

He also developed his own method to decipher the Maya glyphs. He studied the linguistics of the various Maya dialects, expecting that the words and structure of the language would lead him back to an understanding of the glyphs. In the earlier years he emphasized a knowledge of spoken Maya, but in the later period of his life he found it more convenient to use the firsthand documents of the Maya as far back as they could be obtained. Just before he died, he planned to analyze the major Indian languages of Middle America in order to uncover the developmental pattern of each one.

He pointedly omitted consideration of certain materials in his studies. In linguistics he avoided all use of modern ethnological records, preferring the early written documents. And when he worked with Maya glyphs, he refused to consider the many hieroglyphs carved in stone; in this case, he believed that the codices contained the most accurate characters.

The use of old documents stimulated Gates to collect books and manuscripts in preparation for his research. But he had an acquisitive drive which went beyond that of the scholar accumulating data for research; we have already noted his early plan for a concordance of "every word" in Anglo-American law. Early in life he also collected Chinese art and Egyptian texts. At the start of his Maya studies, he copied Bowditch's card index of glyphs in the codices. At Point Loma he acquired a library of theosophist literature. In Mexico he carried on a campaign to acquire every piece of printed matter about the new regime there. At Tulane he proposed to assemble a data bank on all aspects of Middle America. His collecting spirit certainly exceeded the usual scholar's desire to assemble his sources for study.

His most spectacular collecting activity appeared in the library he assembled, which contained almost all of the pertinent published and manuscript records on pre-Hispanic Middle America, with emphasis on the linguistics of that region. From 1911 to 1916 he used every effort to complete the collection, either with handwritten or, more often, photographic copies of manuscripts he could not buy. He worked with the Eastman Kodak Company to devise a paper better suited to reproduce the pages by photography. He boasted that he possessed 95 percent of all the literature on the subject. For some unexplained reason, authorities at the Spanish Archives in Seville refused him access to that rich storehouse, even though other Americans carried on research there. Once he planned to send an expensive photocopying camera to Seville for the use of several scholars, ostensibly with the hope that the instrument could be used to provide copies of documents for him. But he never gained access to the archives.

He went to considerable trouble and expense to assemble his library. He examined dealers' catalogues from several continents, searching out choice items for purchase, and he carried on a large correspondence for the same purpose. In 1915 alone he spent twenty-five thousand dollars for books and manuscripts, simply because he could not bear to pass up any item he did not own; but the expenditure was excessive and strained his financial resources.

Not satisified with what he had acquired, he believed that old manuscripts still existed in Middle America. So he hired Frederick J. Smith to search for them and buy them. For fifteen months Smith traveled through Chiapas, Tabasco, the Yucatán peninsula, and Guatemala, though he had small success in ferreting out unknown documents. Dubious that Smith had done his best, Gates, as we have noted, traveled over the same area and found very little. So he blamed the Europeans and Americans of the nineteenth century for exporting quantities of manuscripts from those countries with the connivance of corrupt officials. A little later, when a woman managed to find a few documents in Guatemala, Gates was unable to buy them from her, but he later believed that eventually he secured the important items at second or third hand.

In the early 1920s he decided to limit his holdings to Maya linguistics and history. So he sold off the non-Maya part of his library, which went to Tulane. But after selling part of his holdings, he sometimes began to recollect the items or copies of them. Over the years he sold parts of his library a number of times and then proceeded to reassemble the same group of documents. With relative ease he could make photographic copies of rare manuscripts, and he sold sets of those copies to the Library of Congress, the Peabody Museum, and the American Museum of Natural History. He considered his library an investment which could be turned into cash when necessary. He was not, however, so much a speculator as a bibliophile with a passion for collecting.

Why he never prepared a catalogue of his own holdings is a mystery. Surely the cost was not the reason. At most, he owned seven thousand items; perhaps he believed that he knew his books and that a catalogue was unnecessary. But the lack of that tool caused trouble on several occasions. When he put up his non-Maya items for sale, the auction was delayed partly because a catalogue had to be prepared. After his death, the same problem cropped up again.

Some observations occur in regard to his passion for gathering together books and documents. Today he is usually remembered and sometimes praised for the excellent library he assembled and reassembled on pre-Hispanic Middle America. There is no doubt that his original purpose was to have on hand the pertinent sources for his research, a desirable luxury if one can afford it, as Gates could. But books and manuscripts are only the tools for research; and one wonders whether he distinguished between the tools and research itself. By 1916 he had just about completed the collection on Maya history and linguistics; in the decades that followed, however, there is little evidence that he made much creative use of his rich possessions. Perhaps Gates did not realize it, but his library seems to have fulfilled a possessive need more than it inspired a drive for research. Had Gates remained a bibliophile without aspiring to scholarship, he might have enjoyed a better reputation and saved his ego from painful bruises.

Two other characteristics of the man remain to be noted, the nature of his public statements and the kind of books he printed. He had a way of making public announcements about his work which promised striking progress in Maya research. When he returned from Guatemala at the end of 1922, he announced that he expected to decipher the glyphs soon and disclose the high state of ancient Maya culture. At the same time he brought from Guatemala a Quiché Indian, Cipriano Alvarado, and installed him at his farm in Virginia. Gates told the newspapers that he had devised a new scientific method to reach the root of language. The method he did not disclose; unless it was the fact that he recorded Cipriano's native speech on a smoked paper cylinder. Alvarado soon became homesick and was allowed to return to Guatemala. Gates never announced any results from recording Alvarado's speech.

On accepting the post at Tulane in April 1924, Gates again indulged in premature announcements. He said he had found evidence of a civilization in Central America as old and advanced as that of ancient Egypt. In addition, he would lead an expedition to Middle America in the summer of 1924, presumably to investigate the newly discovered civilization. Perhaps these were no more than ideas which came to him on the spur of the moment; he never led the expedition, and he did not refer again to the civilization he had discovered. In the same news release, he casually explained that he planned to decipher glyphs, instruct the Indians, and restore the Maya language and literature. The statement is puzzling in its generality, for he failed to explain how he expected to accomplish those aims. In the following year, 1925, a newspaper reported that he was on the verge of deciphering the glyphs; this time he coyly admitted that it might require months or years to carry out the task, but the smile on his face indicated that he believed he was on the threshold of success.[11]

After he joined the staff of the Johns Hopkins University, he gave two interviews to the press which suggested that he had found the key to understanding the glyphs. With the publication of his *Outline Dictionary of*

Maya Glyphs in 1931, he declared that he had made the first translation of a number of isolated glyphs. He had assembled some twenty-five hundred hieroglyphs from the major codices and determined the affixes, which he believed to be the key to decipherment. In addition, his research included the study of seven major branches of the Maya language, which yielded the structure and syntax applicable to the glyphs. Anyone perusing this announcement would have been led to believe that Gates had solved the problem of decipherment—but not so! Four years later, on publishing the Gomesta manuscript, Gates hailed the document as the Rosetta stone which would resolve the meaning of the glyphs. Curiously, this announcement dealt entirely with the manuscript and failed to reveal how he had been able to use the document for actual decipherment.

Unfortunately, Gates's approach to the deciphering of the Maya characters did not yield fruitful results. He cannot be criticized for having failed in the attempt, but one wonders how a person who considered himself a scholar could ignore the caution which must accompany serious research and could issue statements expressing expectations rather than accomplishments.

His publications fall into two general categories: reports on his travel and research, and the reproduction of documents. His travels have been treated earlier in this chapter. Here his scholarly contributions will be briefly mentioned. By and large, it appears to a layman that his productions fall far short of reasonable expectation. It is difficult to point to a single work that qualifies as a significant contribution to the knowledge of Maya history or linguistics. He gave summaries of other scholars' work, and he presented purely descriptive essays like that on the distribution of Maya linguistic stocks. If his writings are viewed in the perspective of his entire career, they appear to be by-products of his general attempt to decipher the glyphs. Because that attempt failed, his writings remain but minor items.

We may note two of his publications which might be

considered original works. *An Outline Dictionary of Maya Glyphs* was conceived within a narrow scope. In 1901 Gates copied Charles P. Bowditch's index file of all identifiable glyphs appearing in the three major codices. Gates excluded consideration of glyphs from any other source. He said that the *Outline,* issued at thirty-five dollars a copy in 1931, was designed for the use of students. The text, however, follows no logical arrangement, and the uninstructed reader finds the volume difficult to understand. Hermann Beyer, a respected scholar of linguistics at Tulane, gave the volume a merciless review. The book, he said, must have been written two decades earlier and not been revised in the light of scholarship during that period. Moreover, Gates studied only the latest glyph forms—those found in the codices—and ignored the older forms on the monuments. With a brief nod of approval, Beyer acknowledged that Gates had produced some new variants of day and month signs, but this was the only favorable point he made in the entire review. He showed how Gates condemned theorizing in other writers but considered it acceptable when he engaged in it himself. All told, the volume has too many errors; in fact, Beyer devoted many of the thirty-five pages of the review to listing mistake after mistake in a wearisome catalogue. He ended with a savage thrust: the volume was too simple for the advanced student, too complicated for the novice, and unreliable and impracticable for both groups.

In turning to Gates's reproduction of documents in Middle American history and linguistics, we face another odd situation. One would suppose that these volumes were designed to make scarce records more easily available. That is true but in a very limited way. Gates issued the books in small editions and placed a high price on each copy. Some of the volumes sold for ten to eighteen dollars each, the *Outline Dictionary* and the Landa for thirty-five dollars each, the Madrid Codex for forty dollars, and the Dresden Codex for sixty dollars.

Some facts about the English translation of the Landa

illustrate the bibliophile's spirit. He issued a total of eighty copies on Whatman handmade paper, with the illustrations colored by hand; seventy of those copies he put up for sale at thirty-five dollars each. In addition, he ran off fifteen copies on ordinary paper for review purposes only, with the stipulation that they could not be sold. When the first edition was exhausted in three months, a rare occurrence with his publications, he issued an uncolored "library" edition at ten dollars per copy, designed for students and the general public. We must not forget that he was asking these prices during the depression of the 1930s.

Gates had no intention of imitating the Duc de Loubat, who distributed his facsimiles to numerous educational institutions without charge. It is only fair to Gates, however, to observe that his books are a pleasure to handle. He used handmade paper, employed attractive type, and set the text within wide margins. Here the bibliophile triumphed.

His most unusual publications featured the reproduction of Maya glyphs in type. He had begun to cast these types before 1900, one for each Maya glyph; and over the years he added more types until he had a font of sufficient size to print major documents. Eventually, he manufactured some two thousand glyph types, and carefully secured a copyright on their use. He considered the type far more useful than the laboriously handmade drawings, and a few scholars agreed with him. But by and large, other scholars, especially J. Eric S. Thompson, warned against the use of those printed editions. Even Linton Satterthwaite, who considered the Dresden Codex useful in the printed edition, agreed that in the end the serious student must compare Gates's version with a facsimile edition if he wished to be on firm ground.

The manner in which Gates reproduced his earliest document in type is described at length on the title page of the Codex Pérez, that is, the Peresianus: "Redrawn and slightly restored, and with coloring as it originally stood, so far as possible, given on the basis of a new and minute examination of the Codex itself. Mounted in the form of the original. Accompanied by a reproduction of the 1864 photographs; also by the entire set of glyphs, unemended but with some restorations, printed from type. . . . Drawn and edited by William E. Gates, Point Loma, 1909."

In several instances he had bad luck with his books. He issued Landa's classic account of Yucatán in 1937 in the first English translation. To Landa's illustrations he added others, but failed to distinguish the source of each picture. It is said that he followed the advice of T.A. Willard in omitting the Spanish text and elaborate editorial notes. This English translation had the virtue of making the Landa text available to a wider audience. J. Eric Thompson, in fact, gave the book a mildly favorable review. But four years later A.M. Tozzer published his English translation of Landa with encyclopedic notes, summarizing the pertinent literature on all subjects mentioned in the text, and with helpful concordances, and indexes. The Tozzer edition justly became the standard reference work and quickly superseded Gates's publication.

A similar fate befell the Badianus Aztec Herbal. Gates had been interested in botany since the 1920s; a decade later he announced that he was studying "the medico-botanico-pharmacological field," as he described it. The Badianus Herbal, though Aztec instead of Maya, fitted the category exactly, and so he published the document in the original and in translation in two volumes in 1939. One year later Emily Emmert edited a version of the same work in one volume, excellently presented with color illustrations, at a reasonable price. Annoyed with the competition from the Emmert volume, Gates hastily prepared a popular edition of the herbal to sell for $3.75, but he died before it was issued.

If he had bad luck with the Landa and Badianus books, he blundered unpardonably in publishing the Gomesta manuscript in 1935. Gomesta was supposedly a sixteenth-century Spaniard who claimed that he owned "books" written in Maya hieroglyphs and that the meaning of those characters had been explained to him by the natives; Gomesta translated some of the glyphs into Spanish. Gates took all of this at face value, and announced in the introduction of the volume as well as in a press release that he had found the key to decipherment.

This incident revealed two serious deficiencies in the scholarly attitude of Gates. He had chosen a life of isolation beyond the orbit of the major Maya scholars of his day; he had, moreover, made enemies of many of them. As a result, he did not know the gossip and small talk current among the leading scholars in the field. In this instance, Gates also exhibited the streak of naïveté that ran through his nature. Somehow he had failed to absorb the critical spirit, the attitude of suspicion, doubt, and inquiry that puts the normal scholar on guard when he encounters a document which appears too good to be true. The most surprising part of the story is that in spite of all his handling of manuscripts Gates was not aware of the peculiarities of seventeenth-century handwriting.

Copies of the Gomesta document had been circulating among scholars for some time. The Carnegie Institution distributed photographs of it to its staff workers, asking for a critical appraisal of the work. Unlike Gates, no one rushed forward to acclaim it as a great discovery. At Tulane, Blom examined those photographs and also showed them to two scholars in the department.

After Gates's book appeared, Blom published the exposure of the Gomesta manuscript, obviously taking delight in revealing this glaring blunder on the part of his old enemy. He traced thirty characters in the document back to older works by Pío Pérez and Daniel Brinton, and he showed that the fabricator of the document did not know Spanish of the sixteenth and seventeenth centuries or the style of handwriting at that period. Blom ended his account with the observation that anyone who accepted this "blatant and childish fabrication" was "incredible."[15] Gates wrote a reply to the attack, but thought better of it and did not publish it.

In still another instance, Gates did not know that his old

friend and enemy Morley would unwittingly score a victory against him. Gates planned to write a comprehensive account of Maya civilization, but it never advanced beyond the planning stage. At the same time Morley started to compose a similar book; it appeared in 1946 as *The Ancient Maya* and became very popular.

All told, Gates's publications leave one with mixed feelings. He did pioneer work in attempting to convert Maya glyphs into type, though the effect did not satisfy scholars. It cannot be denied that he issued handsome volumes, for the physical appearance of the printed page exhibits exquisite taste. On the other hand, the contribution of his own writings appears to be minimal; and his editions of documents simply added one more series of rare books to the library shelves and collectors' catalogues. Perhaps he should have aspired to be no more than a bibliophile.

Any evaluation of Gates must come to grips with the man's personality. His troubles were caused not by others conspiring to deprive him of recognition but by himself. He exhibited two closely related traits: a lack of self-discipline and a craving for power. Refusing to train himself competently in a field of investigation, he felt inferior, and the inferiority in turn bred a desire to dominate. His inveterate compulsion to collect provided the easiest way to achieve a sense of power through personal possession. The fact that he was interested more in the control of raw materials than in wisely exploiting them for fruitful research suggests that possession compensated for the failure to gain recognition in other ways.

His basic trouble came from an unconscious sense of personal inadequacy. He was thirty-five years old when he began Maya studies, and he refused to undergo the discipline necessary to prepare for a successful pursuit of the subject. So he set up his own methods and procedures, disdained the work of the professionals decade after decade, and became a hermit scholar. He accumulated the pertinent resources for research, but he put off using those materials for years. Without results to command respect from the professionals, he resorted to periodic statements that he was about to achieve a breakthrough on decipherment. It is true that he faced serious problems in Guatemala and at Tulane; in both instances, however, he resorted to the assertion of personal authority to hide his lack of administrative ability. In the 1930s, when he finally settled down to research and publication, he was in his seventies. The documents he published, if one accepts the use of Maya type, had the virtue of increasing the available copies of those records. But his own writings, the *Outline Dictionary* and the *Maya Grammar,* reveal his lack of self-discipline, and his acceptance of the Gomesta manuscript betrayed an appalling naïveté. Gates made the error of aspiring to cultivate a scholarly subject while refusing to undergo the necessary rigorous scholarly training.

7

Frans Blom: The Early Years

Frans Blom was a man of considerable gifts and a multifaceted personality. His personal fortunes were marked by a series of ups and downs, but one theme runs like a thread through his varied life: he found spiritual nourishment and satisfaction only when exploring the forests of Mexico. On one occasion he exclaimed, "The sweetest music I know is the sound of the bell-mule at the head of the packtrain, and the singing of the insects in the tropical night."[1] When he was deprived of that experience, his self-confidence crumbled and his spirits withered. It is more than coincidence that the three important episodes of his life took place in the forests of Chiapas. He gained his first interest in archaeology in those jungles; later he went there to recover from personal defeat; and he spent his last years and died in the same locality.

It is not surprising that he differed from other archaeologists of his day. They went on digs, excavated carefully, and put up with the inconveniences of camp life, waiting eagerly to return to civilization. Not so Blom. He carried on no large-scale excavations year after year;

instead, he explored the terrain, located new Maya ruins, and prepared accurate maps of unknown regions. In this respect he resembled John Lloyd Stephens more than his fellow twentieth-century archaeologists.

He also differed from his associates in the way he came to archaeology. No inspiring teacher, no field trips with professionals, no reading of romantic books brought him into the fold. He acquired the fascination for Maya ruins as he wandered through the Mexican hinterland, examining the crumbling structures and copying the curious hieroglyphs. Endowed with a good mind, he introduced himself to the remains of the strange civilization by firsthand experience. Imperceptibly, he moved from acquaintance with Maya studies to comprehension of the subject. After several seasons of fieldwork he agreed to take graduate instruction in archaeology, but there is no evidence that the academic experience made any marked difference in his work. In fact, he rose to notice so rapidly that many a professional who had spent years in training and experience considered Blom an upstart who attained recognition too easily and too fast.

In addition to professional competence, he had an attractive personality which captivated friends and subordinates. When he was in top form, he exhibited "an Old World charm, culture, and courtesy that quickly made him one of the romantic and unforgettable figures of his time in . . . archaeology," according to a friend who worked with him for more than a decade. Blom was "blond, handsome, and vital . . . the ideal natural leader . . . warm and imaginative. . . . "[2] As we shall see, his personality had other facets, but those admirable traits of charm and dynamism carried him far and eventually cast a warm glow over the final period of his life.

He came from a fortunate background. Born in 1893, he was reared in Copenhagen, Denmark, in a family which enjoyed more than moderate prosperity. The training he received prepared him to become a gentleman of the upper middle class, well versed in foreign languages. The family spoke English two days a week, German two days, French two days, and their native Danish on Sundays.

What little we know about his early life is confused in chronology and detail. He was educated at Rungsted Academy. Apparently he devoted some time to the study of art and visited museums in several large European cities for that purpose. He possessed some ability in drawing, though he never turned it to creative artistic use in later life. For a period he fulfilled his military commitment to his country by serving in the navy during several years of the First World War. He gained the degree of Ph.B. from the University of Copenhagen, perhaps in 1917, though the date is not certain. It is unfortunate that we do not know more about his activity with a group of young men who met regularly in the garden of the Hotel d'Angleterre in Copenhagen.

Suddenly he left his native city for an unknown destination abroad. The time of his departure and the reason for it are not entirely clear. In later years either Frans told varying stories or the people he talked with badly garbled the details of what he said. It seems that he left home because his father, a prosperous businessman, insisted that Frans earn his own living, for he refused to enter a career in his father's business. The story that Frans went to Russia and there met a friend who got him a job with an oil company in Mexico is fascinating but apparently without foundation. His relations with his parents remained friendly, and he visited them on occasion in later years.

Beginning in 1919, when Blom was twenty-six, his movements become a matter of record. Early that year he was on the *Mexico,* leaving New York for Veracruz and Mexico City. The fact that he was in that foreign land for months, working only at odd jobs, suggests that he had no prior promise of employment before arriving there. He learned Spanish quickly, and eventually became an explorer for the Eagle Oil Company, with headquarters at Minatitlán, some miles inland from the Gulf of Mexico on the Coatzacoales River. He traveled through the southern part of Veracruz and eventually through Tabasco, Chiapas, and Campeche, looking for oil seepages and managing the travel of geological parties. Necessity forced him to become a muleteer and to acquire the peculiarly pungent language of that breed of men. In working for the oil company, he learned to draw maps and acquired some knowledge of geology. When he wandered through the forests without white men, he used Indian guides and quickly learned about the myths and customs of the natives. Everything he heard and saw went into a diary, supplemented by drawings, maps, and photographs. In the first half of 1922 he visited the Chiapas region, spent some days in April at Ocosingo and Palenque, and had his first meeting with Lacandón Indians, those few surviving descendants of the ancient Maya who still lived in the jungle and followed primitive practices. "The life in these parts charmed me," he explained, "and took more and more hold of me. . . ."[3]

Then he came down with tropical fever, an illness which helped to change his career. Unable to recover in the jungle, he went to Mexico City for medical treatment. The several months he spent in the metropolis brought him to his calling. An engaging man of twenty-nine, possessing a knowledge of foreign languages and the ability to associate with professional and socially prominent people with charm and self-confidence, he made it a point to meet individuals who could help him. He became friendly with Manuel Gamio, head of the Dirección de Antropología, and with Mrs. Zelia Nuttall, a woman of social standing and scholarly repute, who soon considered Blom so promising that she claimed him as her discovery. He submitted his voluminous notes, sketches, and maps to Gamio, who remarked after examining them that Blom was worth more to archaeology than to the oil business. He offered him a job with the Dirección. Gamio knew a promising young man when he met one, and his offer brought the Dane into the ranks of archaeology, though at a smaller salary than he had made with the oil company. As he himself put it, Blom gave up "the famous oil game in order to give all my time to the study of the secrets of southern Mexico and its Indians."[4] And then, on August 2, 1922, he showed remarkable prescience in posting a letter to the right person on the right subject.

The letter, sent to Sylvanus Morley, a specialist in Maya hieroglyphs, appears to be no more than a routine technical description of some of the ruins at Tortuguero, in Tabasco state. Blom referred to a stela southeast of the main structure, with the remark that "the figures are standing sharp in the stone. . . . " "I think," he added, "at least that this stela is very little known." He included "a rough tracing of a sketch" of the glyphs.[5] The drawing was so well executed that Morley could interpret the date at once.

The letter amazed Morley on several counts. The accuracy of the sketch, the careful description of the ruins, and the location of the stela indicated that the writer was more than a run-of-the-mill amateur. Morley yearned, moreover, for date glyphs from that region. For a decade he had scoured the jungle of Mexico and Guatemala, collecting every available carving which yielded a date, but he had not examined Tabasco. Here was a young man who could guide him to the glyphs in that region to round out the chronology of the Maya he was carefully reconstructing. Morley replied with enthusiasm, indicating that he wanted to meet this unknown newcomer to the ranks of Maya archaeology. Incidentally, Blom had to test his patience, because he did not receive an answer for many weeks; Morley was in Río de Janeiro attending a meeting of the International Congress of Americanists. In addition, conflicting commitments of the two men delayed their meeting for almost eight months.

While Blom made friends in Mexico City, he also read the current literature in archaeology. As he thumbed through the periodical *Ethnos,* he found an article by Ramírez Garrido on the ruins of Tortuguero. But Blom realized that he had more information from his recent examination of that site than Garrido presented. So he wrote a two-page note, carefully not criticizing Garrido, which appeared late in the year in *Ethnos*. Although Blom was a mere amateur, the article showed that he was observant, quick to learn, and self-confident, and it marked the beginning of his record of publication as an archaeologist and explorer.

In the meantime, his job with the Dirección de Antropología took him to Palenque. Although he was sent there to determine the measures necessary to preserve the old structures, he went beyond the narrow interpretation of his task and examined the site carefully, made several discoveries, copied hieroglyphs, and threw up a makeshift shelter for the beginning of a museum.

In his report on Palenque, Frans made two remarks which carried significance for the future. "The first visit to Palenque," he observed, "is immensely impressive. When one has lived there for some time this ruined city becomes an obsession."[6] At this early stage of his work, Blom, like his predecessors who had visited the site throughout the nineteenth century, indicated how strongly the Maya ruins captured his interest. And that interest continued until the end of his life. The other remark shows that Blom, also like his predecessors, could fail to investigate a curiosity. When he examined the Temple of the Inscriptions, he noted the carefully cut stone slabs that covered the floor of the building, and especially one slab with plugged holes. "I can't imagine," he wrote, "what those holes were intended for."[7] Twenty-five years later, Alberto Ruz Lhuillier, a Mexican archaeologist, also saw that slab with the plugged holes; on tapping the stone and hearing a hollow sound, he removed the slab and began a four-year task which revealed the finest tomb to be discovered in the Maya area.

When Blom returned to Mexico City, he took up modest living quarters in an old building on Calle Isabella la Católica in the downtown section. In a corner on the third floor was his room, a bright, cheerful place with two windows, old beams, plastered walls, and simple furniture. He had learned to adapt himself to every condition—the crudities of life in the forest, a modest room in the city, or tea at Mrs. Nuttall's baronial Casa Alvarado.

By the time Frans returned to the capital, Morley was in the midst of prolonged negotiations on behalf of the Carnegie Institution of Washington to gain the approval of the Mexican government for a contract to excavate and restore Chichén Itzá. Always planning ahead, he began to think about selecting his field staff for the first season at Chichén. When he visited his friend Gamio at the Dirección, he learned that Blom was a good man, brimming over with enthusiasm. Favorably impressed even before seeing the Dane, he looked forward with eager anticipation to talking with the young man.

The meeting took place on Friday, April 6, at the St. Regis Hotel. Morley described Frans as a blue-eyed, fair-haired Dane, with fine eyebrows, a longish face, and lean in build. As soon as they began to talk of things Maya, Blom's overwhelming enthusiasm completely captivated Morley, who was a superenthusiast on the subject. After lunch they went to the national museum, where Blom pointed to stelae with glyphs from Ocosingo; Morley had never seen those glyphs before, and he was delighted, especially because one had an Initial Series with the complete date. They went on to Blom's room, where he showed Morley the drawings he had made at Palenque and described a new hieroglyphic inscription and a new temple he had discovered there. In addition, he told of sculptured stones he had seen at Toniná and at other places in Chiapas.

Morley determined to have Blom on his field staff. On Saturday the two men met again at Mrs. Nuttall's for tea, and on Sunday they lunched together. As Morley saw it, Blom lacked one essential, a graduate degree in archaeology. By this time archaeology had become a profession, and a promising young man had to compete with the professionally trained men coming from the universities. Morley had made a general arrangement with Professor Alfred Tozzer at Harvard whereby a man could take graduate courses in two fall semesters to earn the master's degree and be free to work in the field in the winter and spring. Although Blom accepted the arrangement, he could not afford to pay the full expense of two semesters at Cambridge, so Morley wrote an urgent letter to Tozzer requesting a scholarship for Frans. About that time Mrs. Nuttall also wrote to Harvard for the same purpose. It is immaterial whether Morley or Mrs. Nuttall secured the aid; more significant is the fact that Blom impressed both persons with his ability and promise.

In the fall of 1923 and again in 1924 he attended Harvard to take courses for the master's degree. The legend that he enjoyed one grand good time taking part in youthful escapades is probably exaggerated. He lived in a room in a cousin's house in Cambridge, and his existence was Spartan because of restricted finances. Aside from the tuition scholarship, he had to pay all other expenses from his savings. It is difficult to understand how he managed. He had to content himself with a modest social life. When writing to a friend, he admitted that he had no knowledge of the popular shows in Boston and that he knew no girls in the area. Apparently he drank occasionally with companions, an activity which carried an additional fillip because it violated Prohibition.

At Harvard Frans met two other graduate students with whom he was destined to work in the future. Oliver Ricketson, Jr., one year younger than Blom, had already had considerable experience in archaeology. A great-nephew of Andrew Carnegie, he was reared with advantages. After attending a private school, he went on to Harvard and received the A.B. in 1916. Then he entered medical school, but World War I interrupted his training. After leaving the service, he abandoned medicine for archaeology and participated in various expeditions in the Southwest. On returning from several trips to the Maya area, he went to Harvard for advanced study, and he and Blom cooperated on the same project for the master's degree. The other graduate student, Oliver La Farge, came from a distinguished family; his grandfather was the famous artist John La Farge, and his father was a highly respected architect. When Oliver attended Groton, he happened to read Grant MacCurdy's book on the Old Stone Age, which directed him to archaeology. Attendance at Harvard and several seasons in the Southwest confirmed his interest in the American Indian. He wavered, however, between archaeology and ethnology. Later on, he interrupted his graduate work to become an assistant to Blom at Tulane.

The only tangible result of the eight months at Harvard was an index of Maya ruins and accompanying maps compiled jointly by Blom and Ricketson. The index lists every known site, with bibliographical references to past publications on each group of ruins. At first glance, the work looks like a mechanical and uninspiring subject for a graduate thesis, but perhaps Tozzer was correct in suggesting the project. Blom, unlike many graduate students, had already acquired field experience; and in addition he had the explorer's fascination for maps and the exact location of sites. The index catered to his interest and at the same time familiarized him with the standard literature on the subject. In later years at Tulane and in San Cristóbal he continued his interest in maps and in recording new sites.

Although Frans made the best of the situation, he was unhappy at Harvard. Classes, lectures, books, and examinations held little interest for a man of thirty who had enjoyed several years of fieldwork. He yearned to talk about practical archaeology with people who knew it at first hand. In the fall of 1923 he was able to speak with Thomas Gann, and he longed for more conversation with his good friend Morley. He bolstered his spirits with the prospect that in February he and Ricketson would be moving over the trails of the Petén to Uaxactún as part of the Carnegie Institution's archaeological project in Central America.

In December, however, that project was seriously threatened. Ricketson wavered as to whether he would lead the expedition, but this was a minor problem compared with the news Morley relayed about the turn of affairs in Guatemala. William Gates, director of archaeology in that country, opposed the Carnegie permit to excavate Uaxactún, and although Morley had secured the necessary permission, no one knew if Gates had sufficient power to have it annulled. During the uncertainty, Morley assured Blom that if he could not go to Uaxactún, he would add him to the staff at Chichén Itzá. At that moment news arrived of revolution in Yucatán; Governor Felipe Carrillo had been overthrown, and a conservative group had assumed power and closed the ports of Yucatán.

For more than a month Blom lived in suspense. The expedition to Uaxactún seemed unlikely, and revolution appeared to eliminate the project at Chichén. His money was exhausted. Would he be paid if the expedition could not get under way? The ever-optimistic Morley continued to assure him that everything would work out all right, though Blom realized that Morley had no firm basis for his bright outlook.

Who can blame Blom for undergoing a fit of depression? "This university makes me feel so damn blue, so write and cheer me up," he appealed to Morley on the drab New Year's Day of 1924. "What is going to be done?" Frans asked on January 3. "Send me some news, even if it is bad. That's better than none." Morley had problems of his own, for all of his staff members were bombarding him with the same question: Would they be able to go to work as planned? Blom poured out his feelings on January 7. "You are right in calling me down," he began, "but I was feeling like a race horse ready for the start, and not allowed to start. My plans for equipment are laid and I was longing to see the things come in, and smell the leather and other nice smells that foretell a new expedition to start." "That is how I feel, the young colt in the corral, eager to get out in the great open for a canter. And you bet your soul I will be standing at the gate waiting for you to open." Three days later Blom asked if he would be paid, because "by the end of the month I will not have a single cent to dispose of."[8]

Not until January 26 did Frans learn that the delays were over and the original plans would go into operation. Gates had resigned in Guatemala, and conditions returned to normal in Yucatán. He received orders to be in New York City on February 1 to embark for British Honduras. At last he was going to Uaxactún.

The members of the expedition, Blom, Ricketson, and A. Monroe Amsden, spent a month traveling to their destination. After arriving in Belize, they crossed British Honduras to El Cayo at the entrance of the Petén, where they acquired twenty-two mules and a gang of native laborers. After the expedition checked in at the Plancha de Piedra Guatemalan customs station, Blom was happy as the mules and natives slowly made their way along the narrow forest trail.

At Uaxactún Frans shouldered responsibility for most of the work. After Ricketson acquainted him with the place and the job to be done, he left for an archaeological project in British Honduras; and eventually Amsden fell sick and had to be sent back to civilization. Blom directed the native workers in numerous tasks. They cleared away the vegetation and erected houses for the future staff and workers; they dug a reservoir for water supply, and cut trails to the different groups of ruins. Blom began to make a survey of the site, copied the glyphs on all the monuments, found the quarry used by the original builders, and excavated a temple.

He demonstrated alertness and ingenuity in making a significant archaeological discovery at Uaxactún. One afternoon he sat on the steps of a pyramid and looked across the bush at three ruined temples in a row before him. On taking some compass bearings, he concluded that the four structures, known as Group E, formed an observatory. From his position, one could see the sun rise over the temple to the left on the longest day of the year, over the temple to the right on the shortest day, and over the middle temple on the equinoxes twice a year. Sometime later another archaeologist, using Frans's discovery as a starting point, found thirteen groups of buildings apparently for the same purpose within a radius of seventy miles of Uaxactún.

After closing the season at the end of April, Blom explored fourteen other sites in the Petén and British Honduras, and returned with much information. He boarded a boat at Belize too late to realize that he was on a rumrunner, and of course when he arrived at Progreso, he was arrested. He quickly gained his release and proceeded to Chichén, where Morley observed that he looked thin.

Events forced him into a difficult decision in the latter part of 1924. In order to earn some money, he put in a brief summer stint with Neil Judd on the U.S. National Museum's expedition at Pueblo Bonito, New Mexico; then he returned to Harvard to complete the requirements for the master's degree. As he listened to lectures and took examinations, he learned that his part-time job with the Carnegie Institution was again in jeopardy. Morley had trouble securing renewal of the concession in Guatemala, though he made provisions to assign Blom to Chichén if the Uaxactún project were suspended. That uncertainty was bad enough; then came news that approval of Morley's budget had been delayed. To make matters worse, Frans had trouble making ends meet at Cambridge. So much uncertainty over a part-time job for a man of thirty-one was too much to bear.

Out of the blue Frans received an answer to his problem: a full-time job with good prospects for the future. William Gates, who had just assumed direction of the new Department of Middle American Research at Tulane University, was having difficulty finding an assistant in archaeology. After several persons refused his offer, he appealed to Professor Tozzer at Harvard, who recommended Blom for the post. Frans, however, knew that Gates was a difficult man to work with—it was common gossip among archaeologists—and so the offer of $3,000 a year and a three-year contract tested his judgment and ingenuity. All told, he handled the situation about as well as was humanly possible.

First, he informed Morley of his intention to take the job

and even sent him a copy of his letter to Gates. Blom remarked that acceptance of the new post would probably end his friendship with Morley and perhaps his association with the Carnegie Institution. At first, Morley was hurt that Frans should think of such a possibility; after all, they were friends on a personal and professional basis and not because of the institutions they worked for. Then Morley advised Blom to consider the matter dispassionately and decide what was best for archaeology and what was best for himself. Although he was wounded at losing Frans from his staff, Morley displayed the finest feelings of sympathy and understanding toward his friend. With gratitude, Blom replied, "It felt good to hear you say it," and added, "Once more, thanks for your letter; it warmed. . . . "[9] Both men realized that they would see little of each other in the future. Blom wanted to say farewell, but he could ill afford the expense of a trip to Washington, D.C. "It will mean that I will have to cut short on other things," he explained, "but I do want to shake your fist before you go south."[10] He made the sacrifice and went to Washington in December to say good-bye. Thereafter, he saw Morley only on rare occasions.

Blom next attempted to arrange the terms of his appointment so as to protect himself against Gates. In this difficult feat he accomplished only partial success. "I take the Gates matter very cold blooded," he assured Morley. "I will simply not go to him if I do not get a legally formed contract with careful stipulation of salary and other conditions." In addition, Blom believed that "the work will sort of be directed by the president of the University. . . . "[11] During the negotiations, Frans wrote rather frankly to President Dinwiddie of Tulane; in his letter of acceptance he referred to his "feeling of uncertainty as regards Mr. G's somewhat unstable temperament. . . . "[12] But Blom apparently received an agreement on no more than his salary and a three-year contract. Gates became his immediate supervisor.

Gates rejoiced over securing Blom and believed that he

had the young man's full cooperation. He boasted that Blom was "ten times Morley's superior. Morley never sees anything but 'dates'; Blom sees everything, topographic and cultural."[13] Two months later, after an interview with Frans, Gates became more enthusiastic. "The Blom matter was delightful," he reported to Dinwiddie. "Once settled he knows he did right, and can't wait to go to work—with us—even with me. Not a bit of friction, and won't be."[14] Gates was a bad judge of other people, and he failed to sense that Blom was playing an astute game with him.

When Frans arrived in New Orleans on February 9, 1925, he addressed one or two clubs, completed preparations for his next task, and after two weeks left on an important mission, which lasted six months. Fortunately, while he and Gates were together during that brief period in February, everything went well.

Blom got off to a good start, leading an archaeological expedition through Mexico. As his assistant, he chose Oliver La Farge, who interrupted graduate study at Harvard to share in the adventure. Blom believed that he would be a good companion, because he had had experience in several expeditions in the Southwest and could ride a horse and manage a boat. Frans assembled all the paraphernalia for the trip and took it to Mexico City, where La Farge joined him. When Blom was still at Harvard, a reporter asked him if he were lonely on trips through the forests of Mexico, and he replied, "Lonely! The day I start on my expedition is the happiest day in my life. After that there is no time to be lonely."[15]

The explorers' itinerary took them from Veracruz, Mexico, to Huehuetenango, Guatemala, through rough terrain and little-explored areas. They investigated the Olmec region of Tres Zapotes and La Venta, sometimes by boat. Gates joined them to examine Comalcalco. After a week, Gates left, and the explorers proceeded to Palenque, Ocosingo, and the adjacent region. They also collected information in Toniná, Chinkultik, and ruins in the neighborhood of Comitán.

As they sat in the plaza of Comitán, talking with Don

Gregario de la Vega, a local worthy, he casually told them that the Indians across the border in Jacaltenango, Guatemala, occasionally held a ceremony in honor of the year-bearer. The matter-of-fact statement electrified the two men, because the year-bearer harked directly back to Classic Maya civilization. In ten days they reached Jacaltenango and confirmed the news. Two years later Blom sent La Farge on an expedition to exploit news of that survival of an ancient ceremony.

Impressive statistics convey something of the extent of the travels of Blom and La Farge: 1,250 miles by horseback, 2,500 miles by water, 1,000 miles by railroad. They collected information on 24 new sites, found 32 new inscriptions, and photographed 73 new monuments.

Although the explorers gathered much archaeological information, the discovery of the fine stucco figures at Comalcalco alone justified the expedition. Late in the day before he planned to leave the site, Frans noted a small room in the undergrowth, apparently in a ruined condition. He planned to examine it the next morning and place it on his map of the site. At that moment, the low rays of the late afternoon sun penetrated the chamber and fell upon a molded headdress. Excitedly, he removed enough rubble to see a fine stucco face. The next day he cleaned out the debris and exposed nine splendidly modeled figures on the wall, full-length stucco carvings of Maya dignitaries, each one a distinct personality. He fully appreciated the aesthetic perfection of the figures and their excellent state of preservation. "They are beauties. . . ," he exclaimed in his diary.[16] At once he wired the news to Gamio. But there was no one in his party with whom to share his excitement. La Farge and Gates showed moderate interest only after witnessing Blom's enthusiasm. Gates, who paid no attention to the progress of excavation, "came up and registered enthusiasm and imbecility," according to La Farge.[17] Only the *jefe político* of the town of Comalcalco appreciated the find, and he had a roof constructed to protect the figures.

The reports of the expedition reveal Blom's deep interest

in nature and in people. Unlike the new professional archaeologists who were beginning to turn out technical reports restricted to scientific details, Frans considered all aspects of the journey an exhilarating experience to be shared with the reader. And so *Tribes and Temples,* the published report on the trip, includes a large amount of human interest material, with the scientific data sandwiched in at appropriate intervals. In this respect Blom unconsciously returned to the style of reporting common in the nineteenth century, and conveyed the trials, joys, and satisfactions which accompanied exploration and discovery.

He recorded personal experience and anecdotes without the least qualm. When he approached Palenque, he voiced joy over retracing the old, well-known trail. On arriving at the ruins, he found that the temporary structure he had erected for his use in 1923 had disappeared, and the palm roof museum and caretaker's hut, which he had also set up, were sagging or falling. But Leandro, the native who had helped him two years before, greeted him with happiness.

Frans was enthusiastic in his appreciation of nature. Early in the expedition, as the party began to climb "through huge, luxuriant forests," he remarked, "Just my old forest—trees, lianas, fern and big trees."[18] A month later, when he was in the Tabasco country, he exclaimed, "The night was magnificent, millions of stars and millions of fireflies."[19] On another occasion, when he was in the highlands, he described the awakening of life in the morning. "Evening in the jungle is beautiful," he declared; "dawn is magnificent." The members of the party arose, wrapped themselves in blankets, and drank coffee. The early rays of the sun struck the tops of the trees, "at first very sparsely and a pale gray. Little by little the light sifted down, and . . . the sun threw a glimmer of gold on the tree-tops. The night insects became quiet, and the birds began to fly around and sing. He who has watched the daily awakening of life in the jungle will never forget it."[20]

Blom also showed a strong interest in people. The

families who provided food and lodging received notice in the diary, and if a family proved pleasant, hospitable, and at all intelligent, he lavished praise on its members. Once he could not resist remarks about the beautiful breasts of a young woman who served the meals; after slightly toning down the original sentence in the diary, he included it in the published account.

Blom's responses to people fluctuated with his moods. When he wished to please or cultivate a person, he exhibited all of the suavity of a European gentleman, usually with notable success. On the other hand, if he were irritated, frustrated, or feeling low, he sometimes engaged in sharp criticism of his friends. These traits appeared on this expedition.

His opinions of Oliver La Farge, his companion on the journey, and of William Gates, his superior at Tulane, were carefully omitted from the published account. The remarks on La Farge, all confined to the diary, come as a surprise. At Comalcalco, when Oliver showed up at the ruins one morning without digging tools, Frans remarked, "I sometimes do wonder what he does fill his head with. He is quick to remember reading, but slow in movement, and impractical and absentminded in the work. I gave him a lecture. . . ." At noon, when Blom sent him back to town to secure the tools and to bring lunch, Oliver forgot a cup which Frans had asked for. And then on May 19 Frans noted that La Farge "is somewhat of a weak sister, and seems to hate hard work. Either he complains because he has eaten too much or because he is hungry."[21]

Perhaps Blom judged La Farge too severely, for it appears from La Farge's diary that the younger man admittedly lacked enthusiasm for archaeology. When they arrived at the ruins of Comalcalco, Oliver remarked, "Big stuff, but leaves me a little cold." On reaching Palenque, Blom led his friend to the Temple of the Cross. It was "a marvellously encouraging sight," wrote La Farge. "But I was humorous about it and he misunderstood it, a pity." By the next day, however, La Farge called Palenque "stupendous," and began to draw some stelae, which helped and pleased Blom.[22]

La Farge never had an unpleasant word to say about his leader; in fact, he reported several instances of his kindness. At Piedra Labrada, they came upon a young native suffering from congested liver. "Frans very nice. Advised doctor in Puerto México . . . and gave cascara sagrada." Some days later when they were staying in a town, Oliver "went on a big private binge second night," spending ten dollars on the spree. When he did not come home, Blom went out to look for him and guided him back. "Darned nice of him," was La Farge's expression of appreciation.[23]

In regard to Gates, Blom made no effort whatever to please, much less to flatter, the man. When the director met the exploring party on several occasions, the published record states the facts as tersely as possible. To avoid referring to him as "Mr. Gates," because he had no doctorate, Frans used the term "Director Gates." In the published record of the expedition, the list of acknowledgments to persons who had aided the enterprise did not include the name of Gates. When Blom and La Farge went to the ruins of Comalcalco, Gates joined the expedition for a brief time. One day Frans noted in his diary that Gates had been resting in the town and was apparently not well. "I am glad he has had a rest," Blom remarked. "He is usually too busy."[24]

Blom had had sufficient experience in dealing with natives for several years to realize that considerate treatment of them ensured their fullest cooperation. At one stage of the journey, he confided to the diary that he did not approve of the rough way German residents in Mexico handled the Indians. "If you are a little kind with them," he observed, "they are very helpful."[25]

The explorers found a remarkable helper in Lázaro Hernández Guillermo, who joined the party at Macuspana near Tortuguero as a mule driver and handyman. "He came walking slowly down the street, a broad shouldered Indian man with excellent Indian features, dressed in sandals, blue cotton trousers, a white cotton shirt, and a broad brimmed Mexican straw sombrero."[26] A man of about forty with a wife and two children, he agreed to join the party for an indefinite time. The next morning, the day of departure, he left his family and appeared with his scanty belongings rolled in a small straw mat.

As the days passed, the manly, humane spirit of Lázaro aroused Blom's admiration. The Indian had more physical endurance than the white men, and he performed every task expertly. When he heard the explorers inquiring about native customs, he quietly indicated that he could also tell them a thing or two on the subject. He never complained, and he displayed a tender regard for the seven animals under his care. Addressing them as "*niños,*" his children, he coaxed them along the trail, and at the end of the day's journey he fed them and washed them down before taking his own rest and relaxation. He looked reproachfully on the white men when they overworked the animals. Mexican muleteers are notorious for the blows and curses they shower on their animals. Only once did Lázaro engage in the practice, but he was ashamed of his action and mumbled to Blom, "Don Pancho, I should not do that!" and, Blom reported, "The rest of the day his head was hanging low."[27]

The two explorers quickly came to like and respect the Indian. They began to address him as "Tata," which meant something like father. As Frans explained, "The name grew out of nowhere, as the natural thing to call him."[28] They had him eat at their table, to the consternation of native families who believed that his place was in the kitchen with the servants. Even in the use of liquor, he showed remarkable control. "He never took a drink while we were on the trail," Blom explained, "but he got himself comfortably mellowed when we reached a village where we expected to rest a few days."[29]

As something of a medicine man in his home village, Tata knew much of Indian lore. When the explorers came back to the United States, they brought him along for a two-week stay in New Orleans, where La Farge attempted to learn the secret rites and customs that had passed down from generation to generation among the Indians.

On the return to the United States, Blom surely enjoyed

the public notice the expedition received. The *New York Times* carried a half-dozen articles reporting the progress of the explorers. When the men appeared in mid August at New Orleans, two lengthy articles summarized their archaeological finds, and ten days later a long release described La Farge's ethnological work in Mexico and Guatemala. In due time the *Literary Digest* noted the finds at Comalcalco as "An American 'King Tut's Tomb.' "

Gates, on the other hand, received very little notice in these reports. In the name of Tulane University he had also organized two other expeditions to carry out plant research in Mexico and Honduras, but those endeavors received only a bare mention on March 29 and no notice thereafter. Moreover, only one of the reports in the *New York Times* emanated from Gates, and it was too brief and vague to be informative. Finally, the official report, *Tribes and Temples,* all but ignored the existence of the director.[30]

The struggle between Blom and Gates was bound to come to a head in short order, because the personal conflict between the two men could not be reconciled. Gates, envious of the public attention the younger man received, insisted on autocratic control over everything in the department. Blom, on the other hand, determined to gain his independence in order to develop archaeological research at Tulane. During the winter of 1925-26 Frans offered his resignation several times in an attempt to force the issue. The administration wisely delayed action, as it waited for Gates to make his exit. Blom knew the strategy of the administration; and he planned to stay on at Tulane once Gates moved out of the picture. The battle moved to a climax in February 1926, when President Dinwiddie assumed direction of the department and authorized Frans to hire La Farge as his permanent assistant. Gates was ousted, and Blom became acting director.

At last Frans secured the independence he had failed to gain when he first came to Tulane. The new position, however, carried a challenge. He must demonstrate ability as an administrator, as an active archaeologist, and as a creative person who could bring fame to the institution and enhance his own professional reputation. In view of the miserly budget under which he operated, he produced an outstanding record during the next decade.

8

Frans Blom: Tulane and Na Bolom

At the age of thirty-three, Frans now entered upon his productive career, which continued during the remaining thirty-seven years of his life. First, he served at Tulane University as head of the Department of Middle American Research, and later he carved out a unique place for himself in exploration and social service in Chiapas, Mexico.

Before turning to the details of his work at Tulane, it is necessary to consider his private life during those years. He lived in the Pontalba Apartments on Jackson Square in the heart of the French Quarter of New Orleans, where he quickly joined a circle of friends, some of them artists and writers. With good looks and dashing spirit, he fitted in perfectly with the bohemians who enjoyed dinners, parties, and informal gatherings with sparkling conversation and drinks to provide relaxation. Here he was far away from the middle-class atmosphere of the university and the surrounding residences of proper New Orleanians. He had the best of two worlds simultaneously, working at the university and living in the freer atmosphere of the French Quarter. His circle included a varied assemblage of individuals, among them the Louisiana regional writer Lyle Saxon, Dorothy Dix, Sherwood Anderson, and the writer and artist William Spratling.

It did not take Blom long to adjust to the spirit of the Quarter. In 1926 when Spratling published a book of caricatures, Blom appeared as the third subject. The sketch depicts the archaeologist, with magnifying glass nearby, lifting the roof from a tropical hut, while a dark-skinned, scantily clad native girl flees from the doorway. It is a good-humored drawing, suggesting of course that Frans examined far more than stelae and hieroglyphs in his expeditions.

Although the faculty at the university looked dubiously on his residence in the Quarter, many a young woman in the city hoped that she might attract his serious attention. He could also exert his charm on older, more worldly-wise women. In the early 1930s, the seventy-one-year-old Mrs. Gilmer, widely known for the advice-to-the-lovelorn column she published under the name of Dorothy Dix, took a three-week tour with him among the ruins of Yucatán. She exclaimed that "going to Mexico with Frans Blom is like being shown over heaven by an archangel."[1]

In his work at Tulane, Blom had a way of getting the most from his staff. He gave his subordinates full latitude to exercise their own judgment and initiative in carrying out the tasks he assigned them. This approach produced more work and perhaps more devotion than would have been likely under rigid supervision. Even at the end of the 1930s, when Blom's position became precarious, his staff tried to aid him in keeping his job.

There was another side to Blom's nature—one that is difficult to assess. Although Ricketson was at Uaxactún only a few days, he and Frans did not get along well together, and Amsden reported that in off hours he found Frans a bit difficult. There is, moreover, the suggestion that sometimes the Dane failed to control his temper. An administrator of another institution remarked to a friend that Blom needed advice in drawing up a good archaeological program at Tulane and that he showed too many signs of impatience. When Morley complained that Hermann Beyer, who worked at Tulane in the 1930s, had cut up rubbings of glyphs loaned to him for research, Frans answered his old friend with a remarkably abusive letter. In exposing the Gomesta manuscript as a fake—an act which humiliated Gates, who accepted the work as genuine—Blom could have been somewhat less direct without lowering his professional standards.

When it came to conducting an expedition through the jungles of the Maya country, however, he displayed unusual efficiency and success. He insisted on careful attention to every detail, followed plans as closely as possible, traveled light by living off the land, and conducted the entire operation with an air of military precision.

His first marriage began happily, to all appearances. After a romance which began on a trip to Yucatán, in 1932 he married a young woman from a wealthy family in New York City. Their elaborate wedding, held in a garden chapel on a Long Island estate, was conducted by an Episcopalian bishop. The union appeared auspicious.

Mary came to live with her husband in New Orleans. She made an effort to adapt to the community, but she was in a difficult position. A wealthy woman who derived her income from a well-known cosmetics company, she had attended the best boarding schools and had become accustomed to the social life of the rich. The bright red foreign sports car she brought with her attracted attention and perhaps envy. Frans moved her into his apartment in the Quarter, and she redecorated it with feminine and more formal taste. She made a conscientious effort to fit into the various circles of life in New Orleans—the university group, the city's social elite, and Frans's pals in the Quarter—each of which had its own atmosphere, customs, and local peculiarities. Mary found New Orleans quite strange. She sought advice and tried to do what was expected of her. Unfortunately, she could not comprehend, much less adopt, the Orleanians' habit of frankly expressing their opinions about everything and everyone. She was not gregarious by nature, and in the end she was considered aloof and withdrawn.

After some years, if gossip can be trusted, the marriage gradually dissolved because Frans and Mary began to find other individuals more interesting. Although she accompanied him to Guatemala in 1937, the next year she went to Reno and secured a divorce on the grounds of cruelty. The end of the marriage came at the worst time for Blom, for he was already despairing over his job. Forty-five years old and sadly in need of a faithful partner to support him through his troubles, he enjoyed no more than intermittent, short-lived friendships.

We have only occasional glimpses of other aspects of the man. In dress he followed accepted middle-class standards, except that on campus he appeared in an Indian-style shirt and white cotton trousers, with a red sash about the waist. Generally, he appeared clean-shaven, which was the only acceptable custom of the period. A photograph taken in 1928, however, shows him sporting a beard and mustache, perhaps as a joke. On expeditions he often did not bother to shave, as was the case in Mexico when he cruised for the oil company. A few weeks out on the first Tulane expedition of 1925, La Farge reported that "Frans is raising a powerful red stubble."[2] When a journalist visited his New Orleans apartment in the mid 1930s, she described him as blond and intelligent, living among piles of English and Spanish books, rapidly smoking Turkish cigarettes, and consuming quantities of coffee. She made no mention of Mary.

During the years at Tulane Blom demonstrated the ability to carry on four major activities almost simultaneously—expeditions, publications, exhibitions, and fund raising. He is generally remembered for the expeditions sent out while he was director of the department.

As a result of the news that ancient practices still

prevailed in Guatemala, he sent La Farge and Douglas Byers, a Harvard friend of the latter, to look into the matter in 1927. After four months of study, the men returned in May with a significant discovery. They learned that the Indians in the neighborhood of Jacaltenango still made use of the old Maya religious calendar. The details of their investigation appear in *The Year Bearer's People,* a study of importance.

By a streak of good fortune Blom led a six-month expedition through the Maya country of Mexico, Guatemala, and the Yucatán Peninsula in 1928. The money for the venture came from an unusual source. The children of John Geddings Gray, a Louisiana engineer, decided to underwrite an archaeological expedition in memory of their father. With a party of seven persons and a train of fourteen saddle and pack mules, Frans started at Tapachula in the southwestern tip of Mexico and moved gradually north until he reached Chichén Itzá. The rugged route he chose, his acquaintance with Indians along the way, and his archaeological finds were the highlights of the expedition.

The route passed through some of the worst terrain in Mexico, filled with extensive wastes and thick forests, much of it even without trails. Ten days out of Tapachula the party climbed six thousand feet up a steep and rocky path along the side of Tacaná volcano. To reach the town of Motozintla, they had to descend a treacherous one-way mule trail to the gorge of the Cuilco River. After fording the zigzag river twenty-eight times, they emerged on the plain of Tierra Caliente and, parched with thirst, plodded across the scorched earth. They welcomed a week's respite in Comitán, where they rested themselves and their mules and witnessed a great fiesta in honor of the local patron saint. Turning eastward, the party then visited the Maya site of Chinkultik.

As they progressed, the country changed, though trials continued to plague them. Even with the aid of ten Indian trail cutters, the ascent of still another mountain appeared almost impossible. Rain made the new trail slippery. One mule after another staggered, lost its footing, and rolled off the trail until a tree stopped its fall. Fifteen times the men had to unload a fallen animal, bring it back to the treacherous trail, and repack the cargo.

This was the life Blom relished. He seemed to greet problems with eagerness and gain satisfaction from solving them. They encountered another mountain, then a perpendicular cliff of four hundred feet, and a cascading river in the valley below; day after day he sent out small parties to find a way down into the valley and across the river. At last they crossed on rafts, traveled some distance, and faced another swirling stream. The timely appearance of a few Indians in dugouts solved that problem. When they reached the Río Jataté, one of the few landmarks on the map, a sudden hurricane swept over the camp, scattering their tents, and every man had to lie flat on the ground, clutching his personal equipment.

The first part of the expedition, with the worst trials, was over. Signs of civilization began to appear, and finally they entered the town of Ocosingo. For more than a week they relaxed, rested the mules, repaired saddles, and enjoyed good food. When the journey resumed, they crossed the great Tzendales forest, the home of the Lacandón Indians, inhabited by jaguars and wild hogs, and reached the Usumacinta River. In mahogany dugouts they coursed down to Yaxchilán, and then struck due east to Flores in Lake Petén. On the way to Tikal a man fell sick, so Blom made the trip to the ruins of Tikal with only one companion. On his return they sent the sick man home, and the entire party went to Bacalar. From there they cut straight through the region of the *sublevado* Indians and gambled with the likelihood of trouble. Unwelcomed though unharmed, they reached Chichén Itzá, the end of the journey.

The expedition yielded several archaeological discoveries. At Pestac, near Toniná, Frans encountered a large carved stone with dot and bar inscriptions whose value was determined by position—a practice found hitherto only in the codices. Then out from Chinkultik, the explorers visited a burial cave used by the ancient Maya, and found bones, skulls, and pottery shards everywhere. This discovery had more macabre interest than historical significance. Blom also came to an interesting conclusion about one aspect of early Maya civilization. Archaeologists had credited the Toltecs with the introduction of the ball court to the Maya of Yucatán. Frans, however, found ball courts in numerous Maya sites which had been abandoned before the Toltec influence could have appeared; so he concluded that the ball court was indigenous to the Maya and perhaps had originated among them.

By persistently following a story of one of his local guides, Blom made another discovery. Hunting for honey, the guide had found a small cache of old pottery and pieces of textiles in what he called a cave. At the designated spot, Frans scaled a twenty-foot cliff and found a small hole, from which he retrieved several pieces of cotton cloth which he believed to be some fifteen hundred years old. According to later analysis, however, the fabric was considerably newer than that.

Financially, the expedition overran its budget. Sometimes Blom receives credit, and rightly so, for conducting the journey so well that he was able to sell his mules at the end of the trip for more than he paid for them. The other side of the story involves a miscalculation. When he explored Chiapas in 1925, he paid one dollar per hundred pounds of corn for his animals. But by 1928 the oil business and civilization had come to Chiapas and raised the price of corn to eight or ten dollars per hundred pounds. With his animals consuming from one hundred to one hundred and fifty pounds a day, Blom was in the red by the end of the journey, despite the sale of the mules.

Blom had good reason to consider the expedition a success. In covering 1475 miles over a period of 200 days, he had mapped unknown territory, secured the first motion pictures of Lacandóns, discovered unrecorded Maya sites, and made some interesting finds. He was at his best in exploration. On every major expedition he extracted useful information about the early Maya, and in addition he recorded new areas and new sites for future investigators to examine.

Two years after the Gray Memorial Expedition, Frans had another opportunity to show that he could make the most of work in the field, this time at one site. Officials planning the Century of Progress Exposition, to be held in Chicago in 1933, commissioned him to make molds of the Nunnery at Uxmal for a reproduction of the structure at the exposition. Not only did he carry out the major task, but he also ranged all over the site and into the country for miles around to find ruins. He turned up twenty-three groups of unknown structures, recorded nineteen new stelae, and added five hundred years to the history of Uxmal.

He and his party also made a number of minor discoveries. A careful examination of buildings revealed the use of false perspective. The original builders had slightly modified the rectangular plan of the inner court of the Nunnery and gradually raised the floor level so as to direct major attention to a particular temple. In addition, the steps on some structures sagged slightly at the ends so as to correct the beholder's perspective. Accidentally, members of his party also found that the walls of a number of buildings had a slight outward inclination as they moved upward, apparently designed to throw deeper shadows on the decorative carvings. Blom's men also demonstrated the practicality of photographing inscribed stelae with bright artificial light at night in order to make the lines of low-relief carving stand out. Although this was announced as a discovery, Frans and his men did not realize that Maler had accomplished the same thing with more primitive methods at the end of the nineteenth century. With some modifications, the Nunnery was reproduced at the Century of Progress Exposition in 1933, and Maya archaeology was the richer for Blom's activity at Uxmal.

The two remaining expeditions of the 1930s failed to produce such striking results. The Danish government provided funds in 1935 for an expedition, led by Blom, to examine the northwestern sector of Honduras. Tegucigalpa, San Pedro Sula, and Copán connected the routes the party covered, sometimes by mule and at other times by air. The mule journey through the Chemelecón Valley yielded small archaeological fare, probably because a number of earlier explorers had combed the area.

Blom's last major trip during the years at Tulane comes as a surprise, because it had no archaeological purpose. A Central American tourist agency commissioned Blom to collect information for a series of pamphlets on Guatemala. Maurice Ries, a writer, and Dan Leyrer, a photographer, accompanied Frans on a six-week trip through the country to gather firsthand information. In the flight over the Petén, Frans counted a hundred unknown mounds, though he had to forego the experience of exploring the archaeological features of the region. The jaunt failed to produce results, for the projected series of pamphlets was never published; and so the three men had no achievement to chalk up to their record except a pleasant trip to Guatemala.

In addition to making expeditions, Frans also participated in professional meetings, where his fellow scientists announced and discussed their discoveries and interpretations. As the director of the Department of Middle American Research, he organized and conducted three seminars for scholars at Tulane between 1925 and 1930; and he headed the session on archaeology of the Committee of Cultural Relations with Latin America, which met in Mexico in 1932. Twice he gave papers at meetings of the International Congress of Americanists. In 1934 he attended the International Congress of Anthropological and Ethnological Sciences and presented reports on the map of Maya sites and on the new quarterly *Maya Research.* The United States government appointed him in 1938 an official delegate to the second conference of that organization, which met in Denmark; at that meeting he described a new museum project for Tulane University, which will be noted later.

Although he preferred the active life of exploration to

the prosaic task of writing, he produced a considerable record of publication. In the decade 1926 to 1936 he turned out an array of articles, some of them of major importance. It can be argued that the list of his writings is not as impressive as it appears at first glance, because many of the items are very brief, some repeat information appearing under other titles, and a number of his papers deal with points of minor interest.

His contributions, nevertheless, are significant. *Tribes and Temples,* written with La Farge, justly brought his work to the attention of fellow archaeologists. The official report of the Gray Memorial Expedition never appeared in print, probably because of the lack of funds; unfortunately, the most readable record of that venture appeared in a periodical with limited circulation. Already in this period he forecast his interest in postconquest history with his excellent account of Caspar Antonio Chi. In the early 1930s he described the ancient Maya ball game; and perhaps his most noteworthy scholarly paper was his treatment of commerce, trade, and monetary units among the Maya, which was reprinted in the *Smithsonian Institution Annual Report.* He launched three series of publications at Tulane: the Middle American Research Series, Middle American Pamphlets, and Middle American Papers. In addition, he edited *Maya Research,* a distinguished professional quarterly, which had to cease publication after several years because of the loss of foundation support.

In addition to compiling technical and scientific reports, Blom wanted to reach the broad public with his enthusiasm for archaeology and his conviction that it could teach valuable lessons about mankind through the centuries. In the epilogue to *Tribes and Temples* he and La Farge expressed the hope that the two volumes "may help to awaken the interest of the public in the history of an ancient American people. . . . "[3] The authors made a point of emphasizing the human interest aspects of the story in that work so as to attract readers beyond the circle of the professionals. *Tribes and Temples,* however, never became popular; unsold copies were still on hand four decades after it appeared.

Over the years Blom made other efforts to reach the informed public, and he showed considerable ability in producing popular writings and lectures on Maya archaeology. His contributions appeared in *Art and Archaeology*, the *Illustrated London News*, the *Pan American Union Bulletin*, the *Gazette des Beaux Arts*, and some newspapers. During the first decade at Tulane he also addressed a number of groups, ranging from college fraternities to library associations. On these occasions he wisely considered the particular interest of his audience, and also carefully wrote out the text of his remarks.

His most ambitious work in the popular field, *The Conquest of Yucatán*, was the only full-scale book he produced in the 1930s. The title is misleading, because he included a general description of pre-Hispanic Maya civilization after relating the story of the Spanish conquest. A more serious blemish was the organization, or lack of organization, of the chapters; only haste and failure to think through the logic of the presentation can explain this obvious weakness. He did, however, use simple language, and he gave a reasonably complete coverage of the story.

In his desire to increase popular knowledge of the Maya, Blom arranged public exhibitions of Maya art and artifacts. The most spectacular appeared in the Century of Progress Exposition, already noted. At the Greater Texas and Pan American Exposition, held in Dallas in 1937, he filled six thousand square feet of space almost entirely with Maya objects, many of them from the collection at Tulane. So successful was the display that it won the grand prize of the fair. The same year he presented an exhibit, "The Maya—Past and Present," at Tulane. And in November and December he provided some items for an exhibit at the Baltimore Museum of Art and wrote the introduction for the catalogue of that display. Subsequently he mounted other exhibitions in New Orleans, Detroit, and at the World's Fair in San Francisco.

The scarcity of financial resources at Tulane forced him to campaign persistently for money to expand the department. He made trips north to meet representatives of foundations, like the Rockefeller Foundation and the

Rosenwald Foundation, whom he hoped to interest in his work. In New York City he arranged evening parties at sponsors' homes to show motion pictures of his expeditions. On one of those occasions, in May 1929, he expected John D. Rockefeller, Jr., as one of the guests. But after the affair Frans felt relieved that the man did not appear, because the rented projector tore the film nineteen times. "I was frantic," he confessed, though he added that the audience appeared to be interested.[4]

During his tenure at Tulane, Blom attracted some $200,000 to augment the operation of the department. If this amount, spread over fifteen years, appears modest or even small today, it was an accomplishment at that time. Ten of his years at Tulane coincided with the depression of the 1930s, when money was difficult to raise. More significant, perhaps, is the fact that the foundation money he secured almost doubled the budget of the Department of Middle American Research.

After becoming director of the department, Blom made repeated attempts to expand its activities by requesting increased funding from the university. In 1929 he proposed a plan to publish the manuscripts in its library, and asked for an additional $10,000. Nothing happened. The following year he submitted a proposal to change the department to an institute (a change in name which did not occur until 1938), listed the specialists needed to carry on different aspects of the work, and arrived at an estimated budget of $201,000. Nothing happened. Three years later, after the replica of the Nunnery at Uxmal gained notice at Chicago, he proposed a full-scale reproduction of that structure for the department's museum, library, and offices. He advised that it should be placed at Claiborne Avenue and Audubon Boulevard Tract, where tourists passing through the city would see it. He estimated the cost at $400,000 for the building and $100,000 as endowment for maintenance. Nothing happened. In 1935 he issued a similar proposal, calling for a reproduction of the Castillo of Chichén Itzá as a five-story building. Again nothing happened.

Finally, in 1938, the administration of Tulane under President Rufus Harris decided to respond to Blom's appeal for a campaign to build the structure. Samuel Zemurray gave $50,000 to finance the drive, and he was made head of the campaign committee to raise $2 million. The university employed a New York fund-raising firm to direct the effort in good Madison Avenue style. After considerable preparation, public announcement of the drive appeared early in 1939. Now the plan called for a reproduction of the Castillo as an eight-story building, air-conditioned and without windows, and for a $1,300,000 endowment. Attractive campaign literature appeared, citing the needs and potentialities of the institute, and conveniently listing the cost of each room in order to attract donors with varying amounts of money. In addition, a list was drawn up of persons in the United States and Central America who might be approached for contributions; in numerous instances notes indicated that the potential benefactor was a personal friend of Blom.

The brochure, prepared by the fund-raising agent, naturally emphasized the achievements of Blom and the needs of the institute. His accomplishments during the years at Tulane were set forth at length, with the implication that here was a scholar and administrator who could direct the activities of the proposed enlarged facilities of the institute.

Frans toured cities in the Northeast and the Midwest in 1939 and again in 1940 to attract donors. Generally, he gave an illustrated lecture on "Explorations in the Land of the Maya." After Tulane sent a group of men to Central America to make another photographic record of the ruins, he used the new film, entitled "Middle America," which had been professionally prepared, with Lowell Thomas as narrator.

Whether he intended it or not, his greatest success in gaining public notice came from his remark that Columbus missed his opportunity on the fourth voyage by not heading south to Yucatán, where he would have found wealth. Frans must have been surprised by the reaction to that offhand remark. Newspapers all over the country quoted the statement, some editorials appeared on the subject, and of course there were rebuttals in defense of Columbus.

In the end, Tulane had staked much of the success of the campaign on Blom himself. It advertised his professional achievements, and expected him to stir up interest by speaking to large groups in cities. As a result, something unfortunate happened, though the exact story is not clear. Frans did not make his best appeal to audiences; he was far more effective in direct contact with individuals. According to rumor, he drank before making public appearances, and eventually his unstable condition prompted President Harris to withdraw him from the tour. Because Tulane could find no other qualified person to take over the scheduled addresses, the campaign came to a sudden halt and ended in complete failure.

The debacle of the building project marked the end, not the beginning, of Frans's personal collapse. There are indications that he began to slip into professional decline during the mid 1930s. The expedition of 1935 produced few archaeological results; moreover, the investigation was on the periphery of Maya culture and not in the Chiapas jungles that Blom found so attractive. Then came the trip to Guatemala in 1937, and it had little to do with the Maya. In addition, an examination of the list of Blom's publications shows a distinct decline in creative articles after 1935. Even his book, *The Conquest of Yucatán,* was not up to his best standards. From 1936 until 1941, when he left Tulane, his publications dealt largely with exhibitions in which he participated. Blom had burned out. The most likely reason was the failure to return to exploration in the forests of Chiapas; he had lost the source of his spiritual nourishment. The last straw was the disastrous failure of the fund-raising campaign.

The sequence of events leading up to Blom's departure from Tulane remains unclear. He stood alone, aloof from the faculty and at times ignoring warnings from his own staff. Cut off from exploration, troubled over the lack of funds for the institute, and conscious of the failure of the building campaign, he apparently took refuge in liquor. Sometime during this period he was demoted from the rank of director to that of associate in archaeology; if the action was intended as a warning to him, it had no effect. President Harris secured his resignation from the university on November 30, 1941, on the grounds of ill health, and accepted it with regret the following day. Blom had reached rock bottom. Alcoholism, defeat, degradation: anyone would have predicted that his career was finished.

For almost two years Frans floundered in the depths of despair. He lingered on in New Orleans, vainly attempting to find employment. Although World War II created jobs in which his versatility in languages and his knowledge of Mexico and Central America could have been useful, he was not a United States citizen and was thus never seriously considered for war work. Presumably, he continued to drink during this period as long as he had the money.

The turning point came in 1943, when he secured a commission in Mexico to make an expedition into the forests of Chiapas. Not only did he return to his beloved Lacandón country, but he met there the woman who was destined to help him build a second career.

Gertrude Duby was forty-two years old. Born in Switzerland, she had trained in horticulture and social work, and made a living as a journalist and photographer. With numerous European languages at her command, she had an international outlook and an abiding interest in social problems. After coming to Mexico in 1940, she investigated working conditions in the textile and tobacco industries, and then turned her attention to the Indians of Chiapas. Although she was attractive in appearance and wore clothes with a flair, she also knew how to work hard, manage affairs shrewdly and economically, direct subordinates effectively, and preside as a charming hostess. It was well known that Frans never allowed women on his expeditions, and yet she joined him without a murmur on his part, an indication of her strong determination.

The two met under prosaic circumstances. It is evident

that they knew of each other before the meeting, but the identity of the matchmaker remains a mystery. Frans left Mexico City by plane on September 24, spent some time in Tuxtla Gutiérrez, and then flew on to Ocosingo. She was already in that settlement, awaiting his arrival. On October 16, the plane, carrying passengers and cargo, swooped down on "the reformed cow pasture" that served as a landing field. Among the people who had gathered for the event was Trudi, as she was always known, who watched the passengers descend. The last one was a tall man with a mane of blond and white hair, who jauntily wore a Chamula-style shirt and Indian knapsack. She knew it was Blom and moved toward him. As she approached, he saw "an attractive looking woman, who certainly did not fit into the picture" of the airfield at Ocosingo, because of "the city-way she was dressed in a tailor-made gray flannel and turban."[5] "You are Frans Blom?" "And you are Gertrude Duby?" That was the end of the meeting, and she thereupon joined the expedition.

Blom was not given to sentiment and made few references to Trudi in his diary except as a companion on the trip. Two days after the meeting, however, when they were on the trail to Toniná, he remarked, "She is the kind of person with whom you can feel in close relation without having to do conversation. I like that gal."[6]

Frans and Trudi lived in Mexico City for seven years, eking out a livelihood through hard work. They made the most of every opportunity to earn a peso. Frans held a minor government position, and he did odd jobs on the side. The couple turned out numerous articles for newspapers and occasionally for magazines. Although the pay was small and uncertain, they were grateful for the income. On three occasions the Mexican Department of Health sent them on expeditions to the Indian country of Chiapas, where Frans enjoyed traveling through his favorite forests, and Trudi studied the condition of the natives. During those years of struggle, it is surprising that he was able to turn out some scholarly articles.

Accustomed to pursuing serious studies, Frans fretted

over the loss of so much time "just to make a living." He conducted classes in English, escorted tourists about, and helped in some academic work, simply "to give me food and a roof over my head."[7] In 1947 he taught a class in summer school—a large class of 220 students, he was proud to explain—and then on weekends hired a Greyhound bus to take students to Texcoco, Oaxaca, and Taxco. "I learn there is money in the tourist business," he observed.[8] At the same time he ground out articles on such topics as the production of chicle for chewing gum, salt making among a certain tribe of Indians, expeditions through the forests, cities and ruins of interest to tourists, and seemingly every possible topic about Chiapas. He succeeded in selling those accounts to Spanish- and English-language newspapers in Mexico as well as to numerous papers and periodicals in Europe.

He and Trudi had a small apartment in the city. Although it was only a two-room affair with kitchen and bath, it faced a terrace full of flowers and commanded a view of a distant volcano, mountains, and nearby Chapultepec Park. Despite the cramped quarters, the Bloms held open house for scientific visitors on Saturdays, and on Sundays they entertained guests with less specialized interests.

When expeditions beckoned, Frans could hardly wait to get on the trail. Actually, he never relished life in the modern city, at least after he moved to Mexico in 1943. He preferred to wander through strange forests, enjoy nature, and let his mind play with ideas in the solitude of the jungle. "Show me a mule and an expense account," he confided to a friend, "and I am on my way. And with no desire to getting rich." He would be satisfied with enough income for "just the rent, the light, the house, etc., and chow."[9]

The trail diary of 1943 teems with personal observations. Now a free man without the problems of Tulane on his mind, Blom felt unhurried, and he filled page after page with comments on each day's events. After climbing a mountain near Ocosingo, he returned to his quarters with satisfaction. "One thing that impressed me this afternoon," he wrote, "as I came down the mountain towards the town was the quiet. There were no noises, no motors exhausting, no automobiles honking mechanical noises. The broad valley lay stretched out at our feet—far away rain clouds—a rainbow light and shadow over the fields. A complete calm that was restful."[10]

On the trail he was all ears and eyes. As he made his way through the woods toward Las Tasas, he noted the sunrise, red-crested woodpeckers, hummingbirds, spider webs across the trail, flowers of every description, a coral-colored mushroom, wild papaya, and spider monkeys.

During that expedition he and Trudi suffered from inconveniences and hardships. It rained often; as a result the trail was a muddy, slippery ribbon through the forest, at some places fallen trees blocked the way, and rivers which they had to cross were swollen. Some nights were bitterly cold; ticks caused infernal itching; and once millions of ants invaded the camp quarters. Frans suffered from an infected leg for weeks, and contracted malaria in the last days of the journey. No complaints, however, came from him; he returned to civilization happy, satisfied, and proud of the exploration he had accomplished.

In 1945 the Bloms undertook the strangest mission of their lives. The Inter-American Indian Institute of Mexico sent them to investigate the ravages of a certain black fly whose bite infected human beings with onchocerciasis, a disease that produced eventual blindness in its victims. Accompanied by a specialist on disease-bearing insects and a handyman, Frans and Trudi went to the southwest corner of Mexico and then struck northward into the mountains to reach their goal. The tribulations on the trail were nothing compared with what they found at Unión Fronteriza. The village, nestling among coffee plantations and natural tropical beauty, shocked them. The municipal agent who attempted to read the letter of introduction they presented faltered because he was going blind. Children emerged warily from their homes and shaded their eyes against the sun; they were going blind. The schoolroom was empty because teachers refused to live in the doomed settlement. Blind adults wandered about the streets, pleading for help for their stricken children. But the Bloms had no aid to offer; medical science, in fact, had not discovered a way to prevent or cure the disease. The bite of the black fly doomed each victim to eventual blindness.

Never before had Frans felt human suffering so keenly. On his return he wrote an impassioned appeal to Manuel Gamio, who had commissioned the study. "It is easy to say there is no remedy for onchocerciasis . . . ," he began. "*I* have seen that the sickness is spreading . . . *I* fear the advance of this evil among ourselves and no doctor has convinced me otherwise . . . no one can convince me that human intelligence can not find a remedy. . . . " To fight the disease, he continued, they must find fanatics as zealous as the Catholic friars of the conquest. "*My cry is:* preparation and prevention. . . . Pardon me, *querido maestro,*" he concluded, "but your commission made me see incredible suffering."[11] The appeal to Gamio is a noble document, the finest thing Frans ever wrote.

Blom had added a new dimension to his experience—concern for the natives of Chiapas—but he had not deserted archaeology. Although it was no longer an exclusive passion, he continued to search for Maya sites. Once, at El Cedro, he heard a man boast of having traversed the region since 1907; "he is our meat," remarked Frans, who expected to gain information about ruins in the area.[12]

Generally, he was content to discover, examine, and record sites. Many of the ruins appeared unpromising for archaeological results. In June 1948, he made a typical entry when he wrote, "Recrossing the Río Naranjo, we came upon an artificial mound in a cow pasture. Nothing special." Four days later he encountered a site at Huaca. "At long last we rode up the edge of a stone-set terrace, and there lay two small stone pyramids about 4 meters high, built of squared rock, apparently without mortar. In front of the westernmost one lay a plain circular altar, split in two. Diameter 1.20 meters. Nothing more, so we turned around."[13] On July 12 he described the ruins at Zapote in similar brief fashion, and concluded, "There is nothing spectacular about these ruins. Their presence only fills out our picture of the Maya in the Zendales region."[14] He did not, however, dismiss these sites as unworthy of notice. In every case he made notes and plans, and often sketched carvings on the stelae he found. In the second volume of *La selva lacandona* he presented all of the data he collected about each site.

During his last twenty years Blom did not produce a record in archaeological research to match the discoveries of his earlier career. Bad luck and lack of adequate funds were primarily responsible. His three-year grant from the Viking Fund for explorations was abruptly cut off at the end of his second year, leaving him without money to write up and publish his results. The excavation of Moxviquil, located near San Cristóbal, had just begun to yield artifacts when the patron of the project died and the subsidy ended. Perhaps the most ironic turn of events occurred in 1943, when he suffered from malaria at El Cedro; Lacandón Indians told him of ancient structures with paintings only three hours away, but he was so ill that he had to be flown back to civilization—and missed discovering the famous murals of Bonampak. That stroke of good fortune was reserved for Giles Healey three years later.

Frans took the opportunity to carry out a double project he had begun at Harvard in 1924-25, a list of all Maya ruins and correct maps of the land where they were located. From 1943 on, he gathered information for both objectives in the state of Chiapas. He made only modest claims for his work in archaeology, saying that he was no more than an explorer who found and recorded unknown Maya sites for future generations to examine. In the name of science he made the information available to all scholars; and as late as 1959 he compiled an additional list of places worth investigating.

His search for Maya sites went hand in hand with the aim of drawing up accurate maps of the unknown areas of Chiapas. "The official maps look fine," he snorted in 1943, "and would be useful as wall decorations or lamp shades, but as maps they are absolutely worthless. Rivers are either marked 25 or more kilometers from where they actually are or in some places run up the mountains!"[15] Good roads on the official maps turned out to be no more than mule trails, and sometimes an apparent town was only a group of abandoned palm shacks. He issued his first map of the Chiapas region in 1953 and included it in the second volume of *La selva lacandona* four years later.

In 1950 the Bloms moved to San Cristóbal in the heart of Chiapas. With a small legacy inherited from his mother, Frans bought a building as his permanent residence at the edge of the town. A local man had constructed the edifice as a seminary to train Mexicans to work with the Indians, but he died before turning it over to the church; his heirs were willing to dispose of it for a modest price. It contained fourteen rooms and three patios. With a few hundred dollars left over from the legacy, Frans installed modern conveniences. The property also included an extensive tract of land, which Trudi quickly cultivated with vegetables and flowers. A shed at the rear housed the horses and mules which provided transportation for the Bloms. In order to give the place a personality of its own, Frans called it Na Bolom, the tiger, and set two tiles, each bearing a copy of a tiger from Tula, into the exterior walls of the building.

Soon after acquiring the house, Frans determined to build up a library of all the important books bearing on Chiapas and made a frank appeal to individuals and institutions to donate books for the project. And the books came in. Within a few years he estimated that 95 percent of the volumes had come as gifts. Appropriately, he called the library after Fray Bartolomé de Las Casas, the early Spanish friend of the Indians.

The Bloms devised ingenious sources of income. Frans fitted up three rooms for paying guests, and started out by charging $2.50 per person for a bed, three meals, and a hot shower. He also collected a fee from curious persons who wished to see the house and the small museum of archaeological objects and Spanish religious pictures he had collected. Trudi made photographs of Indians and sold them to guests; more important, she managed the household with careful economy. Occasionally, they picked up some money from articles written for newspapers.

One of the most important sources of income, irregular and unpredictable as it was, was their work as guides for scientists from abroad who wished to investigate some aspect of the Chiapas jungle. In 1956, for example, Trudi led a group of Canadians on a trip to photograph wildlife in the forest. On her return, Frans had a commitment to guide scientists from the University of California to the northern part of the state in search of amber-preserved prehistoric insects. At the age of sixty-three, he observed to a friend, "These seven or eight hours a day on horseback keep me in good trim."[16]

The Lacandón Indians appealed greatly to the Bloms. Shy and peaceful, those natives carried on the simple existence probably followed by the Maya centuries ago. But their numbers were dwindling. Every time the Bloms made an expedition into the Lacandón country, they carried supplies to the natives. In 1948 they collected medicines from the Mexican Ministry of Health, and from business organizations they received large quantities of combs, mirrors, beads, and seeds.

When Frans and Trudi visited the Lacandóns in 1950, they discovered that the Indians were on the edge of starvation because their crops had failed for three years in succession. Blom shuddered at the sight of the weak, emaciated people, and he described their children as "skeletons in a sack of skin." Angry and determined to save the people, he sent an urgent message for aid, "hoping that something would be done." "And, by God, something was done," he exclaimed to a friend.[17] The government sent money and medicine, and private sources flew in three-and-a-half tons of food. The bewildered natives, amazed at the supplies, filled their canoes and headed for their settlements, while Blom's pack animals carried maize overland to the same destination.

On another occasion the Bloms responded to a tragedy which struck the family of a Lacandón named Bor. When Bor returned one day from searching for food, he found that alligator hunters had descended on his home, abducted one of his sons and his sister and her child, burned his hut, and stolen the implements of his livelihood. His wife survived the attack only to die soon afterward. On learning of the calamity, Frans and Trudi rushed to the place and brought Bor and his two surviving sons to Na Bolom. For months they cared for the stricken man and helped him to regain his sanity. When Bor had recovered and indicated his desire to return to the forests, Frans and Trudi collected tools, seed, and food and secured mules to take him back to reestablish his home. All of that cost money, and Frans had to sell some duplicate artifacts to meet the expense. Thereafter, when any Lacandón needed help, he was welcome at Na Bolom; that practice continues to this day.

Over the years the Bloms pled with the government for two reforms. They insisted that the state should carry on trade for the Lacandóns and protect those natives from unscrupulous merchants. Frans and Trudi also called on the government to create national parks to save the major Maya ruins from destruction.

Frans succeeded in making Na Bolom an object of pilgrimage for scholars. The Pan American Highway made the place accessible by automobile and bus. Everyone who came wanted to see the unique place; some visitors made use of the increasing resources of the library; others showed up to meet the genial host and hostess, and to mingle with other scholars. In the early years Frans or Trudi often guided the casual visitor from room to room and showed slides of their expeditions before the large fireplace in the library. All kinds of people appeared at Na Bolom. In the mid 1950s Frans noted that visitors from twenty-four nations had signed the guest book; a year later he remarked that "more and more scientists turn up anywhere from Toynbee to a professor of oriental art from the imperial university of Tokio, who wanted to spend his sabbatical among the Maya ruins."[18]

He loved the home he and Trudi had created. San Cristóbal, located seven thousand feet above sea level, appealed to him because of its perfect climate, despite some frost in winter. "It's a darned sight better than N.O. any time," he boasted to a friend in New Orleans.[19] He neglected to note that in some seasons of the year the rain could be heavy and continuous for days on end.

Something was always going on at Na Bolom. There were expeditions of his own or those he conducted for visiting groups. There were curious visitors; one man exercised his rattlesnakes in the main patio, to the consternation of the other guests. Frans gloated over the acquisition from foreign archives of thousands of pages on film bearing on the early history of Chiapas. He also carried on considerable correspondence. Whenever anyone, known or unknown to him, inquired about a detail of Chiapas past or present, he wrote a full and generous reply, usually typing the letter himself.

In addition, he published serious articles on archaeology. He described a polychrome plate for the Carnegie Institution, examined the practices of early Maya cremation, investigated the pre-Hispanic amber trade of the region, and turned out a paper on the Maya as engineers. He also became interested in earlier travelers in the region and published several journals of those visitors. His unpublished manuscripts were usually short accounts of other aspects of Chiapas in the past. When books came his way, he read them carefully, and frequently wrote to the publisher if he found mistakes.

La selva lacandona, his major contribution of this period, was a joint work with Trudi. In the first volume, the Bloms' travels of the 1940s, especially the expedition of 1948, are described in great detail, with considerable human interest. The second volume provides a description of the numerous Maya sites they visited, supplemented with maps and sketches. *La selva lacandona,* issued in an edition of a thousand copies, received less notice than it deserves.

Frans's increasing age and his new life-style caused him to adopt a revised set of values. No longer did he strive for professional acclaim. On several occasions he went so far as to declare that he hated publicity about himself, and he made fun of a journalist who planned to write an account of his adventures. His devotion to the forest and his love of nature led him at times to make bitter comments about the superficialities of contemporary civilization. He respected the Indians' way of life and their religion, though he hoped that they might eliminate filthy habits which transmitted disease.

If he simplified his view of life, he retained many of his characteristic traits. When he spoke with serious visitors, he measured his words carefully so as to state facts correctly. In discussing his own travels and research, however, he talked with passion and sometimes with obsession. Humor continued to punctuate his conversation, and many of his letters are far more spontaneous and lively than his published writings. He had only contempt for popular books which boasted of the discovery of a "lost Maya city" in Chiapas. He was amused and at times annoyed that some persons thought he was the mysterious author B. Traven. As in the past, he continued to smoke cigarettes, and in his last years he sometimes neglected his personal appearance and had trouble curbing his tendency to alcoholism. He continued to look very much the gringo; when he visited Mexico City cabdrivers charged the tourist rate until he identified himself as Mexican and haggled over the price in good native fashion.

His thirteen years at Na Bolom brought rich satisfaction. True, he continued to work hard to make a living, but he was within reach of his beloved forests, and he met interesting people and learned of the research of scientists in allied fields. His wife Trudi managed the household well, gained increasing notice for her superb photography, and had a way of creating excitement in everything she did. The Indians loved Frans, and leaders of town and state respected him. Only four years after he moved to San Cristóbal, he was honored with the title First Citizen of Chiapas.

Almost until his death just short of the age of seventy, his striking appearance and the sheer force of his personality commanded attention. When he sat in the throne chair by the fireplace in the library of Na Bolom, blue eyes dancing and white hair flowing, he greeted friends with irresistible geniality and urbanity. Often considered the grand old man, he was more than that: a humanist-patriarch.

Frans Blom's life was a veritable odyssey. Coming from a wealthy family in Denmark, he chose to be an amateur archaeologist in the forests of Mexico, and with little visible change he became a professional. Unfortunately for him, he slipped into the role of administrator, gradually lost the opportunity to return periodically to the tropical jungle, and slumped into personal despair and ruin. He recovered from defeat by going back to Chiapas, where age, experience, and a reconsideration of the values of life broadened his outlook to include interest in the welfare of human beings and joy in congenial social relations. He achieved something rarely granted to a man: Drawing upon experience and hindsight, he had the opportunity to live a second life, close to nature and alive to the fundamentals of social existence.

Notes

Chapter 1

1. Teobert Maler, Peabody Museum Memoirs 5, no. 1 (1911): 42.
2. Ibid.
3. Maler, Peabody Museum Memoirs 4, no. 2 (1908): 4-5.
4. Maler, Peabody Museum Memoirs 5, no. 1 (1911): 6.
5. Maler, Peabody Museum Memoirs 4, no. 2 (1908): 120. Robert Wauchope suggests that the "roaring" animals were more likely howler monkeys.
6. Maler's *Impresiones de Viaje,* on which this paragraph and the four that follow are based, was not published until 1932; this explains why some archaeologists of the later 1920s thought they had discovered Cobá.
7. Maler, Peabody Museum Memoirs 5, no. 1 (1911): 6.
8. Maler, Peabody Museum Memoirs 2, no. 2 (1903): 100.
9. Ibid., p. 104.
10. Maler, Peabody Museum Memoirs 4, no. 2 (1908): 74.
11. Maler, Peabody Museum Memoirs 5, no. 1 (1911): 55.
12. Maler, Peabody Museum Memoirs 4, no. 2 (1908): 120.
13. Ibid., no. 1, p. 48.
14. Ibid., p. 4.
15. Ibid., no. 2, p. 127.

Chapter 2

1. A.P. Maudslay, *Archaeology,* vols. 55-59 of *Biologia Centrali-Americana,* ed. Frederic Du Cane Godman and Osbert Salvin, 59 vols. (London, 1879-1915), 1: "Quiriguá," p. 2.
2. Ibid.
3. Ibid., "Chichén Itzá," p. 2.
4. Ibid., "Palenque," p. 1.
5. Ibid., "Palenque," p. 2; Anne Cary Maudslay and Alfred P. Maudslay, *A Glimpse at Guatemala* (London, 1899), p. 217.
6. The plaster was sent from England to Lívingston in tin-lined barrels. A small steamer took the cargo up the river to Izabal on Lake Izabal, where the plaster was transferred to waterproof sacks for the mule trip over the mountains to Copán. Maudslay estimated that a ton of plaster, bought in England for 50 shillings, cost £50 by the time it arrived in Copán.
7. Maudslay, *Archaeology,* 1: "Quiriguá," p. 4.
8. Maudslay and Maudslay, *A Glimpse at Guatemala,* p. 219; Maudslay, *Archaeology,* 1: "Palenque," p. 4.
9. Maudslay, *Archaeology,* 1: "Menché," pp. 42, 44.
10. When four of her panels were exhibited at the International Congress of Americanists in New York in 1902, she was too modest to present a scholarly paper on the subject; only four years later did she agree to discuss the murals.
11. Maudslay, *Archaeology,* 1: "Palenque," p. 6.
12. Ibid., "Chichén Itzá," p. 5.
13. Maudslay and Maudslay, *A Glimpse at Guatemala,* p. 210.
14. Maudslay, *Archaeology,* 1: "Chichén Itzá," p. 5.

15. Ibid., "Copán," p. 12.
16. Ibid., "Menché," p. 42.
17. Désiré Charnay, *Ancient Cities in the New World* (London, 1887; reprint New York: AMS Press, 1972); pp. 435-36. For a time the site was called Menché; Charnay named it Lorillard City in honor of the sponsor of his expedition; but eventually it became known as Yaxchilán. Maudslay, of course, had not discovered it; Professor Rockstrok of the Instituto Nacional of Guatemala visited the site a year before and told Maudslay about it.
18. The work is a bibliographical curiosity. The text, published in four small volumes, contains 212 pages, with four separate paginations, each to accompany a volume of plates. But the text was actually issued in thirteen parts, not in consecutive order, at various times between 1888 and 1899, though the title page gives the dates as 1889-1902.
19. Maudslay, *Archaeology,* 1: "Introduction," p. 3.
20. Ibid.
21. Maudslay and Maudslay, *A Glimpse at Guatemala,* p. 229.
22. A.P. Maudslay, trans., *The True History of the Conquest of New Spain by Bernal Díaz del Castillo . . .* , 6 vols. (London, 1908-16), 1 (1908), Introduction, p. 1.
23. A.P. Maudslay, "Recent Archaeological Discoveries," *Journal of the Royal Anthropological Institute,* 33 (1913): 12.
24. London *Times,* February 14, 1927, p. 8.
25. Additional sets of the molds had been provided, one for the Trocadero, now the Musée de l'Homme, in Paris, and another for the American Museum of Natural History in New York, through the generosity of the Duc de Loubat.

Chapter 4

1. The report also states that he created a stir among scientists in 1926 by exhibiting a twelve-year-old Maya child at the British Museum.

Chapter 5

1. Spinden to Clark Wissler, October 19, 1918, Spinden File, American Museum of Natural History Archives, New York, N.Y.
2. *The New York Times,* March 20, 1914, p. 20.
3. Ibid., May 10, 1915, p. 4.
4. Ibid., June 30, 1917, p. 9.
5. New Orleans *Times Picayune,* May 6, 1917.
6. *The New York Times,* June 30, 1917, p. 9.
7. Ibid.
8. It is interesting to note that George Kubler, *Studies in Classic Maya Iconography,* Memoirs of the Connecticut Academy of Arts and Sciences 18 (1969), p. 1, begins his discussion with Spinden's monograph, saying that no studies on the subject appeared since 1917 except Proskouriakoff's more restricted *A Study of Classic Maya Sculpture* (1950).
9. Spinden, "The Origin and Distribution of Agriculture in America," in *19th International Congress of Americanists, 1917,* p. 269.
10. Spinden, *Free Exhibition of Industrial Art . . . 1919,* p. 18.

11. On at least one occasion he went so far as to declare that the experience of dead civilizations provided the best guide for modern civilizations if they wished to avoid evil and secure good.

Chapter 6

1. William Gates, *The Spirit of the Hour in Archaeology,* Papers of the School of Antiquity, No. 1 (Point Loma, Calif., 1917), p. 16.
2. Baltimore *Sun,* April 25, 1940.
3. From the records of the academy (Richard Schimmel, Assistant Director, Maryland Academy of Sciences, to the author, November 21, 1973).
4. New Orleans *Item,* May 28, 1924.
5. Ibid., October 26, 1924.
6. New Orleans *Morning Tribune,* June 28, 1925.
7. Gates to Dinwiddie, January 13, 1925, excerpts, Tulane University Archives, New Orleans, La.
8. "William Gates," *Hullabaloo* (Tulane student newspaper), May 14, 1926.
9. Gates, *The Development and the Disruption of the Department of Middle American Research at Tulane University* (1926), p. 3.
10. Gates, *The Spirit of the Hour in Archaeology,* pp. 16, 17.
11. Gates, *Commentary upon the Maya-Tzental Perez Codex. . . ,* Peabody Museum Papers 6, no. 1 (1910): 4.
12. Gates, *The Spirit of the Hour in Archaeology,* p. 15.
13. *Excelsior* (Mexico), May 10, 1925, quoted in G.W. Lowe, "William E. Gates; a Biography," typescript, Provo, U., 1954, p. 40.
14. Not only was Gates at times vague in expressing himself; he could also be totally enigmatic. When Blom and La Farge had returned from their expedition in August 1925, a reporter asked him about the origin of the Maya. "Don't say they are Egyptian," Gates replied. "They are more Egyptian than I am. They are Mayan." He refused to elaborate (unidentified newspaper clipping, August 23, 1925, Tulane University Archives: Clippings).
15. Frans Blom, "The Gomesta Manuscript: a Falsification," *Maya Research* 2 (1935): 248.

Chapter 7

1. Blom to Morley, January 7, 1924, in possession of Mrs. Frans Blom, San Cristóbal, Mexico. Hereafter this correspondence will be referred to as Blom Collection.
2. Maurice Ries to the author, October 10, 1973.
3. Blom to Morley, October 7, 1922, Blom Collection. Blom's account of Palenque, *I de Skore Stove* (Copenhagen, 1923), pp. 181-85, indicates that he was already familiar with some of the archaeological literature of the site.
4. Ibid.
5. Blom to Morley, August 2, 1922, Blom Collection.
6. Frans Blom and Oliver La Farge, *Tribes and Temples,* 2 vols. (New Orleans, 1925), 1: 180.
7. Ibid., 1: 178.
8. Letters in Blom Collection.
9. Blom to Morley, October 20, 1924, Blom Collection.
10. Blom to Morley, November 19, 1924, Blom Collection.

11. Blom to Morley, October 25, 1924, Blom Collection.
12. Blom to Dinwiddie, November 25, 1924, Tulane University Archives.
13. Gates's recommendation, November 7, 1924, Tulane University Archives.
14. Gates to Dinwiddie, January 13, 1925, Tulane University Archives.
15. Boston *Evening Transcript,* October 18, 1924.
16. Blom, "Diary of 1925 Expedition," April 22, 1925, Latin American Library, Tulane University.
17. "La Farge Journal on First Tulane Expedition," April 22, 1925, Latin American Library, Tulane University.
18. Blom, "1925 Diary," March 17.
19. Ibid., April 15.
20. Blom and La Farge, *Tribes and Temples,* 1: 206. Another passage (1: 165), too long to quote, describes a night journey over the savanna; the party continued to travel for twenty-eight hours without sleep. He copied the passage almost verbatim from p. 98 of his diary.
21. Blom, "1925 Diary," April 17, May 6, 19.
22. "La Farge Journal," April 17, May 12, 13.
23. Ibid., March 20, April 4.
24. Blom, "1925 Diary," April 22.
25. Ibid., June 8.
26. Blom and La Farge, *Tribes and Temples,* 1: 140.
27. Blom, "Tata," typescript, p. 9, Latin American Library, Tulane University.
28. Blom and La Farge, *Tribes and Temples,* 2: 247.
29. Blom, "Tata," p. 8.
30. The book betrays some peculiarities. No names of authors appear on the title page. On the reverse of that page the following are mentioned: Blom as director of the expedition, La Farge as assistant, and Lázaro as guide. If the inclusion of Lázaro's name testifies to the explorers' esteem for him, it is strange that Gates, director of the department fostering the expedition, is not mentioned. Incidentally, the passage of three decades did not change Blom's opinion of Gates; in the 1950s he referred to him as "the old nut" (Blom to E.B. Ricketson, November 1, 1955, Tulane University).

Chapter 8

1. New Orleans *Times Picayune,* May 27, 1932.
2. "La Farge Journal on First Tulane Expedition," March 18, 1925, Latin American Library, Tulane University.
3. Frans Blom and Oliver La Farge, *Tribes and Temples,* 2 vols. (New Orleans, 1925), 2: 499.
4. Blom's letter of May 14, 1929, Tulane University Archives.
5. Blom Diary, September 29, 1943, Blom Collection.
6. Ibid., October 1, 1943.
7. Blom to Manuel Gamio, September 17, 1945, Blom Collection.
8. Blom to Dolores Morgadanes, September 29, 1947, Blom Collection.
9. Blom to Carl Guthe, June 27, 1947, Blom Collection.
10. Blom Diary, October 1, 1943.
11. Blom to Gamio, September 17, 1945, Blom Collection.
12. Blom Diary, November 20, 1943.

13. Blom Diary, June 25, 1948.
14. Blom Diary, July 12, 1948.
15. Blom Diary, October 23, 1943.
16. Blom to Edith Ricketson, January 16, 1956, Tulane University Archives.
17. Blom to A.M. Tozzer, May 3, 1950, Blom Collection.
18. Blom to Edith Ricketson, December 18, 1955, Tulane University Archives.
19. Blom to Edith Ricketson, August 11, 1954.

Bibliography

Teobert Maler

A Chronological List of Maler's Works

"Découverte d'un tombeau royal zapotèque à Tehuantepec, en 1875," *La Nature* 7 (1879): 22-23. Spanish translation published in *El México Antiguo* 6 (1942): 1-5.

"Un vêtement royal de l'ancien Méxique," *La Nature* 7 (1879): 207-8. Spanish translation published in *Anales del Museo Nacional de México,* epoca 1, 3 (1886): 1-2.

"Nouvelles explorations des ruines de Palenque," *La Nature* 7 (1879): 299-302.

"Chacmool," *Globus* 35, No. 3 (1879): 41-43.

"Les Palais Sacerdotaux de Mictlan, au Méxique," *La Nature* 9 (1881): 49-50. English translation published in *Scientific American,* supplement, March 5, 1881, p. 4309.

"Notes sur la basse Mistèque," *Revue d'Ethnographie* 2 (1883): 154-61.

"Mémoire sur l'État de Chiapas (Méxique)," *Revue d'Ethnographie* 3 (1885): 295-342.

"Photographs of Copan Expedition." Peabody Museum, Harvard University, Cambridge, Mass., and also Tulane University Latin American Library, New Orleans, La.

"Yukatische Forschungen," *Globus* 68 (1895): 247-59, 277-92; 82 (1902): 197-230. Also as an offprint. English translation, typescript, Latin American Library, Tulane University, New Orleans, La.

Researches in the Central Portion of the Usumatsintla Valley, Peabody Museum Memoirs 2, no. 1 (1901): 9-75; 2, no. 2 (1903): 83-208.

Explorations in the Upper Usumatsintla and Adjacent Region: Altar de Sacrificios; Seibal; Itsimté-Sácluk; Cankuen, Peabody Museum Memoirs 4, no. 1 (1908): 1-51.

Explorations in the Department of the Peten, Guatemala, and Adjacent Regions: Topoxté, Yaxhá; Benque Viejo; Naranjo, Peabody Museum Memoirs 4, no. 2 (1908): 55-127.

Explorations in the Department of the Peten, Guatemala, and Adjacent Regions. Motul de San José; Peten Itza, Peabody Museum Memoirs 4, no. 3 (1910): 131-70.

"Typed Report on Chichen by E.H. Thompson and T. Maler" (n.p., 1910?), Peabody Museum Library, Harvard University, Cambridge, Mass.

"List of Illustrations for a Projected Work," *17th International Congress of Americanists,* 2d meeting, 1910 (Mexico, 1912), p. 486.

Explorations in the Department of the Peten, Guatemala, Tikal, Peabody Museum Memoirs 5, no. 1 (1911): 3-91.

"Chichén," *Revista de Yucatán* (Mérida), July 21 & 28, 1926.

"Bosquejo histórico del Petén-Itzá," *Sociedad de Geografía e Historia de Guatemala, Anales* 5, No. 2 (1928): 204-10; also in *Yikal Maya Than* (Mérida) 9 (1948): 206-7, 220-22.

Impresiones de Viaje, a la ruinas de Cobá y Chichen Itzá, ed. José Rosado E. (printed by the editor, Mérida, 1932). "Cobá y Chichén. . . ," ed. Gerdt Kutscher, *Ensayos e Estudios* (Bonn, Berlin) 4: 1-40. *Impressions of the Trip to the Ruins of Coba and Chicken* [sic]*-Itzá* (English trans., abridged) Greensville, Pa., 1965.

"El dintel de Yaxchilán," *Yan* (Mexico), no. 2 (1953): 135-38.

Teobert Maler: Bauten der Maya . . . 1886 bis 1905 . . . , ed. Gerdt Kutscher

(Berlin, 1971). German and Spanish text. Reproduction of forty plans by Maler.

Wauchope, Robert, *They Found the Buried Cities* (Chicago: University of Chicago Press, 1965), pp. 190-219, gives a selection from Maler's account of his travels.

Works about Maler

Until recently biographical information about the man was scant, confusing, and unreliable. Gerdt Kutscher has filled the gap with a good biographical essay in his edition of *Teobert Maler: Bauten der Maya,* noted above. I have drawn generously from that account. Joseph Louis Capitan's obituary in the *Journal de Société des Américanistes de Paris* 11 (1914-19): 636-37, is of limited use. Vicente Molino, "Teobert Maller [*sic*] . . . ," *Yikal Maya Than,* No. 135 (November 1930): 189-92, reprinted from *Diario del Sureste,* December 11, 1949, is disappointing. Carlos A. Echanove T., "Teobert Maler, Empedernido," *El Nacional* (Mexico), August 15, 1965, supplement, pp. 8-9, is of some use. Information about Maler's personal views and the problems he encountered in the explorations must be gathered from his published reports. Charnay's article, *Journal de Société des Américanistes de Paris* 1 (1904): 289-308, and Perigny's account, ibid. 5 (1908): 95-98, are summaries of Maler's published works rather than commentaries.

His early articles on Mexico, which appeared in European periodicals, 1879-85, seem disappointing today, but they evidence his questioning of popular views and the search for factual data.

Mereille Simoni, *Journal de Société des Américanistes de Paris* 54 (1965): 154-59, discusses the gold Zapotec ornaments found by Maler and points out variations between his paper on them in *La Nature* and the Spanish translation of that article in 1942. Simoni, ibid. 55 (1966): 253, and Alfredo Caso, ibid. 257-60, add further comments.

Werner Fuchss, "Un pionnier suisse au Guatemala: Gustav Bernoulli," *Bulletin de Société Suisse des Américanistes* (Geneva) 11, no. 9 (1970): 32-34, supersedes all other accounts of Bernoulli. Alden R. King, "The Journey of the Tikal Lintels to Basel," *Verhandlungen der Naturforschenden Gesellschaft, Basel* 82, no. 2 (December 1972): 15, adds a note on Maler's activity; Dr. Wauchope kindly called my attention to this item.

Alfredo Barrera Vásquez in *Morleyana* (Santa Fe, N.M., 1950), p. 263, tells of the course Maler offered at his home. T.A. Willard, *Kukulcan* (Hollywood, Cal., 1941), writes briefly of the man; Willard's *City of the Sacred Well,* (New York, 1926), describes Maler's artifacts from the Sacred Cenote. S.G. Morley, manuscript Diary for February 7, 11, March 2, 6, April 1, 1907, American Philosophical Society, describes his meetings with Maler. An account of Edward Thompson is in R.L. Brunhouse, *In Search of the Maya: The First Archaeologists* (Albuquerque: University of New Mexico Press, 1973), chap. 8.

Alfred P. Maudslay

A Chronological List of Maudslay's Words

Diaries, MS., British Museum, London.

"Explorations in Guatemala, and. . . Quiriguá, Tikal, and the Usumacinta," *Royal Geographical Society Proceedings* 5(1883):185-204.

"Ld. Aberdare—Progress of Geography for 1882-83," *Royal Geographical Society Proceedings* 8(1886):385-86.

[Remarks on Cyprian Bridge's "Cruises in Melanesia"], *Royal Geographical Society Proceedings* 8(1886):565-67.

"Explorations of the Ruins and Site of Copán, Central America," *Royal Geographical Society Proceedings* 8(1886):568-95.

[Letter from Yucatán, December 31, 1888], *Royal Geographical Society Proceedings* 11(1889):239-40.

Archaeology, vols. 55-59 of *Biologia Centrali-Americana*, 59 vols., ed. Frederic Du Cane Godman and Osbert Salvin (London, 1879-1915). Reprinted, Boston, 1961.

[Remarks on a paper on New Guinea], *Royal Geographical Society Proceedings* 12(1890):220-21.

"Paper Moulding of Monuments. . . ," *Royal Geographical Society: Hints to Travellers*, 7th ed. (London, 189-), pp. 455-60.

[Remarks on a paper on the Caroline Islands], *Royal Geographical Society Proceedings* 13(1891):133-34.

"The Ancient Civilizations of Central America," *Nature* (London), April 28, 1892, pp. 617-22.

"A Maya Calendar Inscription Interpreted by Goodman's Tables," *Royal Society of London Proceedings* 62(1897-98):67-80.

With Anne C. Maudslay, *A Glimpse at Guatemala and Some Notes on the Ancient Monuments of Central America* (London, 1899). Selection in *Antropología e Historia de Guatemala* 10, no. 1:44-71.

The True History of the Conquest of New Spain by Bernal Díaz del Castillo. . . Translated into English, with Introduction and Notes, 5 vols., Hakluyt Society, series 2, vols. 25-28, 30, 40 (London, 1908-16).

"Plano hecho en papel de maguey. . . ," *Anales del Museo Nacional de Mexico* 1(1909):49-58.

"Exploration in the Department of the Petén," *Nature* (London) 88(1911):247-49.

"A Note on the Position of the Great Temple Enclosure of Tenochtitlan. . . ," *18th International Congress of Americanists, 1912*. (London, 1913), pp. 173-75.

"Some American Problems," *Royal Anthropological Institute Journal* 42(1912):9-22.

"Recent Archaeological Discoveries," *Royal Anthropological Institute Journal* 43(1913):10-18.

"Valley of Mexico," *Geographical Journal* 48(1916):11-23.

"A Note on the Teocalli of Huitzilpochtli and Tlaloc," *Man* 22(1922):27.

"The Maya Sculptures," London *Times*, February 14, 1927, p. 8.

With A.C. Haddon, "Baron Anatole von Hügel," *Man* 28(1928):189-91.

Life in the Pacific Fifty Years Ago (London, 1930).

Letter of Maudslay to British Foreign Office in Wayne M. Clegern, *Maudslay's Central America: A Strategic View in 1886*, Studies in Middle American Economics. Middle American Research Institute, Tulane University no. 29(1968), pp. 73-94.

Selections from Maudslay's writings are given in Robert Wauchope, *They Found the Buried Cities* (Chicago: University of Chicago Press, 1965), 185-89, and Jacquetta Hawkes, ed., *The World of the Past*, 2 vols. (New York: Alfred A. Knopf, 1963) 2:615-19.

Works about Maudslay

Biographical accounts and obituaries appear in the following: early chapters of Maudslay's *Life in the Pacific Fifty Years Ago; The Geographical Journal* (London)

78(1931):1-12 (very helpful); A.M. Tozzer, *American Anthropologist* 33(1931):403-12; A.M. Tozzer, *American Academy of Arts and Sciences, Proceedings* 70(1936):555-58; A.M. Tozzer, *Sociedad de Geografía e Historia de Guatemala. Anales* 13(1936):340-47; also in *México. Museo Nacional de Arqueología. . . Boletín,* epoca 5, 2(1933):63-69; "J.C.C.," *Nature* (London) 127(March 7, 1931):345-46; P. Rivet, *Journal de Société des Américanistes de Paris* 23(1931):242-44; T.A. Joyce, *Man* 32(1932):123-35; and *The New York Times,* January 24, 1931, p. 17. There is a sketch of him in the British *Who's Who* (1914) but not in the *Dictionary of National Biography.*

Cyrus Thomas, "Maudslay's Archaeological Work in Central America," *American Anthropologist,* n.s. 1(1899):552-61, adds little. *Annual Cyclopedia, 1886* (New York, 1889), pp. 24-25, reports on his work at Quiriguá and Copán. *Royal Geographical Society Proceedings* 5(1883):44-45, recounts the meeting of Maudslay and Charnay at Yaxchilán. G.E. Church, "The Ruined Cities of Central America—Review," *Geographical Journal* 15(1900):392-94, gives a descriptive account of *A Glimpse at Guatemala,* without critical comments. *Guide to the Maudslay Collection of Maya Sculpture* (London: British Museum, 1923 [and later editions]) contains an essay on Maya civilization by T.A. Joyce, but tells nothing about Maudslay. Some of his photographs of Maya ruins are in the Field Museum, Tulane University Latin American Library, and the Peabody Museum, Harvard University.

For Adela Breton, see *13th International Congress of Americanists, 1902,* pp. 1x-1xi; her paper is in the 15th Session, 1906, 2:165-69. S.G. Morley's obituary of J.T. Goodman, *American Anthropologist* 21(1919):441-45, provides information on that man.

Elizabeth Carmichael, *The British and the Maya* (London: British Museum, 1973), contains brief accounts of Maudslay, pp. 23-29, Adela Breton, pp. 30-33, and T.A. Joyce, pp. 38-40.

Morley

Morley's diaries, held by the American Philosophical Society, are extensive and informative. Selections from them appear in Robert H. and Florence C. Lister, eds., *In Search of Maya Glyphs: From the Archaeological Journals of Sylvanus G. Morley* (Santa Fe: Museum of New Mexico Press, 1971). The large Morley file of miscellaneous material, Carnegie Institution of Washington, throws much light on the project in Yucatán and his relations with the C.I.W. *Morleyana. . .* (Santa Fe, 1950), offers a readable collection of reminiscences by friends who knew him; the volume is now out of print. Details about his life and a bibliography of writings by and about him can be found in R.L. Brunhouse, *Sylvanus G. Morley and the World of the Ancient Maya* (Norman: University of Oklahoma Press, 1971).

Richard B. Woodbury, *Alfred V. Kidder* (New York & London: Columbia University Press, 1973) gives generous selections from his writings, and Robert Wauchope, *American Antiquity* 31(1965):149-71, provides a good, brief account.

Mitchell-Hedges

A Chronological List of Mitchell-Hedges's Works

Battles with Great Fish (London, 1923).

"The Need for Men," *The English Review,* 41(1925):497-504.

"Among the Horrors, Monsters and Mysteries of Central America's Wilds," newspaper article, 1929; source not identified; copy in Tulane University Latin American Library.

Land of Wonder and Fear (New York & London, 1931).

Tiger (London, 1931). A novel.

Battling with Sea Monsters (London, 1937).

The White Tiger (Atlas Publishing Co., 1943). A novel.

Danger My Ally (London, 1954; Boston, 1954; Boston & London, 1955).

"Blue-Eyed Indians," *New World Antiquity* (London), no. 11 (1954):7-8.

"Some Problems of Middle American Research," *New World Antiquity*, no. 9 (1954):1-3.

Works about Mitchell-Hedges

The British *Who's Who* from the 1920s through the 1950s summarizes the facts of his career. *Danger My Ally* is an interesting example of autobiography, though the reader is not compelled to believe everything in it; reviews of the book appeared in *Time*, August 15, 1955, p. 70, and in *The New York Times*, August 28, 1955, sec. 7, p. 11; the latter is unfavorable. Lady Richmond Brown (Lillian Mable Alice Brown), *Unknown Tribes. Uncharted Seas* (London, 1924) tells the story of the first expedition to examine Lubaantún; Thomas Gann gives his version in *Mystery Cities* (London, 1925). Jane H. Houlson, *Blue Blaze. . .* , (Indianapolis, 1934), recounts the expedition of 1932. For previous discoveries of Lubaantún, see H.J. Spinden, *Arts* 10(1926):270-77. The recent report is by Norman Hammond, "The Planning of a Maya Ceremonial Center: Lubaantún," *Scientific American* 217(May 1972):83-91.

Newspaper articles contribute interesting sidelights to the story of the man and often supplement the autobiography. The New Orleans *Times Picayune*, April 7, 1924, gives the early exaggerated report on Lubaantún; the issue of October 6, 1924 prints Lady Richmond Brown's announcement to explore the site. The index of *The New York Times*, 1922-31, guides the reader to a number of informative items. The obituary of Mitchell-Hedges appears in the issue of June 13, 1959, p. 21. "Archaeologists Are Busy," *Pennsylvania Archaeologist*, pt. 5, no. 1 (1935):3 adds little.

Richard Garvin, *The Crystal Skull* (Garden City, N.Y.: Doubleday & Co., 1973) provides the fullest account of the quartz carving. G.M. Morant, "A Morphological Comparison of Two Crystal Skulls," *Man* 36(July 1936):105-17, carries comments by Adrian Digby and H.S. Braunholtz, and Morant's reply. The findings of this article provide the springboard for the elaborate hypothesis devised by Sibley S. Morrill, *Ambrose Bierce, F.A. Mitchell-Hedges and the Crystal Skull* (San Francisco: Cadleon Press, 1972). Ernett Hillen, "The Mystery of the Crystal Skull," *Weekend Magazine* (Canada), April 7, 1973, 16ff., contains comments by Anna Mitchell-Hedges.

Thomas Gann, who accompanied Mitchell-Hedges to Lubaatún, receives brief biographical treatment in Elizabeth Carmichael, *The British and the Maya* (London: British Museum, 1973), pp. 34-37.

Herbert J. Spinden

A Chronological List of Spinden's Works

Correspondence, Spinden File, American Museum of Natural History, New York, N.Y.

With George F. Will, *The Mandans: A Study of their Culture, Archaeology, and Language.* Peabody Museum Papers 3, no. 4(1906), pp. 81-319; also as an offprint. Reprinted New York: Kraus Reprints, 1967.

"Myths of the Nez Perce Indians," *Journal of American Folk-Lore* 21(April 1908):13-23, 149-58.

"The Nez Perce Indians," *American Anthropological Association Memoirs* 2, pt. 3(1908):165-274; reprinted New York: Kraus Reprints, 1964; also as an offprint.

"The Chronological Sequence of the Principal Monuments of Copan, (Honduras)," in *17th International Congress of Americanists, II, 1910* (Mexico, 1912), pp. 357-63.

"Table Showing the Chronological Sequence of the Principal Monuments of Copan, Honduras," *American Museum Journal* 10(July 25, 1910); also as an offprint, New York, 1910, 38 x 38 cm.

"An Ancient Sepulchre at Placeres del Oro, State of Guerrero, Mexico," *American Anthropologist* 13 (January 1911):29-55.

"The Making of Pottery at San Ildefonso," *American Museum Journal* 11(1911):192-96; also in *El Palacio* 7(1919):183, 185.

"Antiquity of Man in America," *Hearst's Magaine, The World To-Day* 21(January 1912):1618-19.

"Review of Alice C. Fletcher and Francis La Flesche, *The Omaha Tribe,*" *Current Anthropological Literature* 1(1912):186-89.

A Study of Maya Art. Its Subject Matter and Historical Development. Peabody Museum Memoirs 6(1913); reprinted New York: Kraus Reprints, 1970. Revised and enlarged as Part I of *Maya Art and Civilization* (Indian Hills, Col.: Falcon's Wing Press, 1957). The original work was his Ph.D. dissertation, Harvard University, 1909.

"Picture Writing of the Aztecs," *American Museum Journal* 13(1913):31-38; also as an offprint.

"A Chapter of Ancient American History," *Scientific American* (supplement) 77(May 23, 1914):328-31; also in *American Museum Journal* 14(1914):17-31.

"Explorer Invades Central America," *The New York Times,* March 20, 1914, p. 20. Gives quotations from Spinden.

"Stefansson's New New Found Land," *Scientific American* 113(October 2, 1915):289, 306.

"Home Songs of the Tewa Indians," *American Museum Journal* 15(February 1915):73-78; also in *El Palacio* 3(1915):42-47.

"Notes on the Archaeology of Salvador," *American Anthropologist* 17(July 1915): 446-87; also as an offprint.

"Ancient Gold Art in the New World," *American Museum Journal* 15(1915):307-14.

"Indian Dances in the Southwest," *American Museum Journal* 15(1915):103-15; also in *Scientific American* (supplement) 83(1917):8-9.

"Would Excommunicate Germany," *The New York Times,* May 10, 1915, p. 4. Letter to the editor.

"New Data on the Archaeology of Venezuela," *Scientific American* (supplement) 82(August 19, 1916):123.

"Portraiture in Central American Art," in *Anniversary Essays Presented to William Henry Holmes* (Washington, 1916), pp. 434-50; also as an offprint.

"The Pawnee Human Sacrifice to the Morning Star," *American Museum Journal* 16(1916):49-56.

"Review of George F. Kunz, *The Magic of Jewels and Charms,*" *American Museum Journal* 16(1916):243-48.

"The Question of the Zodiac in America," *American Anthropologist* 18(1916):53-60; also as an offprint.

"Pre-Columbian Representations of the Elephant in America," *Nature* (London) 96(1916):53-60.

"The Archaic Type," in Philip A. Means, "A Survey of Ancient Peruvian Art," *Connecticut Academy of Arts and Sciences* 21(1917):390-93.

"On the Greater Use of Indian Foods," *Scientific American* (supplement) 84(July 7, 1917):7; also in *American Museum Journal* 17(1917):189.

"The Invention and Spread of Agriculture in America," *American Museum Journal* 17(1917):181-89.

"Travel Notes in Western Venezuela," *Scientific American* (supplement) 83(June 30, 1917):408-9; also in *American Museum Journal* 17(1917):15-23.

"The Earthquakes and Eruptions in San Salvador, Seismic Disturbances in Central American Republics from June 7th to July 4th Last," *Scientific American* 117(August 4, 1917):76, 88; also in *The American* (Bluefields, Nicaragua), October 16, 1917.

"Nez Perce Tales," *American Folk-Lore Society Memoirs* 11(1917):180-201.

"The Origin and Distribution of Agriculture," in *19th International Congress of Americanists, 1915* (Washington, D.C., 1917), pp. 269-76; also in *Source Book in Anthropology*, comp. A.L. Kroeber and T.T. Waterman (Berkeley, 1920, pp. 245-51; rev. ed. New York, 1931, pp. 227-33); and in *New York Press*, October 1920.

"Recent Progress on the Study of Maya Art," *19th International Congress of Americanists, 1915* (Washington, 1917), pp. 165-77; also as an offprint.

"Notes on the Archaeology of Salvador," *American Anthropologist* 17(1917):446-87.

"Reproductions in Duotone of Scenes and Portraits from the American Southwest," *American Museum Journal* 17(1917):115-23.

Ancient Civilizations of Mexico and Central America (New York, 1917; 2d ed., rev., New York, 1922; 3d ed., rev., New York, 1928; 3d ed. reprinted New York: Biblo & Tannen Booksellers & Publishers, 1968); under title of "The Nuclear Civilization of the Maya and Related Cultures" in his *Maya Art and Civilization* (Indian Hills, Col.: Falcon's Wing Press, 1957).

"Origins of American Agriculture," *Scientific American* (supplement) 80(August 23, 1919):120-31.

"Creating a National Art," *Natural History* 19(1919):622-30; also in *Woman's Wear*, April 17, 1920.

"Field for Soldiers in Foreign Trade," *The New York Times*, May 25, 1919, sec. 3, p. 6.

"The Shattered Capitals of Central America," *National Geographic Magazine* 36(1919):185-212.

Free Exhibition of Industrial Art in Textiles and Costumes at American Museum of Natural History . . . 1919 (New York, 1919). [Spinden's name does not appear on cover or title page.]

"Series of Photographs. . . Exhibition 1919," *Natural History* 19(1919):631-54. Legends by Spinden.

"American Indian Poetry," *Natural History* 19(1919):301-7; also in *El Palacio* 7(1919):34-40.

Quoted passage of Spinden in S.G. Morley, *The Inscriptions of Copan* (Washington, 1920), pp. 208-9.

"Central American Calendars and the Gregorian Day," *Proceedings of the National Academy of Sciences* 6, no. 2 (February 1920):56-59.

"The Stephens Sculptures from Yucatán," *Natural History* 20(1920):379-89; also as an offprint.

"The Great Friar of Paramo," *Natural History* 21(1921):71-73. Poem.

"Shall the United States Intervene in Cuba?" *World's Work* 44(1921):465-83.

"Formal Inbreeding in Human Society with South American Examples," *International Eugenics Congress,* 2d session, New York, 1921; part title, *Eugenics, Genetics and the Family. Volume I: Scientific Papers of the Second International Congress of Eugenics. . . ,* 1921 (Baltimore, 1923), pp. 285-96.

"Yellow Fever—First and Last. . . ," *World's Work* 43(December 1921):189-91.

"The Understudy of Tezcatlipoca," in *American Indian Life,* ed. E.C. Parsons (New York, 1922), pp. 237-50.

Letter to the editor, *The New York Times,* November 19, 1922, sec. 2, p. 6. Against the Bursum Land Bill.

"Can Man Conquer his Parasites? Need of an International Coöperation in Fighting Disease," *World's Work* 42(March 1923):554-60.

"Civilization and the Wet Tropics," *World's Work* 45(February 1923):438-48.

"The Art of Ancient Mexico," *The Freeman* 7(1923):404-5. Commentary on Manuel Gamio, *La población del Valle de Teotihuacán,* 1922, and Enrique Juan Palacios, *Páginas de la Historia de México,* 1922.

Letter to the editor, *The New York Times,* November 2, 1923, sec. 2, p. 6. On deaths of Percy Houghton and Clifford Holland.

"The Archaeology of Brazil," *Art and Archaeology* 15(1923):150.

"New World Correlations," *21st International Congress of Americanists, I, The Hague, 1924* (The Hague, 1926), pp. 76-86; also in *Psyche* 7(1926):62-74.

"Letter from Dr. Herbert J. Spinden. . . ," *Eastern Association on Indian Affairs. Bulletin Number Three* (1924):12-14.

"Lowly Banana Builds an Empire," *The New York Times,* May 18, 1924, sec. 8, p. 6.

"Adventuring in Archaeology. . . ," *The New York Times,* May 25, 1924, sec. 4, p. 9.

"The Mosquito Kings, a Royal Travesty," *The New York Times,* August 17, 1924, sec. 4, p. 9.

"Primitive versus Civilized Ghosts," *Forum* 71(April 1924):531-35.

"What about the Indian?" *World's Work* 47(February 1924):381-84.

Introduction to Robert W. Willson, *Astronomical Notes on the Maya Codices,* Peabody Museum Papers 6, no. 3(1924):vii.

The Reduction of Mayan Dates, Peabody Museum Papers 6, no. 4(1924); also as an offprint. Reprinted New York: Kraus Reprints, n.d.

"A Lover's Lament" and "My Home over There" (Tewa poems), in *American Indian Love Lyrics,* comp. Nellie Barnes (New York, 1925), pp. 37-38.

"The Chorotegan Culture Area," in *21st International Congress of Americanists, 1924,* pt. 2 (Göteborg, 1925), pp. 529-45.

"Engineer's Place in the Modern World," *Harvard Graduates Magazine* 33(June 1925):624-26.

"A Great American Emperor Revealed. . . ," *The New York Times,* May 10, 1925, sec. 4, pp. 14-15.

"Holy City of Early America Revealed. . . ," *The New York Times,* December 6, 1925, sec. 4, pp. 8, 23.

"What is Civilization?" *Forum* 74 (August 1925):162-71, 371-79; also in Maurice Maeterlinck et al., *What Is Civilization?* (New York, 1926), pp. 155-74, with title

"The Answer of Ancient America."

"Toasts," *Forum* 74 (1925): illustrated section, vii-viii. Contains long quotation by Spinden.

"Maya Architecture, a Review of Some Recent Publications," *Arts* 10(1926):270-72.

"The Early History of the Banana," *Unifruitco* 1, nos. 11-12(1926):653-58, 738-41.

"Also the Friendly Tropics," *Forum* 75(February 1926):204-11.

"Maya Ship Battles Sudden Gulf Gale," *The New York Times,* February 24, 1926, p. 4.

"Dr. Spinden Writes of Maya Discoveries," *The New York Times,* April 1, 1926, p. 16. Quotations from him.

"Archaeology: Mexico and Central America," in *Encyclopaedia Britannica,* 13th ed. (1926), 1:193-96.

Preface to Gregory Mason, *Silver Cities of Yucatán* (New York, 1927), pp. v-xvii.

"The Prosaic versus the Romantic School in Anthropology," in G.E. Smith et. al., *Culture: the Diffusion Controversy* (New York, 1927), pp. 47-98.

"Study Dead City of 'Rubber People' . . . ," *The New York Times,* May 1, 1927, sec. 9, p. 16.

"Importancia de la antigua civilisación Maya," *Sociedad de Geografía e Historia de Guatemala, Anales* 3(1927):369-75.

"Can Civilized Man Keep Savage Virtues?" *Forum* 78(September 1927):346-56.

"Ancient Mayan Astronomy," *Scientific American* 138(January 1928):8-12.

"Maya Inscriptions Dealing with Venus and the Moon," *Buffalo Society of Natural Sciences* 14, No. 1(1928):5-59.

"In Quest of Ruined Cities . . . ," *Scientific American* 138(February 1928):108-11.

"Deciphering Mayan Mysteries . . . ," *Scientific American* 138(March 1928):232-34.

"Thank the American Indian . . . ," *Scientific American* 138(April 1928):330-32.

Ruins in the Maya Area. After F. Blom and O.G. Ricketson, Jr., with some additions by H.J. Spinden 1928 and revised by Frans Blom 1929 (New Orleans). Map.

"The Willows by the Water Side," "Sleepy Bird Lullaby," and "That Mountain Far Away" (three Indian poems), in *The Turquoise Trail: An Anthology of New Mexican Poetry,* ed. Alice C. Henderson (Boston & New York, 1928), pp. 133-34. Originally in *American Museum Journal* 19(1919):301-7.

"Problems of Industrial Art and Our National Welfare," *Brooklyn Museum Quarterly* 16(1929):127-28.

"The Population of Ancient America," in *Smithsonian Institution Annual Report for 1929* (Washington, 1930), pp. 451-71; also in *Geographical Review* 18 (October 18, 1928):641-60.

"Spinden's Creed," *The Art Digest* 4, no. 4 (mid October 1929):14. Contains a quotation from Spinden.

"The Fine Arts of the Mayas (Abstract)," *Art and Archaeology* 28(1929):90-91.

"Airplane to Help Find Ancient Ruins," *The New York Times,* August 18, 1929, sec. 9, p. 11.

"Maya Dates and What They Reveal . . . ," *Brooklyn Institution of Arts and Sciences. Museum. Science Bulletin* 4(1930):1-111; also in *24th International Congress of Americanists, 1930* (Hamburg, 1934); also as an offprint.

"Art and Culture of Peru and Mexico, a Review of Several Books," *International Studio* 97(1930):70,72.

With Mrs. Ellen S. Spinden, "The Mystery of the House of the Magician; Sidelights on Studies at Uxmul," *Hobbies, The Magazine of the Buffalo Museum of Science* 2(1930):69-74.

"The Eclipse Table of the Dresden Codex," in *23d International Congress of Americanists, N.Y., 1928* (New York, 1930), pp. 140-48.

"Maya Eclipse Data Held Key Language," *The New York Times,* August 22, 1930, p. 17.

"Indian Artists of the Southwest," *International Studio* 95(February 1930):49-51.

"Lover's Lament," *Golden Book* 20(October 1930):38.

"History of the Study of Maya Hieroglyphs" (n.p., 1930?), typescript, incomplete; in Peabody Museum Library, Harvard University, Cambridge, Mass.

"Indian Symbolism," in *Introduction to Indian American Art,* ed. John Sloan and Oliver La Farge, pt. 2 (New York, 1931), pp. 3-18.

"Fine Art and the First Americans," in *Introduction to American Indian Art,* ed. John Sloan and Oliver La Farge, pt. 2 (New York, 1931), pp. 3-8; also in *Scholastic* 29(October 24, 1935):21-22, and in *Indians at Work* 3(1936):45-48.

"Indian Art on Its Merits," *Parnassus* 3, no. 7 (November 1931):12-13.

"Social Background of the American Indian," *Hospital Social Service Magazine* 23(1931):108-12.

"Chinook Jargon," *West* 27, no. 6 (1931):126-27.

"Says Mayans Created Great Civilization," *The New York Times,* January 25, 1931, p. 22.

"Old Maya Ruins Found," *The New York Times,* May 16, 1931, p. 19.

Exhibition of Persian Art and Its Reaction to the Modern World (New York: Brooklyn Museum, 1931). This work does not bear Spinden's name, but it is credited to him in *Brooklyn Museum Annual Report for 1931.*

"The Language of the Mayas Still a Challenge to Science," *The New York Times,* October 11, 1931, sec. 9, p. 4.

"An Archaeological Junket in Yucatan," *Brooklyn Museum Quarterly* 18(1931):133-38.

"International Congress of Prehistoric and Protohistoric Sciences Field Excursion in the Vicinity of Cambridge and Oxford," *Brooklyn Museum Quarterly* 19(1932):151.

"The Royal Tombs of Southern Mexico," *Brooklyn Museum Quarterly* 19(1932):56-62.

"The Language of the Mayas," *Mexican Life* (Mexico) 8(August 1932):21, 60.

"Monte Alban Tomb is Rich in Promises," *The New York Times,* January 24, 1932, sec. 9, p. 5.

"Indian Manuscripts of Southern Mexico," in *Smithsonian Institution Annual Report for 1933* (Washington, D.C., 1935), pp. 429-51; also as an offprint.

"What Can Never Happen Again," *Brooklyn Museum Quarterly* 20(1933):17-18.

"Origin of Civilizations in Central America and Mexico," in *The American Aborigines, 5th Pacific Science Congress,* ed. Diamond Jenness (Vancouver, Canada, 1933), pp. 217-46.

With Mrs. Ellen C. Spinden, "The Place of Tajin in Totonac Archaeology," *American Anthropologist* 35(1933):255-70.

Songs of the Tewa; Translated by Herbert Joseph Spinden . . . (Exposition of Indian Tribal Arts, 1933). Includes an essay on American Indian poetry, pp. 7-70. For reviews, see *Book Review Digest, 1934* (New York, 1935), p. 884.

"Recent Archaeological Discoveries in Central America and Mexico," *The World Today, Encyclopaedia Britannica* 1, no. 3 (February 1934):49-52.

"Old Manuscripts Reveal Mexican History," *The New York Times*, February 27, 1934, p. 15.

With Mrs. Ellen C. Spinden, "An Excursion to Mexico," *Brooklyn Museum Quarterly* 21(1934):81-85.

Handbook of Brooklyn Museum School Service . . . (New York: Brooklyn Museum, 1934-36).

Crediting Ancient America [N.Y., 1934]. Address to Middle States Association of History Teachers, April 27-28, 1934.

"Review of J. Eric Thompson, *Mexico before Cortez*," *The Yale Review* 23(Winter 1934):423-24.

"Review of J. Scott, ed., *The Polar Regions*," *Brooklyn Museum Quarterly* 22(1935):97.

"Review of Charles R. Knight, *Before the Dawn of History*," *Brooklyn Museum Quarterly* 22, no. 2(1935):96.

"Curatorial Reports. American Indian Art and Primitive Cultures," in *Museums of the Brooklyn Institute of Arts and Sciences, Report for the Year 1935*, pp. 15-22.

"Primitive Arts of the Old and New World," *Brooklyn Museum Quarterly* 22(1935):163-71; also as an offprint.

"Maya Pots and Skyscrapers," *Three Americas* 1, no. 5 (October 1935):26-28.

Tabular View of Maya Chronology (New York: Brooklyn Museum, 1935). Chart, 41 x 70 cm.

"A Digest of Recent Work in Maya Astronomy," mimeographed, American Anthropological Association, December 29, 1935, n.p.

"America before Columbus," *Scientific Monthly* 42(1936):176-78; also in *The Missouri Archaeologist* 2, no. 2 (1936):3-6; also as an offprint.

"First Peopling of America as a Chronological Problem," in *Early Man: International Symposium*, ed. George Grant MacCurdy (Philadelphia and New York, 1937), pp. 105-14; also as an offprint.

"Huaxtec Sculptures and the Cult of Apotheosis," *Brooklyn Museum Quarterly* 24(1937):177-88; also as an offprint.

"The Mayas, America's First High Civilization," *Pan American Union Bulletin* 72(September 1937):672-76.

Foreword to *African Negro Art from the Collection of Frank Crowinshield* (New York: Brooklyn Museum, 1937).

"Waters Flow, Winds Blow, Civilizations Die," *North American Review* 249(September 1937):53-69.

"Sun Worship," in *Smithsonian Institution Annual Report for 1939* (Washington, D.C., 1940), pp. 447-69.

Masks, Barbaric and Civilized (Brooklyn Museum, 1939). Catalogue of an exhibition.

"Pueblo Bonito," *Region III Quarterly* (Santa Fe) 1, no. 2(1939):4-6.

"The Archaeology of the Northern Andes," *New York Academy of Science, Transactions*, series 2, 1, no. 5(1939):83-87.

"Pottery Design of the Chorotegans," *Brooklyn Museum Bulletin* 1 (1939):1; also as an offprint.

"A Final Word on Maya Correlation" (1940?), mimeographed, n.p.

"Time Scale for the New World," in *American Scientific Congress, Proceedings, 8th Session, 1940* (Washington, D.C., 1942), 2:39-44.

"Weaknesses of Mexican Chronology" (n.p., 1940?), typescript, carbon; in Peabody Museum Library, Harvard University, Cambridge, Mass.

"Los mayas; la primera alta civilisación de América," *Ah-kin-pech* (Campeche)

4, no. 46 (December 10, 1940):25-26; also in *Yikal Maya Than . . .* (Mérida) 2, nos. 157-58(1941):160.

Art Finds a Way: the Story of Human Skills (Brooklyn Museum, 1940). Catalogue of an exhibition.

"Art Finds a Way," *Brooklyn Museum Bulletin* 2, no. 2(1940):1.

"Diffusion of Maya Astronomy," in *The Maya and Their Neighbors* (New York, 1940), pp. 162-78; reprinted New York, 1962.

"Nicaraguan Pottery Designs by David Sequiera," *Parnassus* 12, no. 1(1940):20-21.

"The Zodiacal Calendar of the Maya" (1941), mimeographed, n.p. Address to 40th Annual Meeting of the American Anthropological Association, December 29, 1941.

America South of U.S.: As Revealed by Art . . . Exhibition (New York: Brooklyn Museum, 1941).

"Cronología y cosmología Maya-Tolteca," *Sociedad Mexicana de Antropología, México* 2(1942):74.

"Conferencia del Doctor Herbert J. Spinden," *Universidad nacional de la Plata. Instituto del Museo. Revista del Museo de la Plata* (1942):134-41.

"La serie supplementaria y la correlación 'A'," *Sociedad Mexicana de Antropología* 3(1943):311-19.

Top of the World, Arctic Lands in Human History. Handbook of the Exhibition . . . , 1944 (Brooklyn Museum, 1944).

A Documentary Exhibit of the Opening of the Pacific (New York, 1945).

"Maya Builders," *American Institute of Architects, Journal* 6(August 1946):55-58.

"Chorotegan Influences in Western Mexico," *Sociedad Mexicana de Antropología.* 4(1948):34-35.

"An Olmec Jewel," *Brooklyn Museum Bulletin* 9(February 1947):1-12.

"New Light on Quetzalcoatl," in *28th International Congress of Americanists, 1947* (Paris, 1948):505-12.

"Mexican Calendars and the Solar Year," in *Smithsonian Institution Annual Report for 1948* (Washington, D.C., 1949), pp. 393-405.

"Ecuadorian Carpets—Indian or Spanish?" *El Palacio* 55(1948):3-8.

"Linguistic Evidence of Racial Equality in Intelligence," *Eugenical News* 15(1949):48-51, 55-56; also as an offprint.

Westward Ho . . . Exhibition (Brooklyn Museum, 1949).

Tobacco Is American: The Story of Tobacco before the Coming of the White Man (New York: New York Public Library, 1950).

"The Indian Trail from the Time of the Mayas to the Colonial Period," in *Highways in Our National Life: A Symposium,* ed. Jean Labatat and W.J. Lane (Princeton, 1950), pp. 49-65.

"Old Collections Find New Home," *Brooklyn Museum Bulletin* 11(Summer 1950):1-3.

"Power Animals in American Indian Art," in *Indian Tribes of Aboriginal America: Selected Papers from the International Congress of Americanists, 29th Session,* ed. Sol Tax (Chicago, 1952), 3:195-99.

"Mayan Architecture," *Collier's Encyclopedia . . .* (1954), 15:582-84.

"How Did the Ancients Do It? . . . ," *Natural History* 64(May 1955):232-39, 278; abbreviated version under title "Engineering Marvels of the Ancients," *Science Digest* 38(November 1955):53-58.

"Los Toltecas en Guatemala," *Sociedad de Geografía e Historia de Guatemala, Anales* 29(1956):18-23.

"Maya Astronomy and the Electronic Calculator," *Homenaje al Doctor Alfonso Caso* (Mexico, 1956), pp. 343-51.

Maya Art and Civilization, rev. & enlg. (Indian Hills, Col.: Falcon's Wing Press, 1957).

"Discussion of Miss Proskouriakoff's Paper," in *Middle American Anthropology,* ed. Gordon B. Willey (Washington, D.C., 1958), pp. 36-42.

"Alfred Marston Tozzer 1877-1954," *National Academy of Sciences of the United States of America. Biographical Memoirs* 30(1957):383-97.

Introduction to *Art of the Maya Civilization . . . Exhibition . . . ,* (New York: Martin Widdefield Gallery, 1957).

"The Personality Figurines of Campeche" (n.d.), mimeographed; copy in American Museum of Natural History, New York, N.Y.

"Lectures on Art," MS (n.p., n.d.) American Museum of Natural History, New York, N.Y.

"Notes on Rio Grande Pueblos" (n.d.), 2 vols., typescript, American Museum of Natural History, New York, N.Y.

"Notes on the Woolwa or Southern Sumo, Nicaragua," MS (n.p.), 1920, American Museum of Natural History, New York, N.Y.

Drawings and reports on Puerto Rico, MSS (n.d.), American Museum of Natural History, New York, N.Y.

"The Historical Position of the Toltecs" (n.p., n.d.), typescript, incomplete; in Peabody Museum Library, Harvard University, Cambridge, Mass.

"The Totonacs" (n.p., n.d.), typescript; in Peabody Museum Library, Harvard University, Cambridge, Mass.

"The Status of the Olmeca" (n.p., n.d.), typescript, carbon; in Peabody Museum Library, Harvard University, Cambridge, Mass.

Works about Spinden

Biographical information is difficult to find in print. The *National Cyclopedia of American Biography* (1937-38), pp. 73-74, provides the fullest account. A sketch appeared in *Who's Who* beginning in 1916-17; the obituary in *The New York Times,* October 24, 1967, adds little. *Art and Archaeology* 28 (1929):189 gives a brief notice. On rare occasions Spinden referred to his past in his articles. Personal traits are known from scattered sources. Letters to the author from Mrs. Ailes Spinden, Mrs. Frederick H. Zimmerman, J. Eric S. Thompson, and interviews with Dr. Gordon Eckholm, Dr. Junius Bird, and Dr. Harvey Shapiro provided useful information. Jane Corby, in "Curator of Culture," *Brooklyn Eagle,* April 15, 1939, describes his activities at that time.

Spinden wrote relatively little about his travels. For the expedition of 1914, see Morley's MS Diary, American Philosophical Society; *Santa Fe New Mexican,* April 11, 1914; *The New York Times,* March 20, 1914, p. 20 and October 24, 1914, sec. 4, p. 5. On the secret service mission of 1917-18, Morley's Diary provides the information; see also Morley File, Carnegie Institution of Washington. *The United States Navy Register, 1918,* gives Spinden's official status. The story of his sudden departure from San Salvador comes from Boaz Long in *Morleyana* (Santa Fe, 1950), pp. 118-20. Spinden described his methods of exploration in his *Scientific American* article "In Quest of Ruined Cities," 1928.

The Mason-Spinden expedition can be followed in numerous articles in *The New York Times,* 1926; in Mason, "The Shrines of a Vanished Race," *World's Work*

53 (November 1926):75-89, and more fully in Mason's book, *Silver Cities of Yucatán* (New York & London, 1927); a selection from Mason's book is in Robert Wauchope, *They Found the Buried Cities* (Chicago: University of Chicago Press, 1965), pp. 241-65. For information about Gregory Mason, see *Who's Who,* 1928-29, and an unsatisfactory obituary in *The New York Times,* December 1, 1968, p. 86. His *Green Gold of Yucatán* received a review in the same paper, October 24, 1926, sec. 3, p. 6, and his *Silver Cities of Yucatán* was reviewed in the *Times* April 13, 1927, p. 16 and April 24, 1927, sec. 3, p. 6.

On antidiffusionism, see Spinden's writings, 1916 and 1927. His rebuttal to Opsjon is in *The New York Times,* July 7, 1926, p. 27 and was reprinted in the *Journal de Société des Américanistes de Paris* 18 (1926):368; Spinden's reply to Walde-Waldegg's claim is also in *The New York Times,* April 8, 1932, p. 23. One Cleanthis Zoaris, in *The New York Times* April 24, 1932, sec. 3, p. 2, replied to Spinden by saying that perhaps some of King Minos's mariners had crossed the Atlantic to Central America.

In general, brief articles summarizing Spinden's views have been omitted here. Mention might be made, however, of "Find American Date Recorded 613 B.C. Mayas Ahead of Einstein," *The Monthly Evening Sky Map* (Brooklyn) 18, no. 208 (April 1924), and of "The Mayans['] Remarkable Knowledge of Astronomy," ibid. 22, no. 264 (December 1928), which asserts that Spinden found the Maya 70 percent correct in recording eclipses. A long announcement by the Peabody Museum of his explanation of the Maya's use of the Venus calendar is interesting for the notice it received in newspapers, for example, *The New York Times,* December 28, 1925, pp. 1,2.

Many other activities and opinions of Spinden can be followed by using the index of *The New York Times.* "Jaguar Sky-God," *Brooklyn Museum Quarterly* 21 (1934):28-32, reports a lecture by the man. Brief items on his research are in *El Palacio* 30 (1931):218-19; 39 (1935):60-61, 89-91; 47 (1939):21-22. The official title of the Meriam Report is *The Problem of Indian Administration* (Baltimore: Johns Hopkins, 1928). Spinden's criticism of Christian leaders who opposed Indian dances is in *Eastern Association of Indian Affairs. Bulletin Number Three,* p. 14. See also statements by John Collier and F.W. Hodge on the same subject, *The New York Times,* December 16, 1923, sec. 8, p. 6 and December 20, p. 16. The letter by Edith M. Babb, which started the controversy, is in *The New York Times,* December 2, 1923, sec. 9, p. 8. David H. Kelley, "A History of the Decipherment of Maya Script," *Anthropological Linguistics* 4, no. 8 (1962):12-13, gives an estimate of Spinden's work on hieroglyphs.

For assessment of his publications, see George B. MacCurdy on *A Study of Maya Art,* in *Current Anthropological Literature* 1 (1912):145-54, and S.G. Morley on the same book, ibid., 154-57; G.H.C. on *Songs of the Tewa,* in *Brooklyn Museum Quarterly* 21 (1934):108-9, and notices summarized in *Book Review Digest, 1934* (New York, 1935), p. 884. Hermann Beyer, *Apuntas acerca de un nuovo manual de Arqueología Mexicana* (Mexico, 1918), pp. 3-17, lists criticisms of Spinden's *Ancient Civilizations of Mexico and Central America.*

William Gates

The following abbreviations are used: "Tulane LAL" for Tulane University Latin American Library, and "Tulane Archives" for Tulane University, Archives Collection.

A Chronological List of Gates's Works

Gates Correspondence, MS., Brigham Young University, Provo, U.

Gates Folder, MS., Tulane Archives.

Maya and Tzental Calendars (Cleveland, O.: privately printed, 1900).

Codex Perez: Maya Tzental (Point Loma, Cal.: privately printed, 1909). Gates printed a few copies in 1905.

Commentary upon the Maya-Tzental Perez Codex with a Concluding Note upon the Linguistic Problem of the Maya Glyphs, Peabody Museum Papers 6, no. 1 (1910):13-64; also as an offprint, Point Loma, Cal., 1910.

"Copan and Its Position in American History," *Pan American Magazine* 13(1912):37-44; also in *El Sendero Teosófico* 2, no. 2 (1912):100-14, and in *The Philosophical Path* 1 (1911):419-26.

Codex Cortesianus. Madrid Codex (Point Loma, Cal., 1911).

"El sistema de Cronología Azteca," *El Sendero Teosófico* 3, no. 3 (1912):208-12.

"Concepts linguistiques dans l'Amérique ancienne," *Congrès International d'Anthropologie et d'Archaeologie Préhistoriques, Compte Rendu,* 14th Session, 2 (1912):341-48; English translation, pp. 421-26; also in *The Philosophical Path* 3 (1912):421-26, and as an offprint, Geneva, 1912.

The Spirit of the Hour in Archaeology, Papers of the School of Antiquity, no. 1 (Point Loma, Cal., 1917); also in *The Philosophical Path* 9 (1915):425-41.

Early Chinese Painting, Papers of the School of Antiquity, University Extension Series Number Five (1916).

"Mexico Today," *North American Review* 209 (1919):68-83.

"The Four Governments of Mexico," *World's Work* 37 (1919):68-83, 570-80, 654-65; 38 (1919):58-68, 214-26.

"Solution of the Mexican Imbroglio," *Forum* 62 (1919):415-26.

"The Distribution of the Several Branches of the Mayance Linguistic Stock," in S.G. Morley, *The Inscriptions of Copan* (Washington, D.C., 1920), pp. 605-15.

Department of Middle American Research. Session of 1924-25 (n.d.), New Orleans.

Gates to Dinwiddie, Charlottesville, Va., January 13, 1925, excerpts, typescript, bound in copy of *The Development and the Disruption . . . ,* Tulane LAL.

The Development and the Disruption of the Department of Middle American Research at Tulane University at New Orleans (March 1926).

Editor, *Maya Society Publications.* See individual entries below.

The Dresden Codex (n.d., n.p.). Prospectus.

Editor, *Maya Society Quarterly* 1 (1931-32).

"The Thirteen Ahaus in the Kaua Manuscript . . . ," *Maya Society Quarterly* 1 (1931):2-20.

"Glyph Studies," *Maya Society Quarterly* 1 (1931):32-33.

"A Lanquin Kekchi Calendar," *Maya Society Quarterly* 1 (1931):29-32.

An Outline Dictionary of Maya Glyphs, with a Concordance and Analysis of Their Relationships, Maya Society Publication no. 1 (1931). An edition of 207 copies. A half-dozen copies of the same title were printed in 1910.

The Dresden Maya Codex Reproduced from Tracings of the Original Colorings and Finished by Hand, Maya Society Publication no. 2 (1930). An edition of 75 copies.

Codex Ixtlan: Zapotec, Maya Society Publication no. 3 (1931).

Codex Meixuiro: Zapotec, Maya Society Publication no. 4 (193-).

Codex Abraham Castellanos: Zapotec, a Geographic Lienzo, Maya Society Publication no. 5 (1931).

An Aztec Maguey Manuscript, Maya Society Publication no. 6 (193-).

"The Birth of the Vinal," *Maya Society Quarterly* 1 (1932):38-44.

"Glyph Studies," *Maya Society Quarterly* 1 (1932):68-70.

"Pokonchí Calendar," *Maya Society Quarterly* 1 (1932):75-77.

"Era of the Thirteen Gods and the Nine Gods, Book of Chuyamel," *Maya Society Quarterly* 1 (1932):78-92.

"The So-called Maya Alphabet," *Maya Society Quarterly* 1 (1932):187.

"The Mayance Nations," *Maya Society Quarterly* 1 (1932):97-106.

"The Specific Type of Word and Syntax Formation in the Mayance Family," *Maya Society Quarterly* 1 (1932):150-53.

"Glyph Studies," *Maya Society Quarterly* 1 (1932):153-82.

The Madrid Maya Codex; being the Combined Troano and Cortez, Maya Society Publications no. 12 and no. 21 (1933).

"Naciones Mayances," *Sociedad de Geografía e Historia de Guatemala, Anales* 10 (1934):401-12.

The Gomesta Manuscript, of Hieroglyphics and Customs: End of the 16th Century, Maya Society Publication no. 7 (1935).

The Maya Calkini Chronicle . . . , Maya Society Publication no. 8 (1935).

Arte, Vocabulario y Doctrina en Lengua Cholti, 1685, Maya Society Publication no. 9 (1935).

Plantas Medicinales de Yucatán. Manuscript of the Late 18th Century with Colored Illustrations of the Plants, trans. and ed. Elizabeth C. Stewart, Maya Society Publication no. 10 (1935).

Chilan Balam de Tekax, Manuscript in Maya, Maya Society Publication no. 10 (193-).

Arte de la Lengua Ixil . . . , Maya Society Publication no. 14 (1935).

Boturini Tarascan Calendars, Maya Society Publication no. 15 (193-).

Doctrina en Lengua Kekchi, Maya Society Publication no. 16 (193-).

Planetary Calendar in Nahuatl, Maya Society Publication no. 17 (193-).

Rural Education in Mexico and the Indian Problem. A Lecture . . . , Mexico, 1935. Excerpts in *Weekly News Sheet* (Mexico), March 8, 1935, pp. 1-2.

The Maya Society and Its Work, Maya Society Publication no. 19 (1937).

Yucatán before and after the Conquest by Friar Diego de Landa with Other Related Documents, Maps and Illustrations. Translated with Notes, Maya Society Publication no. 20 (1937).

To the Board of Trustees of the Johns Hopkins University (Baltimore, 1938).

De la Cruz-Badiano Herbal of 1552, Maya Society Publication no. 22 (1939). Latin text and illustrations.

De la Cruz-Badiano Aztec Herbal of 1552; full English Translation, Maya Society Publication no. 23 (1939). Also popular edition prepared but not issued.

A Grammar of the Maya; being a Complete Grammar of the 16th Century Language, Maya Society Publication no. 13 (1938), 105 copies. Second ed., 1940.

"The Acanceh Frieze," proposed as Maya Society Publication no. 24; never completed or published.

Three manuscript papers, Tulane LAL.

The following catalogues of parts of his library:

The William Gates Collection . . . (New York, 1924). Leaflet advertising the sale.

The William E. Gates Collection (New York, 1924). Catalogue of the books that Tulane purchased.

The Gates Collection of Middle American Literature . . . (Baltimore, 1944?). One volume in seven parts.

Works about Gates

Brief biographical accounts are in *National Cyclopedia of American Biography* (New York, 1934), pp. 254-55, with a portrait of Gates; *American Historical Review* 46 (1940):254; and in obituaries of April 25, 1940, in the *Baltimore Sun, The New York Times,* The *New York Journal and American,* and the *New York Herald Tribune.* The only longer account is by Gareth W. Lowe, "William E. Gates: A Biography," typescript, 77 pages (Provo, Utah, 1954). Lowe's use of Gates's correspondence provides an important contribution on the subject; a revised edition is in progress. I have drawn upon Lowe's account throughout the chapter. Material from other sources, however, must be used to fill out the portrait of the man.

Fugitive bits of information can be found in other places. Emmet A. Greenwalt, *The Point Loma Community in California, 1898-1942: A Theosophical Experiment* (Berkeley & Los Angeles: University of California Press, 1955) provides a good picture, though the account of Gates's activity in the community is meager. For the first visit to Mexico, Gates gave his views in the articles listed above, which he wrote after his return. The anonymous criticism is in *The Mexican Review,* clipping, Tulane LAL. The organization of the first Maya Society was reported in *The New York Times,* May 2, 1920, sec. 2, p. 6; a typed list of officers and members, presumably prepared in 1922, is in the F.W. Hodge Papers, Southwest Museum, Los Angeles, California.

The story of Gates's relations with Morley and the Carnegie Institution comes from Morley's manuscript Diary, American Philosophical Society, and is told in R.L. Brunhouse, *Sylvanus G. Morley* (Norman: University of Oklahoma Press, 1971). Lowe is particularly good on this subject, giving excerpts from Gates's correspondence. J. Eric S. Thompson also supplied the author with interesting data. Information about P.E. Shufeldt comes from *El Palacio* 55 (1949): 310; C.L. Lundell, "Archaeological Discoveries. . . ," *American Philosophical Society Transactions* 72, no. 3 (1933):170*n*, 176; and Morley's Diary.

For the Tulane episode, local newspaper articles collected in a scrapbook, Tulane LAL, provide the story; items from *The New York Times* can be located in the index of that paper. The Gates and Blom folders, Tulane Archives, are indispensable and enlightening. An account of Samuel Zemurray, a man worthy of a full biography, is in John Kobler, "Sam the Banana Man," *Life,* February 19, 1951, pp. 83-94, and with more background in Charles M. Wilson, *Empire in Green and Gold* (New York, 1947). Gates's aims for the department appear in newspaper articles in the scrapbooks noted above and in the leaflet *Department of Middle American Research. Session of 1924-25.* One version of his introduction to the public is in *Tulane News Bulletin* 4 (May 1924).

Some of Gates's writings provide pertinent material. *The William Gates Collection* (1924) contains a good autobiographical account, and *The Gates Collection of Middle American Literature. Sections A-G* (1944) has occasional illuminating notes under some entries. *The Maya Society and Its Work* gives Gates's views about his research and publications.

For his public announcements, see the newspapers already noted, and *The New York Times,* December 18, 1922, p. 3; *Scientific American* 145 (December 1931):400-401, and 152 (May 1945):276-77.

The major reviews of Gates's publications include the following: Hermann Beyer on the *Outline Dictionary* in *American Anthropologist* 35 (1933):659-94; J. Eric S. Thompson on the Landa, *American Anthropologist* 40 (1938):309-10; Blom's exposure of the Gomesta manuscript in *Maya Research* 2 (1935):234-47; Linton Satterthwaite on the *Codex Dresden* in *American Journal of Archaeology* 56 (1952):242-43. "G.B." on the *Maya Grammar* in *Journal of Philosophy* 35 (1938):667-69 admitted he did not know hieroglyphs and devoted his remarks to the philosophy of language.

Gates figures in Ross Parmenter, "The Identification of Lienzo A. . . ," *Middle American Research Institute, Philological and Documentary Studies* 2, no. 5 (1970), Publication 12, pp. 180-95. See David H. Kelley, "A History of the Development of Maya Script," *Anthropological Linguistics* 4, no. 8 (1962):15 for the single head Gates identified.

Frans Blom

Because of the extensive nature of Blom's published and unpublished works, the following is only a selective bibliography.

The location of manuscript items is indicated as follows: Na Bolom (materials in possession of Gertrude Duby Blom, Na Bolom, San Cristóbal de Las Casas, Mexico); MARI (Middle American Research Institute); Archives (Tulane University Library); LAL (Latin American Library, Tulane University); and Peabody (Library of the Peabody Museum, Harvard University).

A Chronological List of Blom's Works

Correspondence of Blom. Na Bolom, MARI, and Archives.

Unpublished articles by Blom. Na Bolom, Peabody, and LAL.

"Las ruinas de Tortuguero," *Ethnos,* 2 epoca, 1(1923):77-78.

I de store Skove; Breve ta fra Meksiko (Copenhagen, 1923).

"Las Chanacas of Tecuanapa," *Journal of American Folk-Lore* 36(1923):200-203.

"Report of the Preliminary Work at Uaxactun, Guatemala," *Carnegie Institution of Washington Year Book,* no. 23 (Washington, D.C., 1924), pp. 217-19.

"Notes from the Maya Area," *American Anthropologist* 26(1924):403-13.

"Diary of Frans Blom on the First Tulane Expedition to Middle America," MS, typed, LAL, MARI.

With Oliver Ricketson, Jr., *Index to Ruins in the Maya Area* (Boston, 1925), mimeographed.

"Tata, a Prince of an Indian" (n.d., n.p.), typescript, LAL. Internal evidence indicates that it was written some years after the 1925 expedition.

"El observatorio más antigua del Continente Americano," *Sociedad de Geografía e Historia de Guatemala, Anales* 2(1926):335-38.

With Oliver La Farge, *Tribes and Temples. . . ,* 2 vols. (New Orleans, 1926-27).

"Masterpieces of Maya Art. The Tomb at Comalcalco. . . ," *Art and Archaeology* 24(1927):222-27.

"San Clemente Ruins, Petén, Guatemala (Chichantún)," *Journal de Société des Américanistes de Paris* 20(1928):93-101.

"Caspar Antonio Chi, Interpreter," *American Anthropologist* 30(1928):250-62; in Spanish, *Icach* (Institución de ciencias y artes de Chiapas, Tuxtla Gutiérrez), no. 11(1963):17-20.

"Index to Maya Ruins. . ." (n.p., 1928), typescript, Peabody.

Ruins in the Maya Area. After Blom and Ricketson, with some additions by Herbert J. Spinden, 1928, and revised by Blom (New Orleans, 1928). A map.

"John Geddings Gray Expedition Field Letters," MS, (1928), 5 vols., LAL.

"John Geddings Gray Expedition," MS, (1928), 2 vols., LAL, MARI.

"Exploraciones en el departamento del Petén, Guatemala," *Sociedad de Geografía e Historia de Guatemala, Anales* 6(1928):182-88.

Preliminary Report of the John Geddings Gray Memorial Expedition, 1928 (New Orleans: Tulane University, 1929).

"Remarks on the Classics of Middle American Research," typescript, LAL. Address before the Louisiana Library Association, April 19, 1929.

"La importancia de las investigaciones arqueológicas en la América Latina," *Nueva Patria* 1, no. 2 (February 1929):7-8.

"Preliminary Notes on Two Important Maya Finds," in *23d International Congress of Americanists, 1928* (New York, 1930), pp. 165-71.

"Uxmal, the Great Capital of the Xiu Dynasty," *Art and Archaeology* 30(1930):199-209.

"Uxmal Notes," MS, LAL.

"Trails and No Trails. Concerning the John Geddings Gray Memorial Expedition, 1928. . . ," *Holland's, The Magazine of the South* (Dallas) 49 (February 1930):10-11, 29-30, 33, 35.

"Index to Maya Ruins," *American Anthropologist* 32(1930):572-74.

With other authors, "Summary of Archaeological Work. . . 1929 and 1930," *Pan American Bulletin* 65(1931):400-414; also in a Spanish edition.

"Reconstructing a City of Ancient America," *Discovery* (London) 12(May 1931):149-51.

"Ancient Skyscrapers and the World's Fair," *Commerce* (Chicago), March 1931, pp. 14, 27-28.

"Archaeological and Other Maps of Middle America," *Ibero-Amerikanische Archiv* 6(1932):1-5; also in *Ibero-American Review* 6(1932):288-92.

The Maya Ball Game Pok-ta-pok (Called Tlachtli by the Aztecs), Tulane University, Department of Middle American Research. Research Series no. 4 (1932):488-530.

"Maya Numbers," *Proceedings of the Louisiana Academy of Sciences* 1, no. 1 (1932):7-13.

Commerce, Trade and Monetary Units of the Maya, Tulane University, Department of Middle American Research. Research Series no. 4 (1932):531-56; also in *Smithsonian Institution Annual Report for 1934* (Washington, D.C., 1935), pp. 423-40.

The "Negative Batter" at Uxmal, Tulane University, Department of Middle American Research. Research Series no. 3 (1932):557-66.

"Maya Books and Sciences," *Library Journal* 3(1933):408-20.

"L'Art Maya," *Gazette des Beaux Arts* 10 (December 1933):321-40.

With S.S. Grosjean and H. Cummins, Historical Background on *A Maya Skull from the Uloa Valley,* Tulane University, Department of Middle American Research. Research Series no. 5(1933):7-14; also in *Revista Conservadora del Pensamiento Centroamericano* (Managua) 15 (March 8-11, 1968); and in *Sociedad de Geografía e Historia de Guatemala, Anales* 10(1933):32-36.

"Proposed Museum and Library for the Department of Middle American Research. . . ," MS, September 15, 1933, LAL.

With other authors, "Summary of Archaeological Work in Middle America, 1931, 1932, 1933," *Pan American Bulletin* 67(1934):861-82.

Editor, *Maya Research,* 3 vols., 1934-36.

"A Ruined City with a Confusion of Names," *Maya Research* 1(1934):133-37.

"Short Summary of Recent Exploration in the Ruins of Uxmal, Yucatan," in *24th International Congress of Americanists, 1930* (Hamburg, 1934):55-59.

"A Hitherto Unrecorded Building at Labná, Yucatán," *Maya Research* 2(1935):189-90.

"History below the Surface; Talk. . . ," Tulane University Chapter of Sigma Xi, November 6, 1935, New Orleans. Mimeographed.

"The 'Gomesta' Manuscript, a Falsification," *Maya Research* 2(1935):233-48.

"More Fakes," *Maya Research* 2(1935):249-50.

"Blom Diary, Honduras, 1935," MS, MARI.

"A Checklist of Falsified Maya Codices," *Maya Research* 2(1935):251-52.

"Maya Calculation and Construction," *The Military Engineer* 27(1935):1-5.

"The Ruins of Cópan and the Earthquake," *Maya Research* 2(1935):291-92.

"Notas sobre 'The Temple of the Warriors at Chichén Itzá, Yucatán' por Earl Morris, Jean Charlot and Anne Axtel Morris," *Maya Research* 2(1935):203-15.

The Conquest of Yucatán (Boston, 1936); reprinted (New York: Cooper Square Publishers, 1971). Spanish translation, *La vida de los Maya* (Mexico, 1944; Guatemala, 195- and 1967); Danish translation, *Mayalandete erobring* (Copenhagen, 1945). For reviews, see *Book Review Digest, 1936* (New York, 1937), pp. 98-99.

A Museum and Library for the Department of Middle American Research. . . (n.p., 1936). A brochure.

"A Visit to Quiriguá . . . (after 1852) from the Original Manuscript of Dr. Carl Scherzer. . . ," *Maya Research* 3(1936):92-101; in Spanish, *Sociedad de Geografía e Historia de Guatemala, Anales* 13(1937):447-57.

"Codex Tulane the Most Original Pictorial Manuscript in the U.S.A.," *Anthropos* 31(1936):238-39.

"The Maya of Central America," *The Art of the Maya . . . Baltimore Museum of Art* (Baltimore, 1937).

An Exhibit arranged by the Department of Middle American Research of Tulane University Entitled "The Maya–Past and Present" ([New Orleans], 1937).

"A Selective Guide to the Material Published in 1938. . . ," in *Handbook of Latin American Studies, 1938* (Cambridge, Mass.: Harvard University Press 1939), pp. 10-19.

"Middle America," in *Golden Gate International Exposition. Department of Fine Arts. Division of Pacific Cultures* (San Francisco, 1939), pp. 146-48 plus photographs and catalogue of the exhibition.

"Coronel Modesto Méndez, Explorador del Petén. . . ," *Sociedad de Geografía e Historia de Guatemala, Anales* 16(1940):167-79; also in *Antropología e Historia de Guatemala* 7(1955):3-17.

Diary of an expedition, 1943, MS, Na Bolom.

"El lienzo de Analco, Oaxaca," *Cuadernos Americanos* (Mexico) 34, no. 6 (1945):125-36.

R.P. Fray Tomas de la Torre–Desde Salamanca, España, hasta Ciudad Real, Chiapas. Diario de viaje, 1544-45 (Mexico, 1945). Prologue and notes by Blom.

"Apuntes sobre los ingenieros Mayas," *Irrigación en México* 27, no. 3 (1946):5-16.

With Gertrude Duby, "Darkness to All Who Dwell There," *Natural History* 55(1946):231-32, 237, 239.

Diary of an expedition, 1948, MS, Na Bolom.

[Reports on his activities,] *The Teosintli* (Rochester, N.Y.), June 1948-November 1962, passim.

With Gertrude Duby, "Entre los indios lacandones en México," *América Indígena* (Instituto Indigenista Interamericana) 9(1949):155-64.

With Gertrude Duby, "Preliminary Explorations in the Lacandón Zone, Chiapas," *Boletín Indigenista* (México) 9(1949):80-83. Spanish and English text.

"A Polychrome Plate from Quintana Roo," in *Carnegie Institution of Washington. Notes on Middle American Archaeology and Ethnology*, no. 98 (Cambridge, Mass., 1950), pp. 81-84.

Diary of an expedition, 1950, MS, Na Bolom.

Juan Ballinas–el desierto de los Lacandones. Memorias 1876-1877 (Tuxtla Gutiérrez, Mexico, 1951). Introduction and notes by Blom; photographs by Gertrude Duby.

Mapa de la selva lacandona (San Cristóbal, Chiapas, 1953).

"Ossuaries, Cremation and Secondary Burials among the Maya of Chiapas, México," *Journal de la Société des Américanistes de Paris*, 43(1954):123-26.

"La lápida de Chiapas," *Ateneo* (Chiapas) 5(1954):41-44.

"El retablo de Teopisca en Chiapas," *Anales del Instituto de Investigaciones Estéticas* (Mexico) 23(1955):39-42.

With Gertrude Duby, *La selva lacandona*, 2 vols. (Mexico, 1955-57).

"Vida precortesiana del indio Chiapeneco de hoy," *Estudios Antropológicos publicados en Homenaje al Doctor Manuel Gamio* (Mexico, 1956), pp. 277-85.

"La vida de los Mayas," *Nicaragua Indígena* (Instituto Indigenista Nacional), 2 epoca. 2(1957):73-77; 3(1958):14-20.

"Historical Notes Relating to the Pre-Columbian Amber Trade from Chiapas," *Amerikanistische Miszellen (Mitteilungen aus dem Museum für Volkerkunde in Hamburg)* 25(1959):24-27.

"Notas sobre algunas ruinas todavía sin explorar," *Sociedad Mexicana de Antropología* 8(1961):115-25.

With Gertrude Duby, "Proyecto para declarar 'Parque Nacional' al territorio en que encuentran las ruinas Mayas de Yaxchilan," *Icach* (Instituto de ciencias y artes de Chiapas, Tuxtla Gutiérrez), no. 11 (1963):15-16. Written 1959.

"Hernán Cortés e el libro de trajes de Cristoph Weiditz," *Icach*, no. 11 (1963):7-14.

With Gertrude Duby, "The Lacandons," in *Handbook of Middle American Indians*, ed. Robert Wauchope and Gordon R. Willey (Austin: University of Texas Press, 1969) 7:276-97.

"Selva Lacandona. Notas Topográficas," n.d., Na Bolom.

Robert Wauchope, *They Found the Buried Cities* (Chicago: University of Chicago Press, 1965), pp. 295-307, provides a selection from Blom's writings.

Works about Blom

Until a detailed biography of the man appears, information must be gathered from various sources. The basic facts appear in several obituaries: J. Eric S. Thompson, *Estudios de Cultura Maya* 3(1963):307-14; Douglas S. Byers, *American Antiquity* 31(1966):406-7; Frans Termer, *Sociedad de Geografía e Historia de Guatemala, Anales* 36(1963):577-83, and also in *Antropología e Historia de Guatemala* 16(1964):82-86; and an appreciation and description by Gertrude Duby Blom, *Siempre* (supplement), November 13, 1963, p. viii. Other sketches are brief or disappointing. His first marriage and divorce are reported in *The New York Times*, May 7, 1932, p. 12; June 16, 1932, p. 25; August 6, 1938, p. 3.

For Blom's relations with Morley, the Morley Diaries, MS, American Philosophical Society, and the Blom correspondence, Na Bolom, are indispensable. Karl Ruppert in *The Maya and Their Neighbors* (New York, 1940), pp. 222-31, reported groups of structures at other cities similar to the arrangement of the observatory temples Blom found at Uaxactún.

His activities at Tulane must also be culled from diverse items. Blom folder, Archives, and scrapbooks for the 1930s, LAL, provide much interesting, if miscellaneous, material. The few reports of the Department of Middle American Research, 1924-25, 1928, and 1932, give the official version of his work. Newspaper articles supplement the scrapbooks. *The States* (New Orleans), April 27, 1926, treats Blom and Tulane. Helpful reports are in *The New York Times* and can be traced in the index of that newspaper.

For the expedition of 1925, see useful items in *The New York Times.* The account of Lázaro Hernández ("Tata") comes from the relevant passages in *Tribes and Temples* and from Blom's MS "Tata. . . ," LAL.

Until recently Oliver La Farge received no major treatment. That situation is remedied in part by D'Arcy McNickle, *Indian Man: A Life of Oliver La Farge* (Bloomington & London: Indiana University Press, 1971), which is based on the La Farge manuscripts. A briefer treatment is by Douglas Byers in *American Antiquity* 31(1966):408-9. La Farge's diary of 1925, LAL, is invaluable for his reaction to Blom; he provided a readable account of the same journey in "The Land of Gog and Magog: Exploring the Lost Mayan Civilization and Their Wild Descendants," *Scribner's* 79(1926):607-16. Oliver La Farge, *Raw Material* (Boston, 1945), is disappointing; a more informative summary of his work on the expedition is Kenneth Barr's article in *The New York Times,* August 30, 1925, sec. 8, p. 6. The official record of the 1927 expedition is La Farge and Byers, "The Year Bearer's People," Middle American Research Series no. 2 (New Orleans, 1931).

The Gray Memorial Expedition is best related by Blom himself in "Trails and No Trails. . ." (1930). "F. Webster McBryde, Beta Phi (Tulane). . . ," *The Delta of Sigma Nu,* May 1929, pp. 545-50, gives the story by a student who was a member of the expedition.

The expedition to Uxmal in 1930 received several notices in *The New York Times.* Sam Leyrer, "A New Method Used in Photographing Maya Hieroglyphics," *Maya Research* 2(1935):60-63, explains how the night pictures were made.

For the expedition of 1935, see two articles by the Danish representative on the trip, Jens Yde, "A Preliminary Report of the Tulane-Danish National Museum Expedition to Central America, 1935," *Maya Research* 3(1936):25-37, and "Archaeological Reconnaissance of Northwestern Honduras," Middle American Research Series no. 9, also as an offprint, Copenhagen, 1938, reprinted from *Acta Archaeologia* 9.

Other aspects of Blom's work in New Orleans are scattered. The scrapbook for 1937, LAL, contains material on the fair at Dallas. The exhibit at the Baltimore Museum of Art received notice in a number of the art magazines.

The project for the reconstruction of the Castillo on the Tulane campus is explained in *The Middle American Research Institute . . .* [1939?] and in the accompanying *Cost Leaflet for 1939 Campaign;* another leaflet is entitled *Something New between the Americas* [1939?]. The scrapbook for the 1939 campaign, LAL, provides pertinent newspaper clippings.

On Blom's second life in Mexico from the 1940s, there are various descriptions. José Pérez Moreno, "El Maravilloso Mundo de la Selva," *Todo, La Mejor Revista de México,* no. 806, February 17, 1949, pp. 20-21, 66, tells of the Bloms' earlier trips through Chiapas. M.F. Knight, "Frans Blom, Archaeologist and Explorer," *Christian Science Monitor,* January 21, 1950, p. 12, describes the couple when they lived in Mexico City. Julia Hernández, "El Paraiso de los Blom," *El Libro y el*

Pueblo (Mexico) 19 (February 1957):61-66, recounts a tour of Na Bolom. Their humanitarian work for the Indian receives good treatment in F.M. Denbaugh, "The Lacandons," *Américas* 12, no. 1 (January 1960):31-35. An interview with the Bloms appears in "Entrevistamos a Pancho Blom al cumplir 65 años en Na Bolom de Jovel," *Icach* (Textla Gutiérrez), no. 14 (January-June 1965):43-48. William Hagney, "From the House of the Jaguar," *Science of Man* (Garden Grove, California) 1, no. 2 (April 1962):88-95, is informative. *Homenaje a Frans Blom. . .* (San Cristóbal, 1966) contains tributes to the man.

The Bloms' interest in the jungles of Chiapas receives the most detailed treatment in their *La selva lacandona*. The MS diaries of the expeditions of 1943 and 1948, Na Bolom, give a fine description of the travels through the selva. One should not overlook the books by Gertrude Duby: . . .*Los Lacandones, su pasado y su presente* (Mexico, 1944); *Hay razas inferiores?* (Mexico, 1944 and 1974); and *Chiapas indígena: texto y fotografías* (Mexico, 1961).

Index